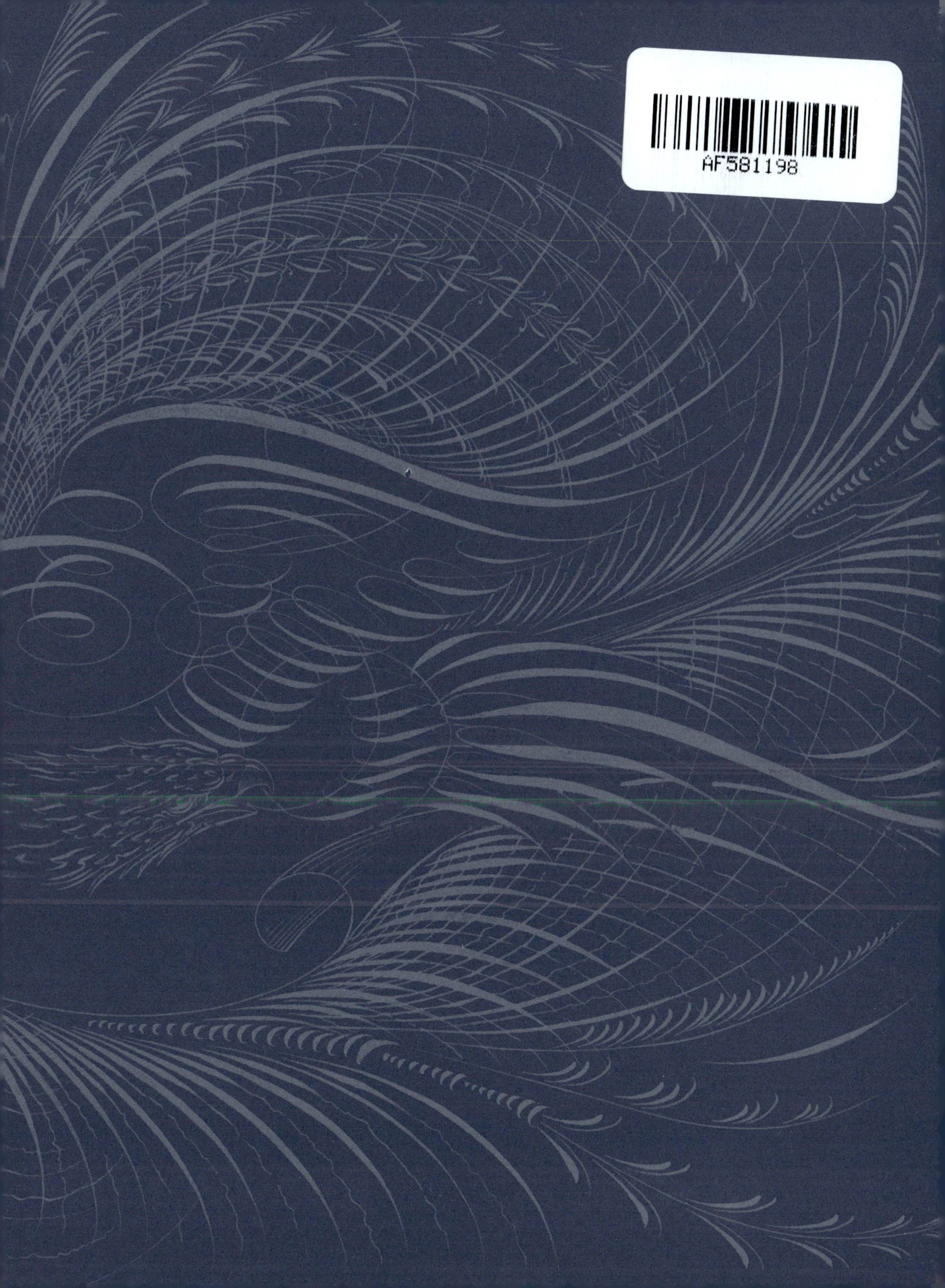

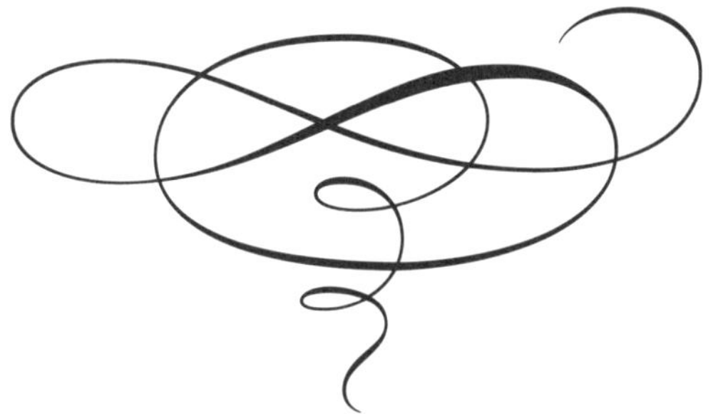

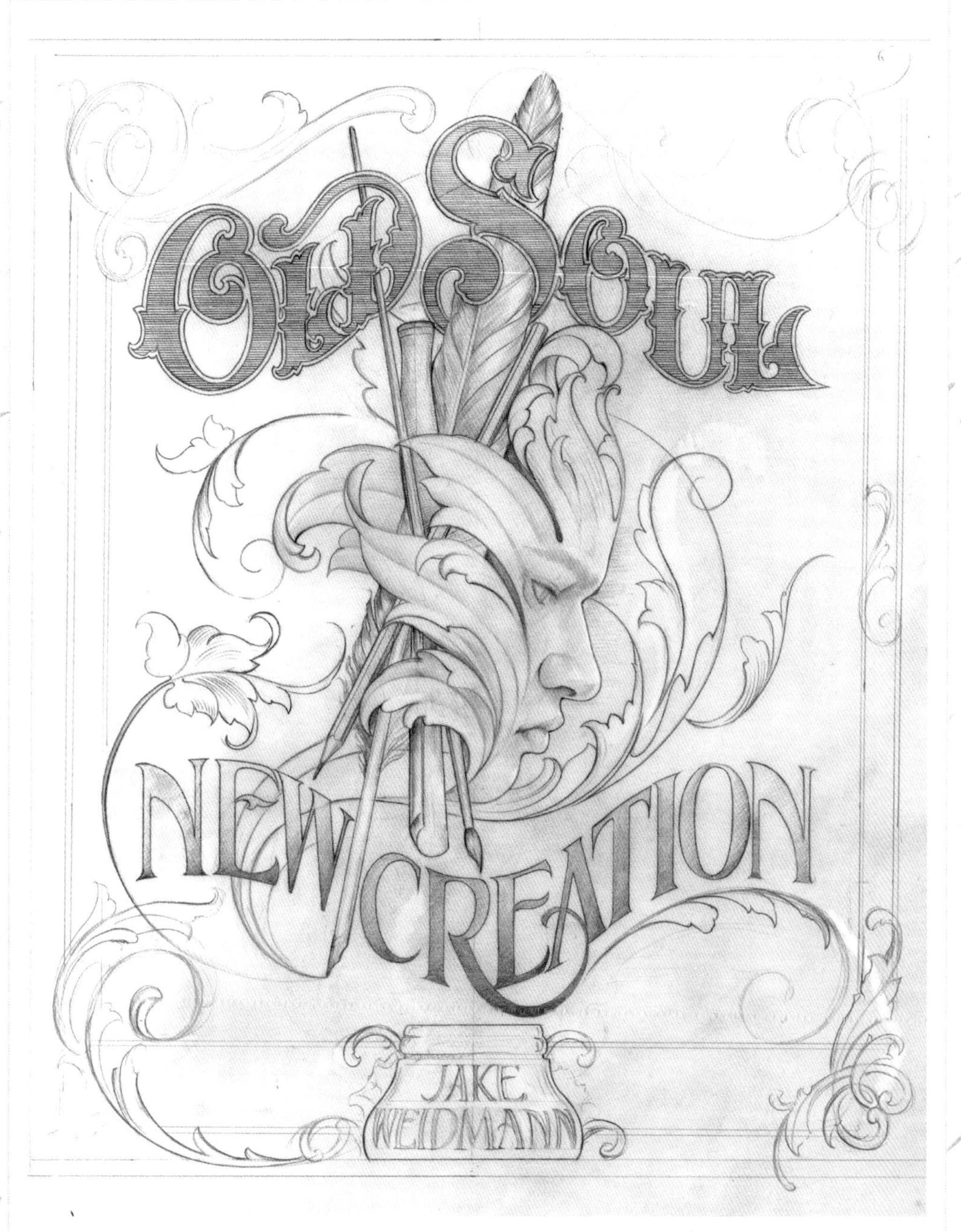

THOMAS NELSON
Since 1798

Old Soul, New Creation

Published in Nashville, Tennessee, by Thomas Nelson. Thomas Nelson is a registered trademark of HarperCollins Christian Publishing, Inc.

Photography by Jake Weidmann.

Thomas Nelson titles may be purchased in bulk for educational, business, fundraising, or sales promotional use. For information, please email SpecialMarkets@ThomasNelson.com.

ISBN 978-1-4002-4685-4 (eBook)
ISBN 978-14002-4684-7 (HC)

Printed in Malaysia

25 26 27 28 29 SEM 10 9 8 7 6 5 4 3 2 1

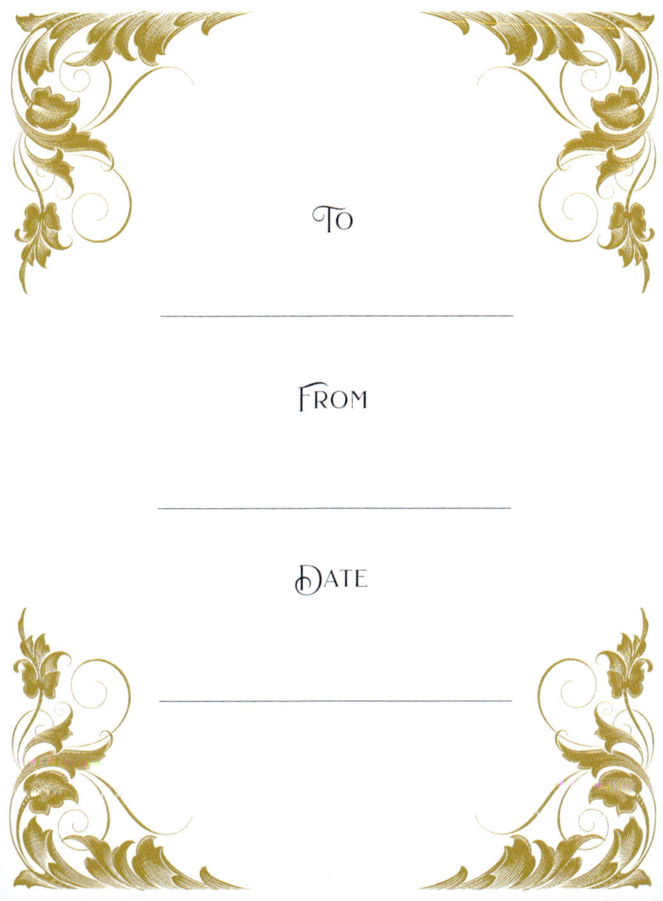
To
From
Date

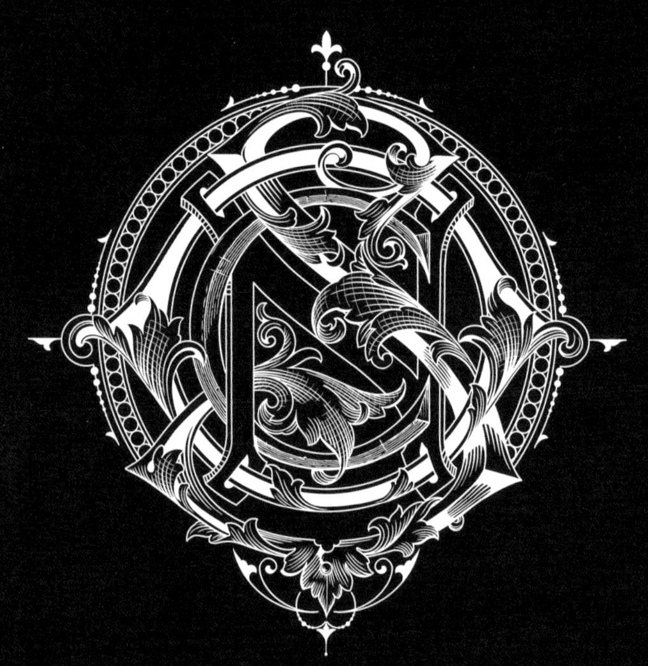

To my beloved wife, Hannah,
and my dear children, Emma, Henry, and Eloise.
All that I do bears some measure of you,
for I carry your hearts in my hand.

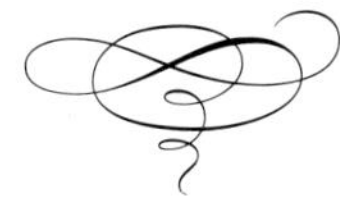

Jake Weidmann
ARTIST
AND
MASTER
PENMAN
FINE·ART
CALLIGRAPHY
LETTER DESIGN

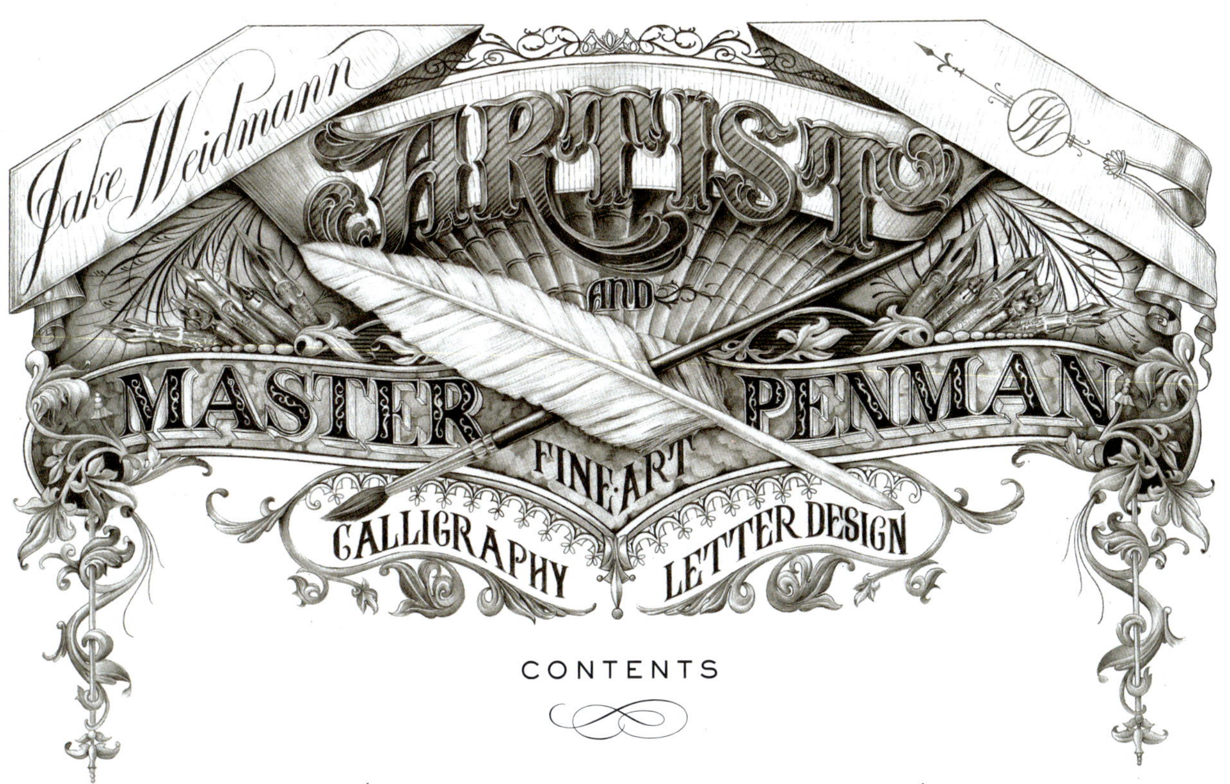

CONTENTS

Introduction

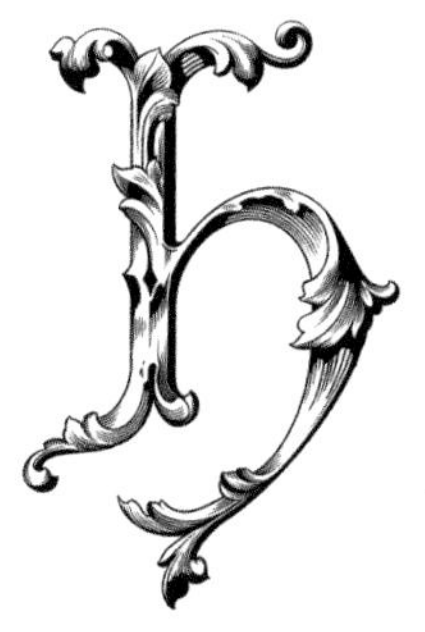

i there. My name is Jake Weidmann. And I am an artist. That might sound self-serious or perhaps even egotistical, but in many ways, it's more a confession than an introduction. You see, it took me a long time to come to grips with the calling God had on my life. Indeed, if C. S. Lewis could refer to himself as "the most reluctant convert" following the years he spent as an atheist arguing against a Christian faith he would ultimately claim, love, and defend, then I might as well be called "the most reluctant creative." Be it insecurity, disbelief, fear of failure, impostor syndrome, or the like, I always found reason to discredit one of my deepest and longest-held passions. In fact, I still wrestle with fears and doubts from time to time. Perhaps you know those feelings too. Perhaps you know them only too well. If so, then, my friend, this book is for you.

Despite that reluctance, I am nevertheless writing to you as someone who is truly living their dream. Yet for decades my dream remained only that. I relegated myself to the sidelines, held back—even suppressed—in favor of other passions and pursuits. My dream hardly seemed realistic. The pursuit of art as a vocation almost never does. And so it wasn't even my first choice. It was more like my last resort. But here's the thing: Art chose me long before I chose it. And I don't say that easily, given all that art has given me—and through

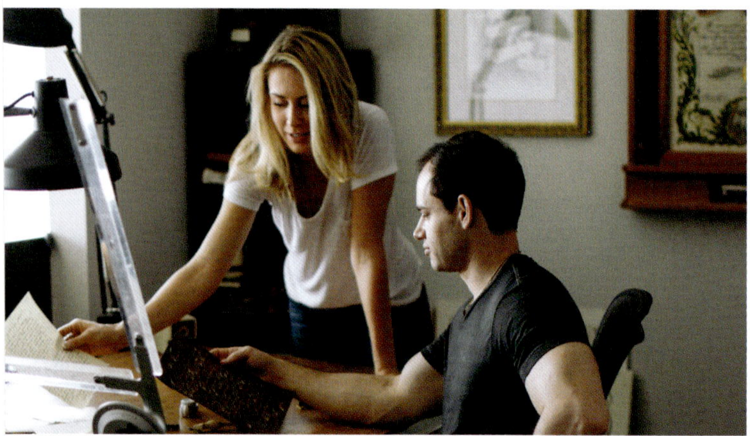

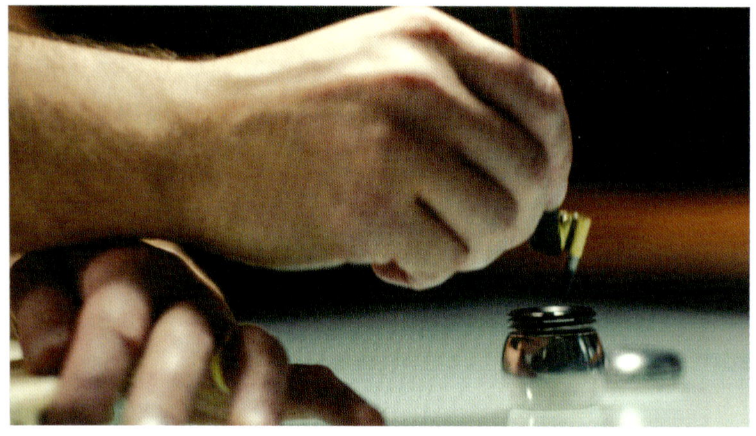

always seen—eventually breaking through a cloud. I finally knew who I was. Major events converged in quick succession, breaking the curse of self-doubt and sending me headlong into my calling. Within a few months, fresh out of college, I completed my certificate as the youngest Master Penman in history, moved into the art studio of my dreams, and acquired a few gracious patrons who would help unearth in me what had been buried for years. I finally knew what God has always known.

Since the dawn of my art career, I have done and seen so many things that I know would not have been possible any other way. Through my art I have met incredible people—chief among them being my wife, Hannah, whom I began dating after she came to my very first public art show. (The finer details await in later pages.) The grace I had cultivated in my hand as a Master Penman served the highest purpose in wooing her heart through our exchange of wax-sealed letters. Once married, Hannah joined me in the beautiful business of art making. Ever and always side by side, we have followed God's calling on our lives as creators, which has led us to many places and continues to offer us opportunities far beyond our wildest imaginations.

But even then, it has hardly been one triumph after another. We have experienced seasons of great struggle. Once or twice I've even wanted to quit. Being in business for oneself is not always what it's cracked up to be, especially with a family in tow. "Do what you love and you'll never work a day in your life," they say. Well, I don't know who "they" are, but I'd like a word. Hannah and I work tirelessly in the businesses we have built together. And yes, by and large the work is fulfilling. But there is a great deal that is far from glamorous: bookkeeping, customer service, order fulfillment, and hey, the trash needs to be taken out every so often, so add *janitor* to that list of roles as well. Even the creative side involves the various pressures of time management, budget constraints, and (occasionally!) anxious clients. Yet I would not have it any other way. All this work—from the sacred to the mundane, from the fun to the *un*fun—has shaped me and is still shaping me. Indeed, as I reflect upon the pieces that adorn the pages of this book, each of which have had their shares of joy and hardship and everything in between, I can see how they have formed me as much as I have formed them.

So, now comes the big question: What is this long-reluctant artist doing writing a book? The official version is that as a Master Penman I have a deep, abiding love for the written word. Moreover, as an artist I am all about communicating. Also, who wouldn't want to see my work and hear the stories that lay behind them? So, in short, a book makes perfect sense. And yet, there is also a less official version. You may have to lean in to hear it. *Writing this book absolutely terrifies me.* I am *way* outside

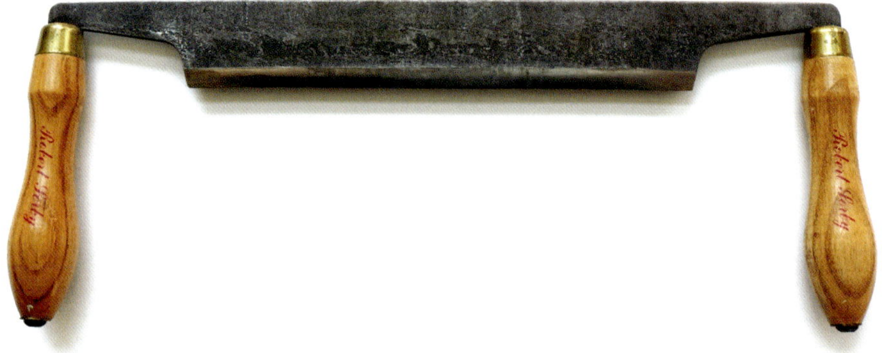

of my comfort zone here. I never imagined I'd become an author. I never even had the desire. But here's the thing: I also didn't think I would become an artist either. Thank goodness this book has a lot of pretty pictures.

More seriously, though, despite my trepidation, I do firmly believe that part of my responsibility as an artist is not only to communicate through art but to communicate *about* art as well. I have spoken often and at length on the symbolism in my work and the process of creating, whether at a conference, a TED Talk, or a private showing. What I haven't done until now, however, was offer a full account of my own personal and spiritual transformation as an artist. And, at this point in my life and career, it seems high time to do so. This means getting autobiographical and personal in ways that I did not anticipate doing. Perhaps I was being held back by my insecurities. Perhaps my inner servant still wanted to hide his talent in the sand.

But wait—surely I've learned my lesson on that score already.

The truth is that I really didn't want this book to be all about me. And here's the good news: It isn't! The real hero, the main character and even the author of my story, is God Himself. J. R. R. Tolkien said the thing that people really love about a narrative is that it ultimately points to the existence of a narrator. May that be so in my own story. I want my life to ring out with all the hallmarks of the loving God who set it in motion and guided it all along the way.

So, welcome to my artist's studio. Hear the wood shavings crunch beneath your feet as you step into my woodshop. Enter the quiet scriptorium where I give life to letters and adorn words with wings. Just know that these creative spaces are sacred to me. They are my tabernacle; they are my temple. I encounter God here, and my

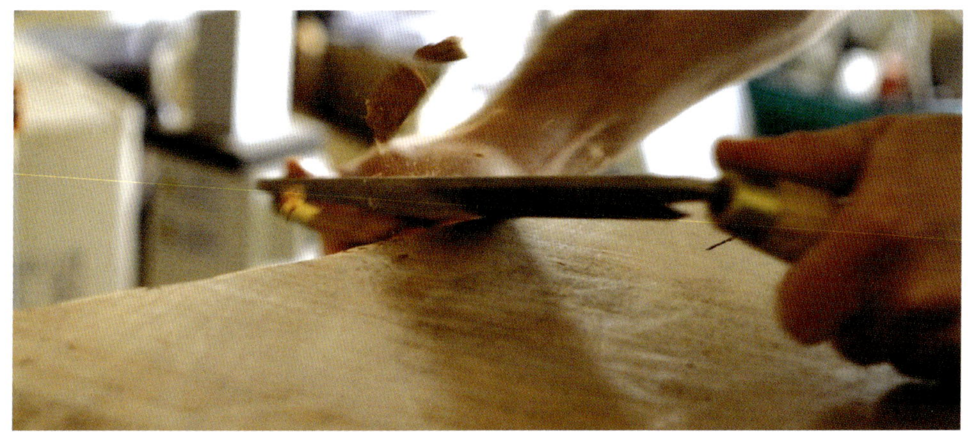

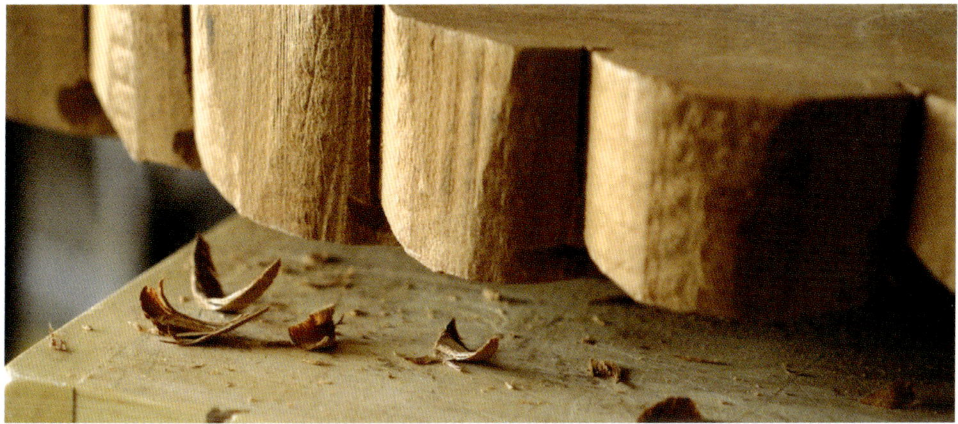

hope is that you encounter Him here too. For as enchanting as the artistic process is to observe, the real Master at work is the Author of my faith and Lover of my soul. After too many years downplaying the role of creativity in my life, the embrace of my calling has only brought me into deeper fellowship with God. I have come to learn that as I create, I do so in imitation of my Creator, whose artistry is evident from the far-flung galaxies to the intricacies of the sparrow's plumage. As I strive to preserve symbols with my hands, He more deeply impresses the symbol of His image—*imago Dei*—upon me. I create in the Artist's image. And so do you.

As it turns out, then, who *I* am isn't all that significant. At least not on my own. I need God. I need my Creator. He is the One who has so artfully taken the little I have and turned it into much. And that is who *He* is. After all, as we read in

Let bravery bluster you, let passion invigorate you, let the very breath of God inspire and animate you.

Scripture, He reduced Gideon's army and still led him to victory against insurmountable odds; He called forth an outcast to free His people from Egypt; He used a shepherd boy to slay a giant; and He fed the masses with five loaves and two fish.

That is great news because—let's be honest—I haven't given Him a whole heck of a lot to work with. After all, I'm the one with the bright idea to work with ancient tools in a digital age. How's that for a sling and a few smooth stones against the Philistine army? But what I have learned firsthand about the power of our God is that it doesn't matter who you are, or what you can or cannot do. He said, after all, that His strength is made perfect in our weakness, and He means it. If that means that we need to pray in the face of recurring doubt ("Lord, I believe, help my unbelief"), then so be it.

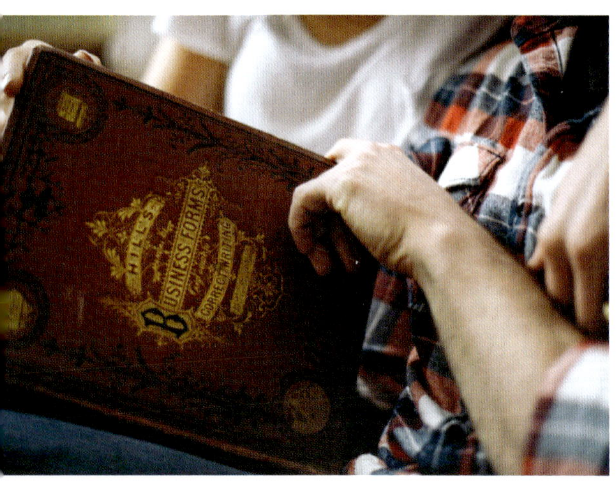

And yes, we're about to get to the artwork, I promise. But before we get there, I want to assure you that just as this book is not all about me but rather about God's work *in* me, so it is also about what I hope and believe God is working in you. You may or may not consider yourself a creative, but, my friend, God is *creating in* you. Will you join Him in that artistry? I pray that you do. I pray that you are released from any reluctance to embrace your calling. I pray the strongholds of the Enemy would fall and that any lingering insecurity would wither to dust. I pray that doubt would be banished and fear in all its nasty forms would be driven far away by the Spirit of the living God.

And I pray, too, that you would discover—if not *re*discover—your God-given creativity in whatever shape it takes in your beautiful life. Do not feel limited to the pen, a paintbrush, or even (gasp) a finger on an iPad. Whatever your hand finds to do, do it with all your might. Let bravery bluster you, let passion invigorate you, let the very breath of God inspire and animate you. And finally, may you see yourself as God sees you: washed in the light of His good purposes. May you sense His presence ever more deeply as you create with your Creator. Don't be surprised if you find He is making a new creation out of you!

So, here ends my confession. Perhaps it is long overdue. Perhaps it is right on time. Either way, I am done hiding my talents in the sand. I am a reluctant creative no more. And even though this book presents quite the personal challenge, I am *so* excited to share it with you. Within these pages you will read the stories behind many of my most important works. And of course you get to enjoy the works themselves! I have poured my heart into each one of them. And I pray that through it all, you join me in seeing the Creator's hand at work throughout.

To God be the glory.

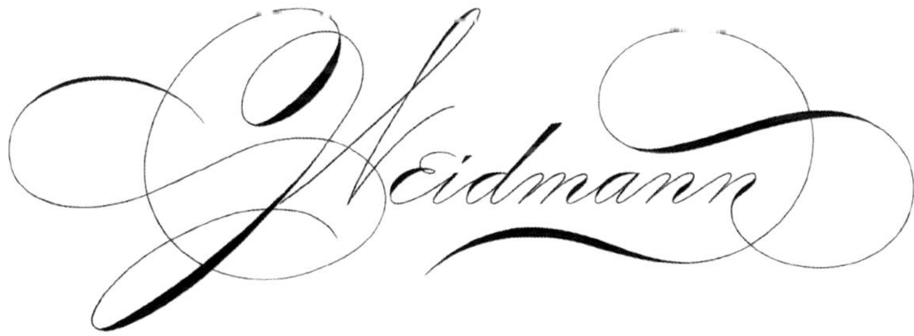

A Prayer of Repentance

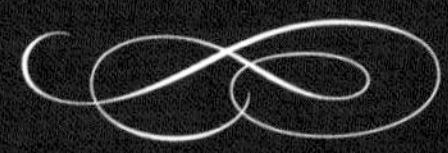

The God of mercy, Elohim Chaseddi, have mercy on me!

For I forged a chain of shame and wore it willingly. I have been a captive in the land of doubt. Like a tyrant king I allowed fear to rule over me. I set limits where You made a way out. 'Twas Thee who sparked the flame of creativity and I the one who snuffed it out. Forgive me, God, for the gifts I have squandered. Forgive me, God, for the talents I covered. Worse than disbelieving in my abilities, I doubted the One who brought them about. But this is my prayer of repentance. This is my cry of revolution. All that was before is behind me, for this is my exodus from the land of doubt. From here I walk the path to freedom. To shame am I no longer bound. I am one with Thee, my maker, and Thou shall teach me to make once again. So let fear's crooked crown tumble down; let my enemies instead bear all dread. I shall walk with Thee in the garden and create with Thee as a friend. Creation's power is a torment to those who wish to destroy. So teach me to wield this weapon for Thy goodness and glory on high.

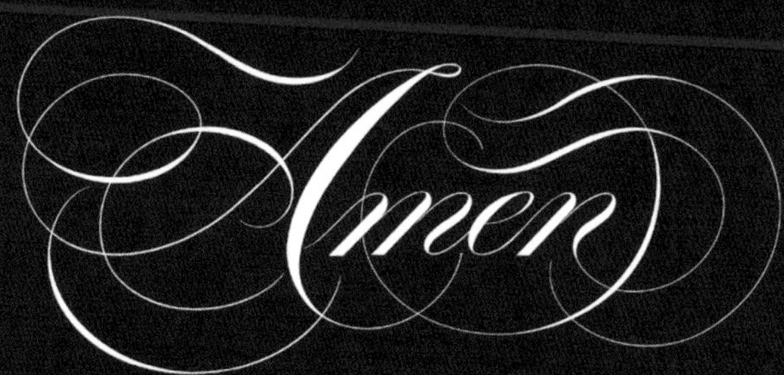

CHAPTER ONE

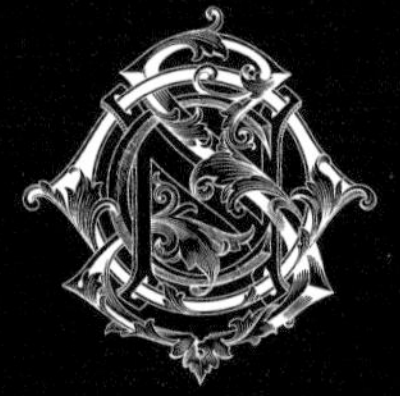

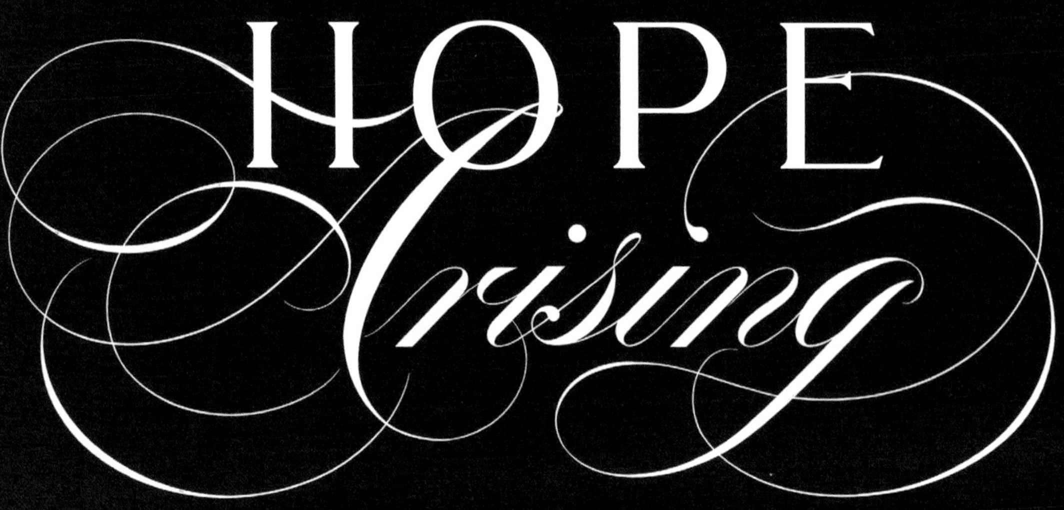

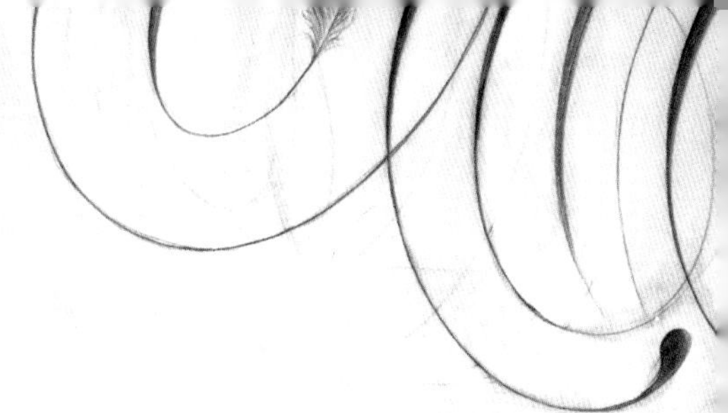

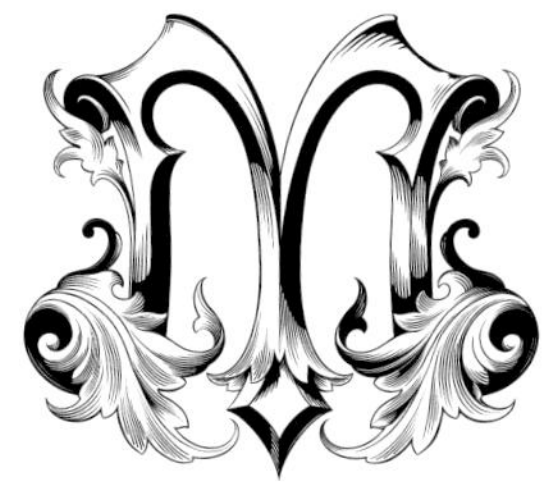

y story as an artist begins on an idle weekday in the spring of 1991. As usual, Mom picked me up from school in her light-blue Chrysler minivan, my two younger sisters already inside. We then made the short commute to our suburban home and pulled into the garage. I unfastened my seatbelt, gathered my backpack and G.I. Joe lunchbox in routine fashion, and pulled open the sliding door. But on this otherwise ordinary day, something felt off. My mom sensed it immediately as we exited the van—a faint smell of burning tainted the air. She cautiously approached the entry into the house and reached for the brass doorknob. It felt warm to the touch. Sure enough, as soon as my mom twisted the knob and opened the door, billows of black smoke came rolling out of the house. In a panic, she ushered me and my siblings into the side yard, then she rushed to the neighbors' house to call the fire department. With sirens blaring, a brigade of firefighters soon arrived, descending on our home with unfurled hoses and outstretched ladders to tame the fiery beast within.

And all the while I sat in our neighbors' backyard, eating cheese and crackers on their sun-faded Little Tikes picnic table, fiddling with my juice box while my home burned. I was just seven years old, hardly grasping the significance of this world-shaking event, even as it filled the air around me with ash.

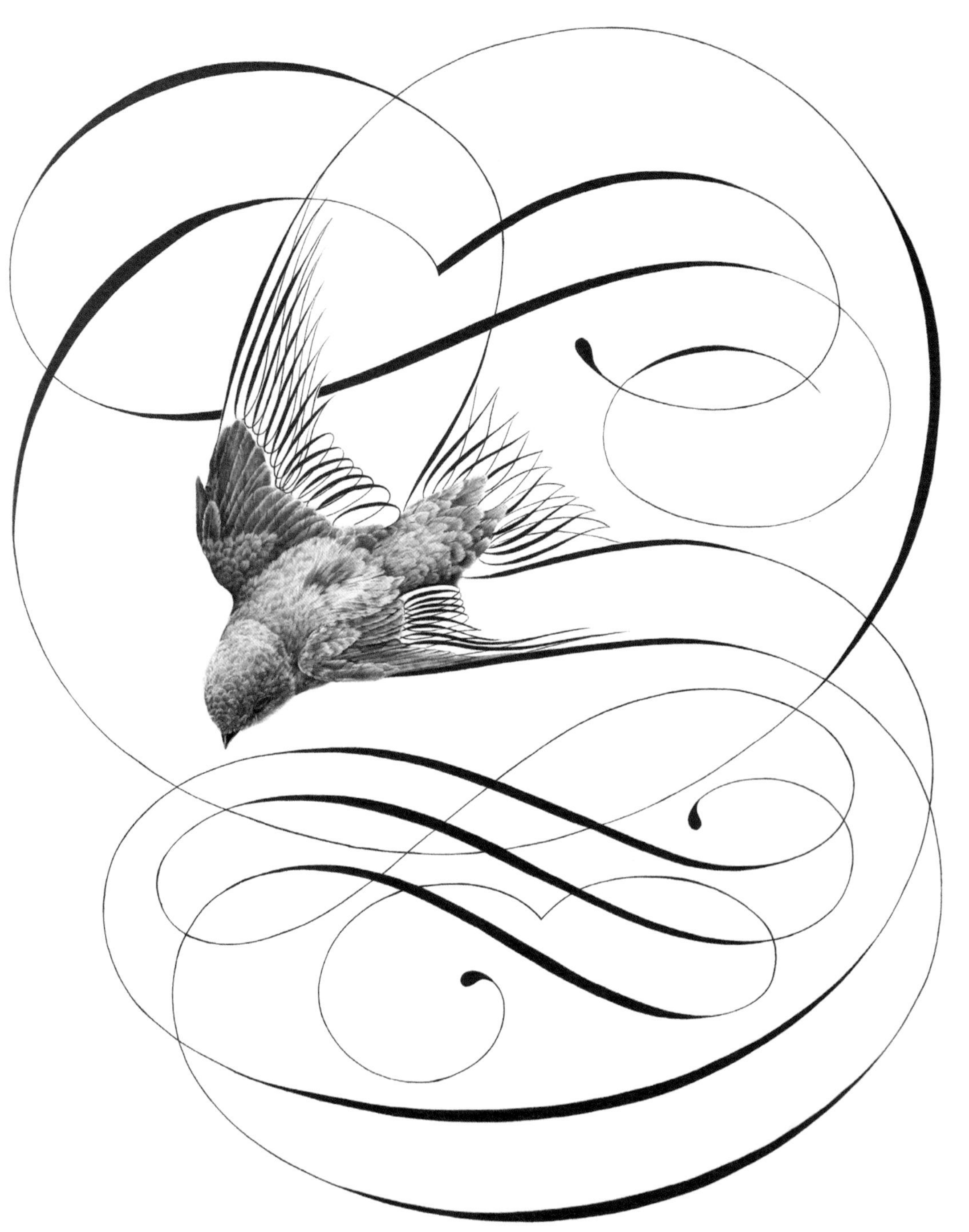

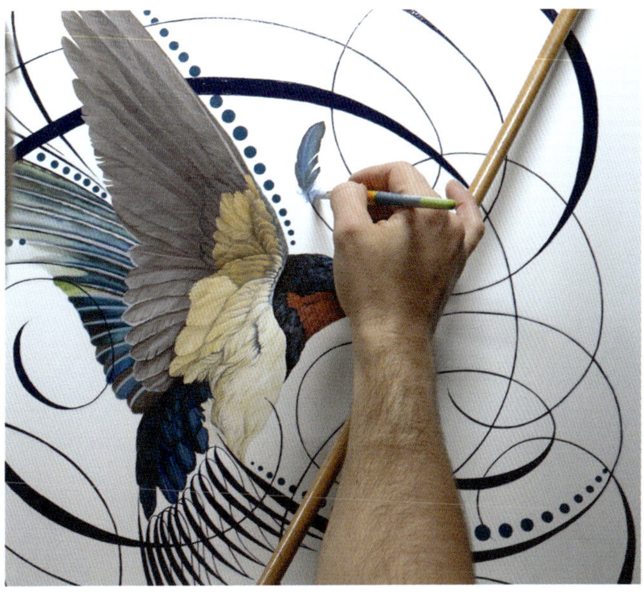

That evening the insurance company arranged to put my mom, dad, and us four kids in a small condo just a few miles away. We walked into the lightly furnished dwelling with little more than the clothes on our backs. My dad was still wearing his suit from work, ash clinging to his polished loafers. We were in a daze. Mom and Dad tried to make the best of things. "We're having an adventure!" my mom exclaimed, obviously covering the quiver of trepidation in her voice with a bit of overwrought exuberance. Kids can sense these things. Nevertheless, we went along with the game. It was like embarking on some grand holiday, only our home wouldn't be the same as we left it upon our return—something I could not fully comprehend at that age.

News of our plight traveled quickly. Some family friends came by with a cardboard box brimming with old toys they had gathered from their own closets and toyboxes. My siblings and I were delighted! But I also knew I had to act quickly. Like any self-respecting middle child in my position, I ensured my rightful place in the pecking order. So, what did I pull from this cardboard box, this charitable treasure chest? A single

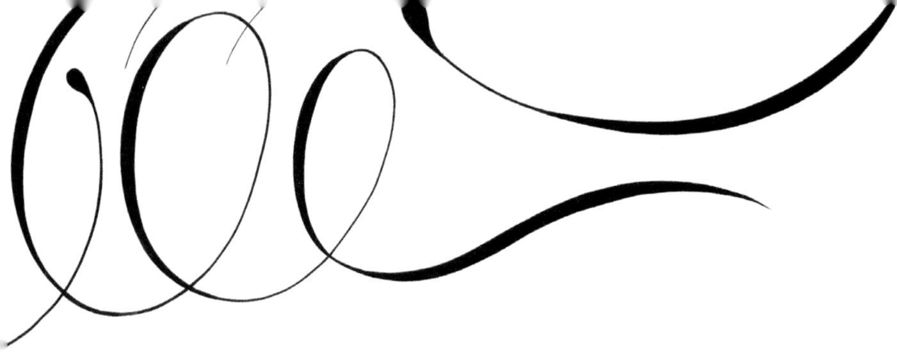

stuffed animal parrot with an elastic band for feet. Scooting myself back from the frenzy, I slipped the elastic onto the first two fingers of my right hand and lifted that lightly loved little bird up into the light: a humble phoenix rising from the ashes of an awful day.

I MADE NOTE OF HIS EVERY DETAIL, SUMMONING ALL THE ACCURACY MY SEVEN-YEAR-OLD FINGERS COULD RECORD.

The next morning I was back at school, still shaken from the day before but clinging to my symbol of hope in the form of my secondhand parrot. We arrived early, so there was still time before class began. I went over to the corner of the classroom to get a sheet of paper from the printer. Perhaps you remember the kind? It was an old dot matrix model from the eighties with an accordion-stacked ream of paper, edged with sprocket holes on either side that fed through the rollers in the printer. I carefully creased the perforated holey edges, tore them from the sides of my paper, and returned to my desk.

In that moment, artistic inspiration filled and animated me. I took out a freshly sharpened pencil and began to draw my newfound feathered friend. I made note of his every detail, summoning all the accuracy my seven-year-old fingers could record. I even portrayed him high in a tree with a nest behind him—a set of hungry chicks within. In some small way, I found comfort in providing him a home even as I was deprived of mine.

I was finishing up the last few details when suddenly I heard someone let out a soft gasp behind me. Turning around, I saw my teacher, Mrs. K., bending down. She carefully lifted the drawing from my desk and began to study it. To me it was a simple drawing, but in her hands it was as if it had been transformed into some precious, ancient manuscript. Rather than tuck it away for safekeeping, she asked if she could hang it on the wall for all to see. I was delighted, if a little reluctant. As much as I liked my drawing, the warmth and encouragement it won me in the glowing eyes of my teacher seemed a fair trade.

Some weeks passed and the drawing didn't reappear. I thought perhaps Mrs. K. had forgotten all about it. And soon I did too. One morning, however, as I went to hang my backpack in the hall, I looked up and noticed a change. There, expertly matted on black construction paper, was my drawing, arranged alongside a slew of others running the length of the hallway. What is more, a blue ribbon hung beside it with a silver foil "1st Place" printed on the top. I rushed into the classroom in a state of confusion and disbelief. "Mrs. K.! Mrs. K.! Did I win an art contest?" Exuberantly, she turned to me and replied, "Yes, Jake! I entered your drawing in a contest, and you won!" Then came the words that would change my life forever: "You are an artist!"

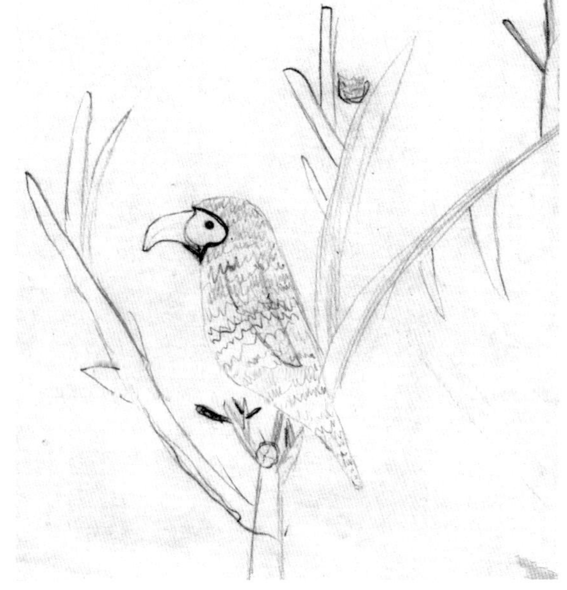

Did I know then what I would become? I have already shared my reluctance to accept this calling earlier in life. But as I look back now, I can see that *even then*, even in the midst of one of the most traumatic times of my childhood, God was working. Even as I created that little drawing,

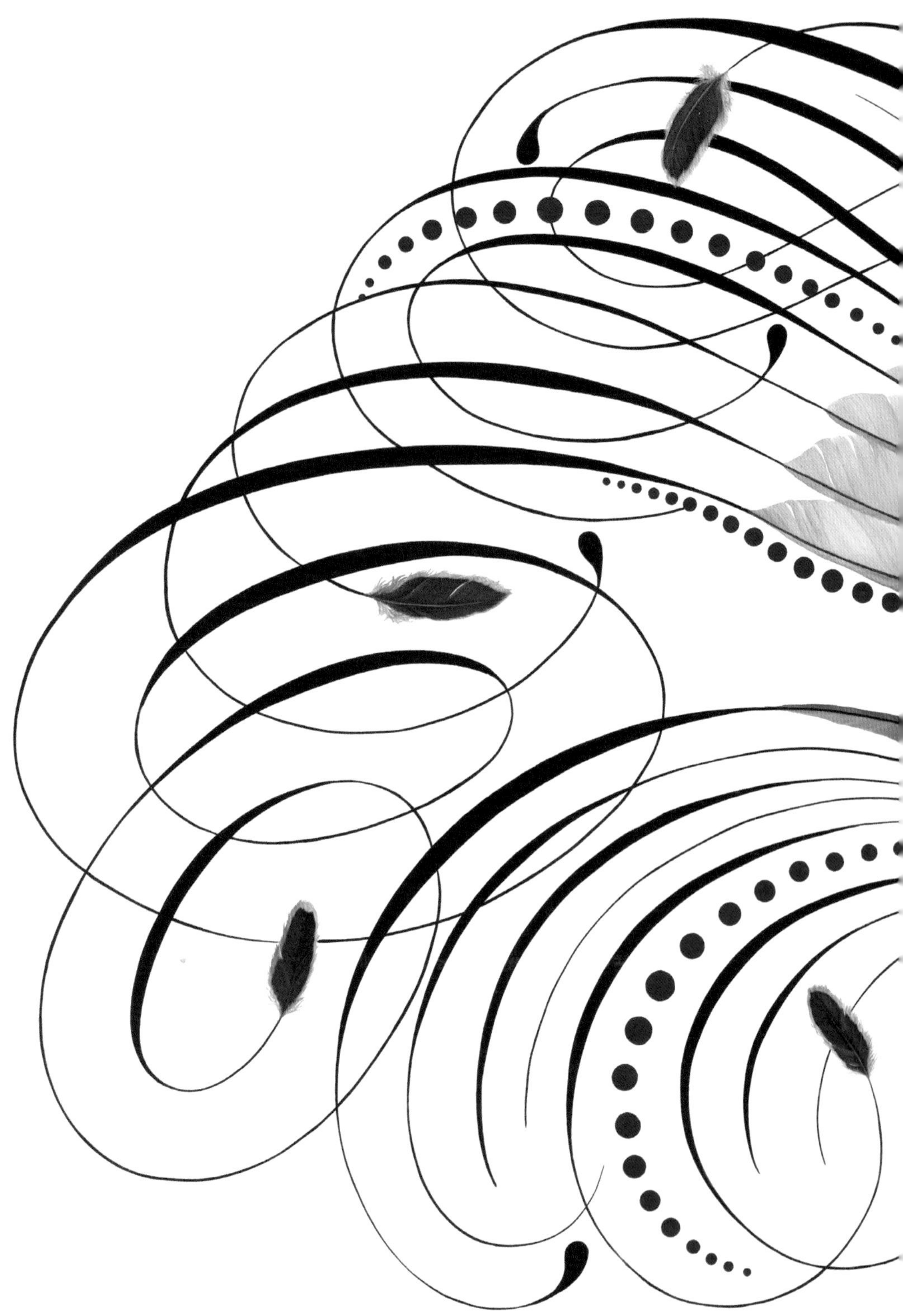

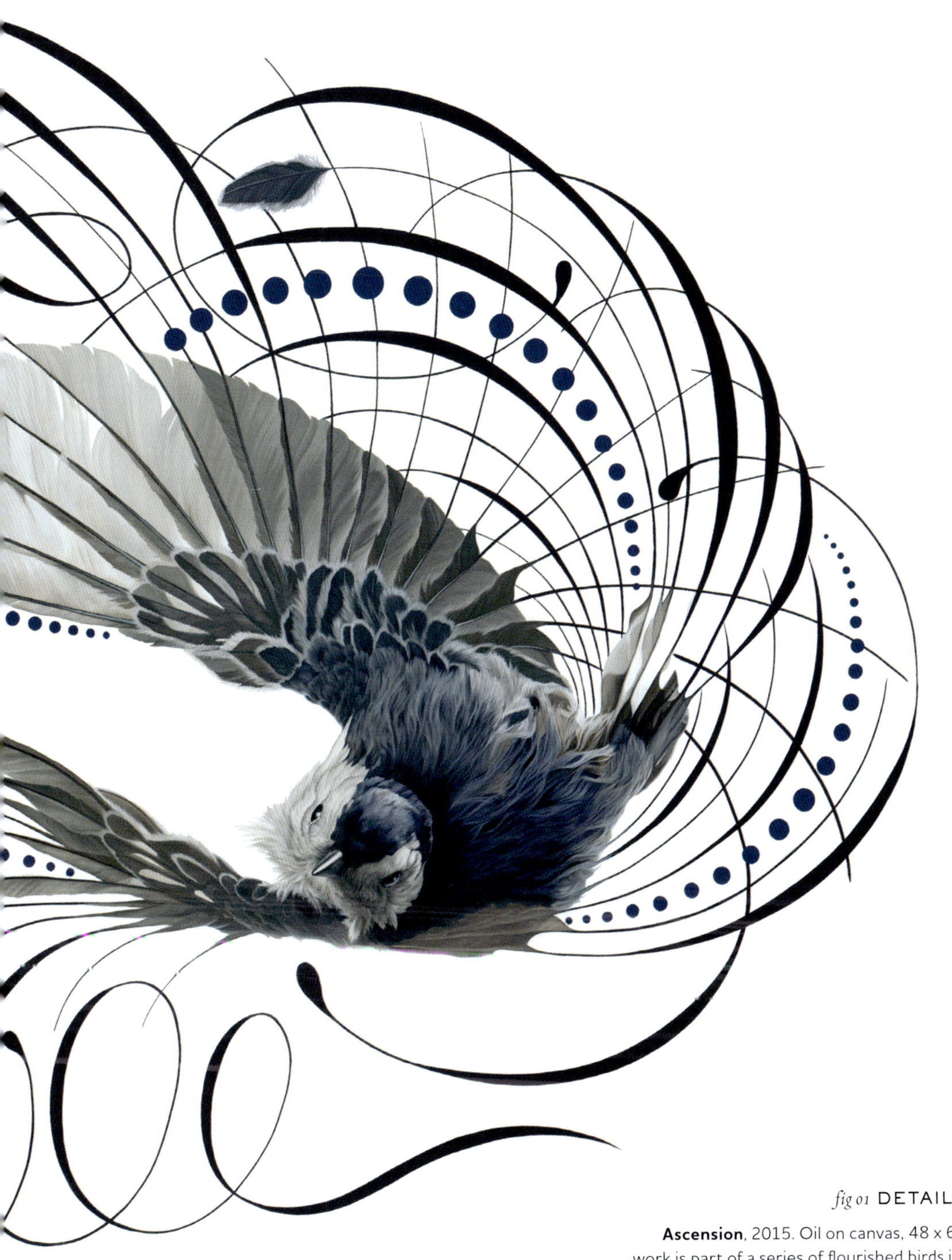

fig 01 DETAIL OF WORK

Ascension, 2015. Oil on canvas, 48 x 66 inches. This work is part of a series of flourished birds in Weidmann's signature style—emphasizing the value and beauty of life as seen though God's eyes (Matthew 10:29).

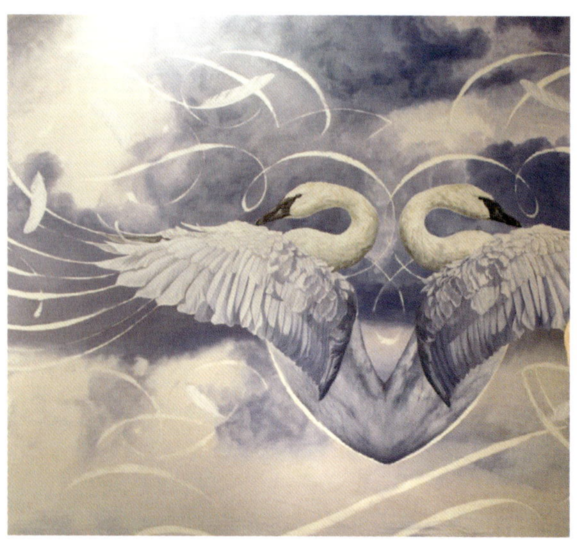

He was creating something in me. In what should have been a season marked by angst, worry, and even fear, He gave me hope.

Is there something in your life that feels as if it's been turned to ash? Perhaps it's something that you cherish, a place where you have felt most at home. Loss is hard. It can feel devastating. But it does not need to feel hopeless. I pray this story of God's provision brings you hope, that you would see the evidence of His purposes even in the midst of loss. After all, Scripture says, "God works all things together for good for the ones who love God, for those who are called according to his purpose" (Romans 8:28 CEB). You may not see it now, but you *will* see, as you look back on this season, that He is working in you as He worked in me—creating something new.

This "new" may be a new spiritual fruit, a new capacity for patience or long-suffering, new humility, new wisdom, new joy. You may feel like

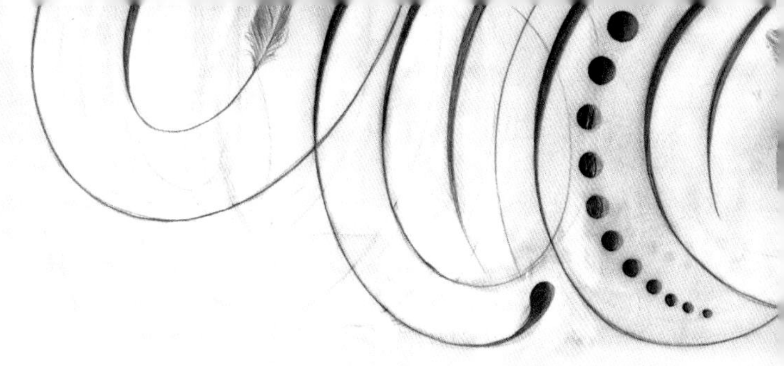

the same old you, but make no mistake: God is making something new in you, bit by bit, till at length you are an entirely new creation in Christ.

Looking Heavenward

Out of the ashes, I took my first artistic flight. Perhaps not quite as grand as a phoenix, exactly, but I was on my way—thanks in no small part to that delightful little parrot with an elastic band for feet. To this day, birds continue to make a regular appearance in my work. I even fancy myself something of an ornithologist. Hannah and I often joke that I have all the makings of a bird-watcher when I get old—complete with brimmed hat and pocketed vest. We certainly live in the right place; the foothills of the Colorado Rockies are a bird-watcher's paradise!

I often race to our back deck with binoculars in hand when I catch a glimpse of a bald eagle through one of our western-facing windows or hear the calls of red-tails or ospreys. In the spring, I await the arrival of swallows, who nest in the eaves of our entryway, and listen for the song of the western meadowlark. These brown-speckled birds with bright yellow breasts are no larger than a robin, which makes them difficult to spot even as their enchanting melody resonates throughout the surrounding hills. These remarkable feathered friends—these gifts of a good Creator—are a wonder to behold. Yet they also offer an illustration of the twofold hope that has grown in me as an artist since that fabled day—a hope to resonate and a hope to transcend.

The recognition of God's artistic call on my life was like the discovery of my very own song. And why sing if not to have that melody resonate? For the chief end of the bird's song is to communicate something of shared meaning, and so it is with my desire in creating art. Like the song of the meadowlark, an art piece for me is a bid

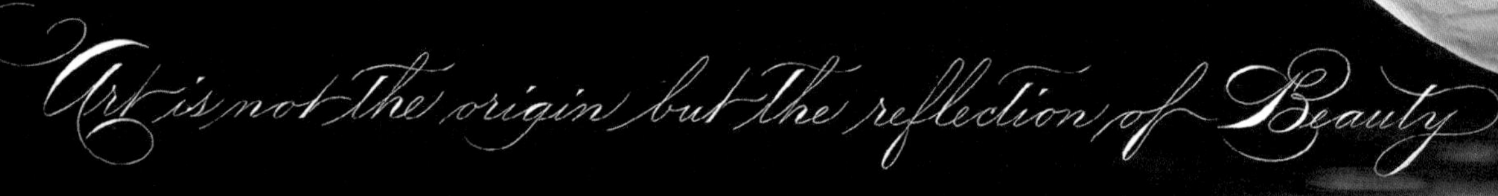

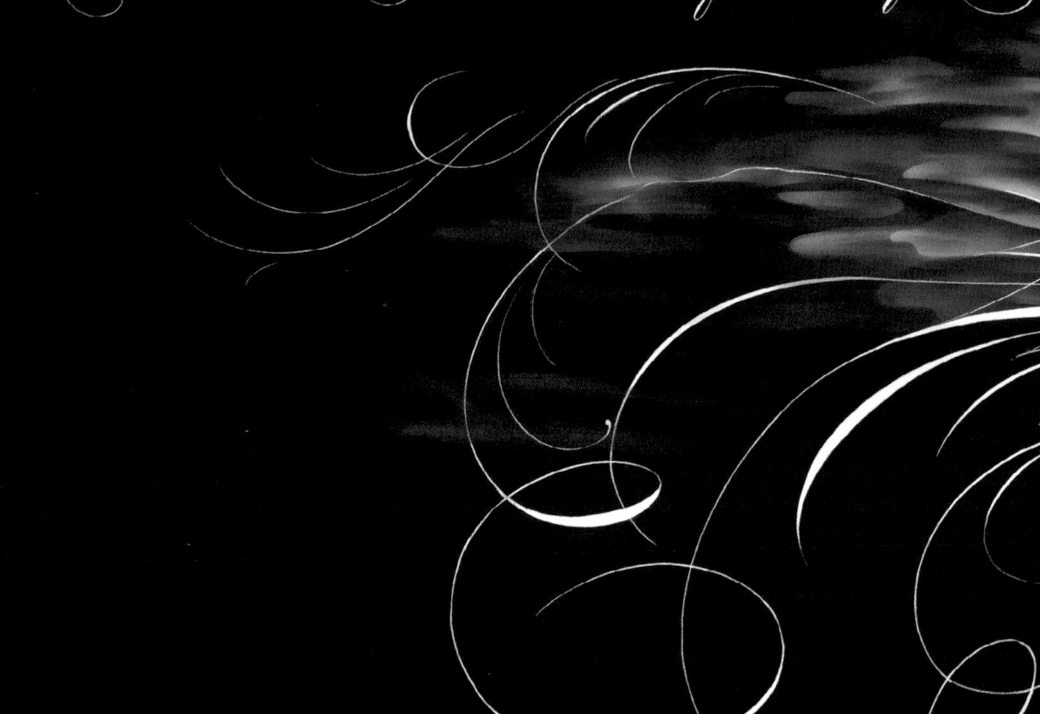

fig 02 DETAIL OF WORK

Reflected Beauty, 2019. Pastel and calligraphy on black paper, 28x40 inches. The swan itself has long been a symbol of beauty, giving life to Weidmann's truthful and poetical phrase penned in Spencerian script: "Art is not the origin but the reflection of beauty."

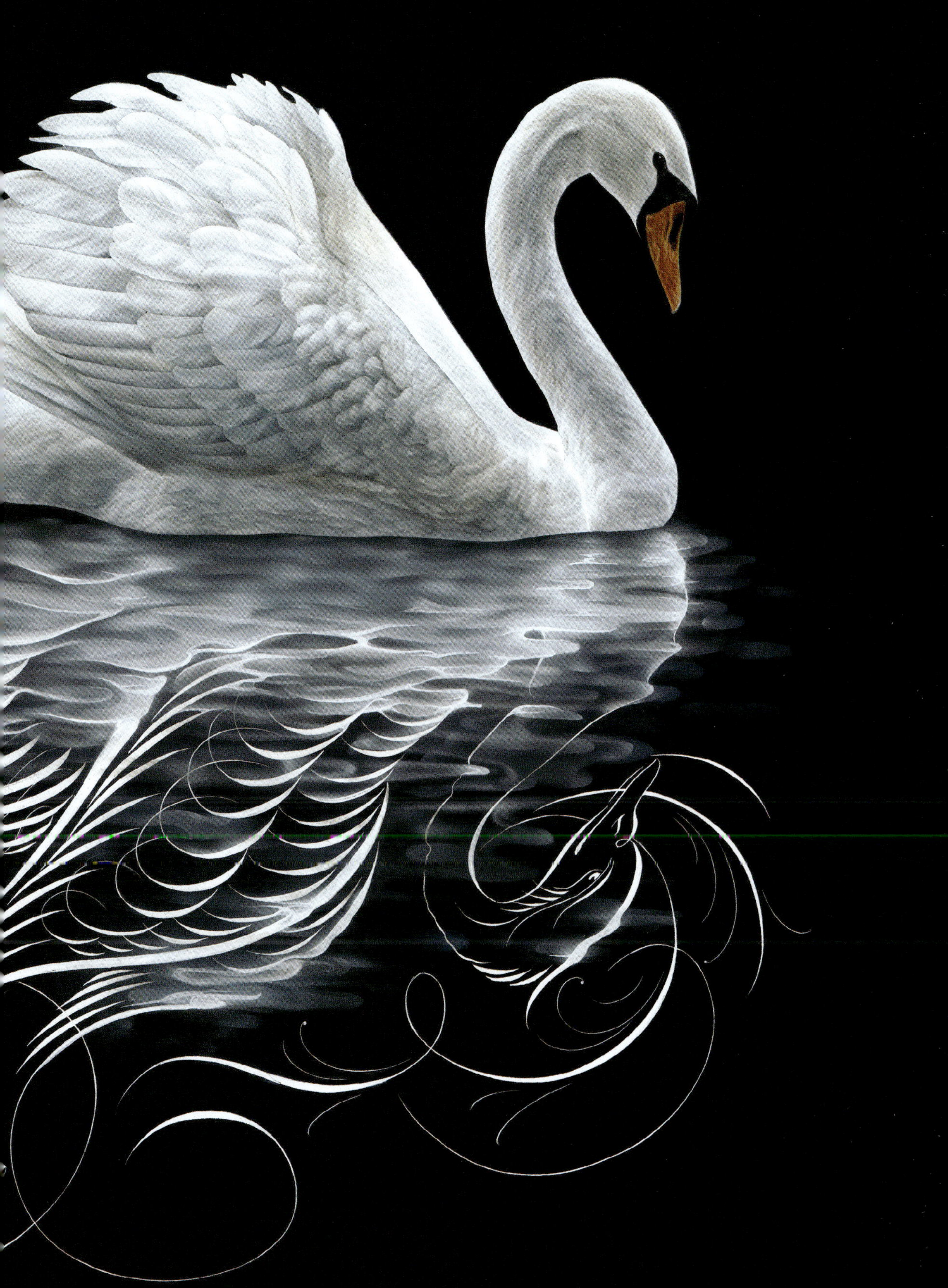

I FOUND MY HOPE NOT ONLY IN CREATION BUT ALSO IN CONNECTION.

for connection sent out far and wide to whoever may receive it. At seven years old, I was reluctant to present my drawing. But once I saw it there on the wall, a change stirred within me. I found my hope not only in creation but also in connection. I wanted my song to resound like those meadowlarks in the surrounding foothills. Indeed, I do not consider my work finished when I lay down the last stroke or even sign my name in the corner. It is only made complete when it is seen and experienced by others. And so I hope for deep and meaningful connection. I want others to pick up the melody, to bring it into harmony with their own.

As I grew beneath the boughs of a loving home—mercifully, home is so much more than brick and mortar, studs and siding, which in one spark can be turned into a tinderbox—I found ample opportunity to explore and develop my artistic voice. Mom and Dad were the perfect audience, providing a safe and encouraging space for experimentation while also providing profound spiritual guidance. No matter how long the process or difficult the execution, I wanted to make them proud. And they were only too willing to receive my next creation. Even today, my mom still cries over my work, and I cherish her every tear.

John Ruskin, the great Victorian art critic, once said, "Every noble youth looks back, as to the chiefest joy which this world's honor ever gave him, to the moment when first he saw his father's eyes flash with pride, and his mother turn away her

fig 03 DETAIL OF WORK

Immanuel, 2014. Oil on canvas, 24 x 36 inches. Jesus was born not to change history but to affect eternity. As Christ entered into this dark world two thousand years ago, so the Spirit enters our hearts today to bring His light and flourish through us.

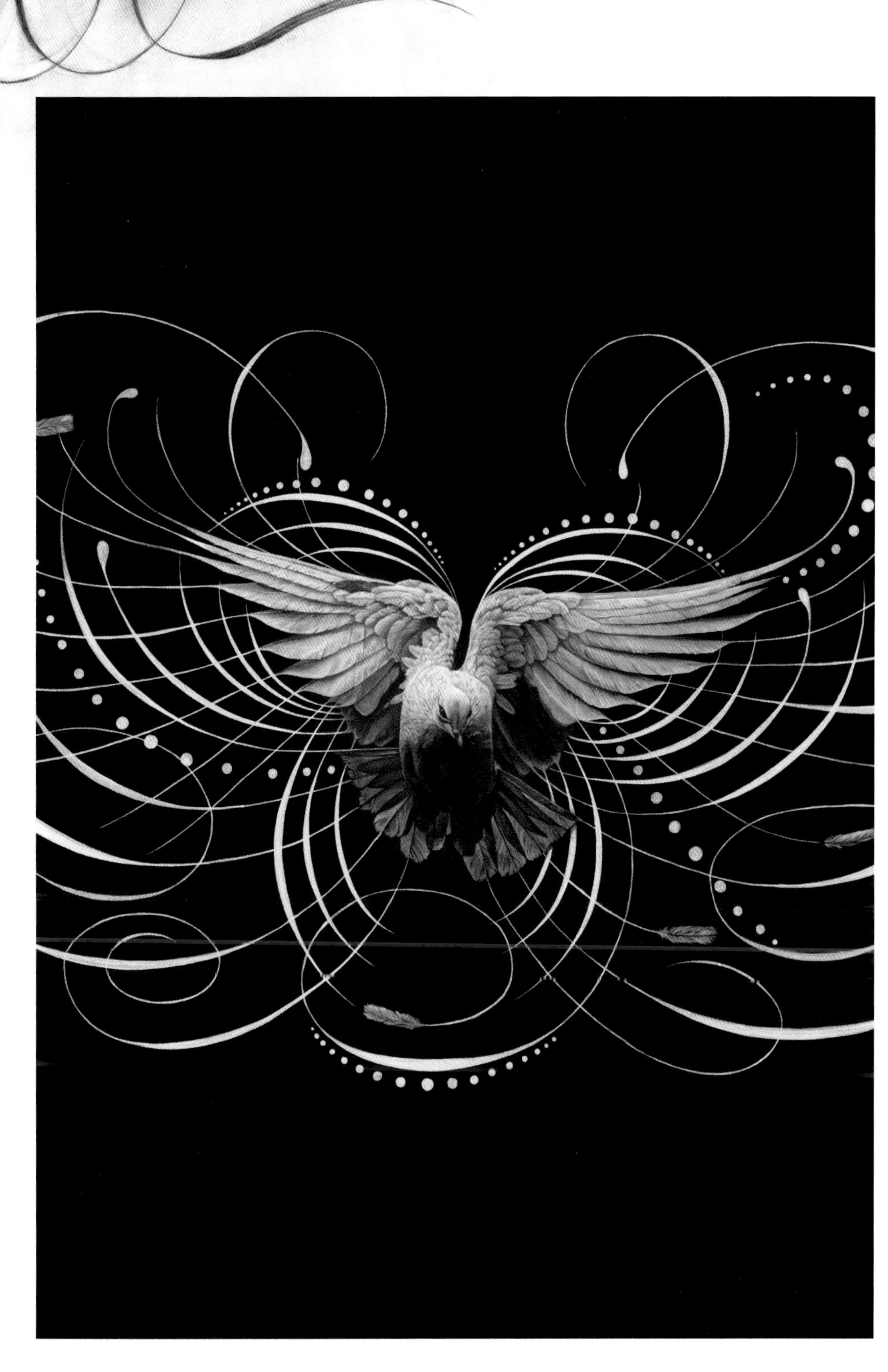

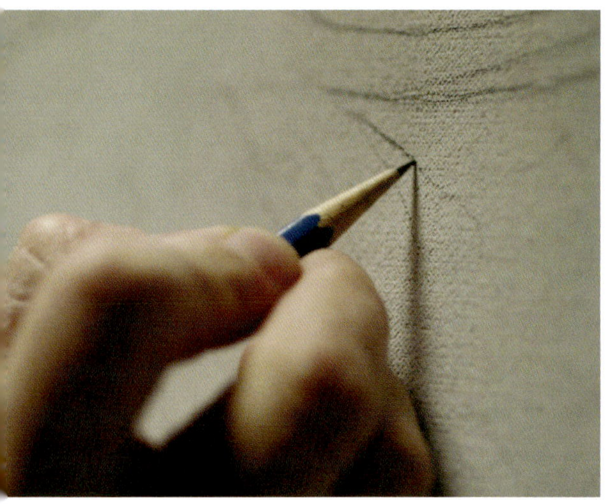

head, lest he should take her tears for tears of sorrow."[1] And though Mom and Dad were not quite so Victorian as all that, they always gave similarly heartfelt responses. They were present and emotionally available. This is important for any young person, particularly those who are creative, but it also revealed to me a deeper truth—one I wish to share with you. God loves and delights in the creative work of your hands. How could He do otherwise? Consider the world He created and filled to the brim with such awe-inspiring beauty. You are a son or daughter made in His image. So let's hope together in resounding not only here on earth but also in heaven. Indeed, who could hope for more?

Like the meadowlark, let our voices resonate. But let's not stop there. Let's also take flight! Let us hope for transcendence! When I create, I aim not only to connect but also to lift others up, to draw them out of their everyday experiences to a higher place. I recognize this might sound audacious, but I believe many of us know what it is to be elevated by a piece of art or music. Whether alone or in a crowd, we find our spirits rise within us. Heaven feels close enough to touch. I do not know how or why. But I nevertheless hope my work inspires that same connection with others—to be a means of transcendence.

I also hope that I would experience that same transcendence as I work. There have been moments in my studio—my tabernacle—when I have felt the Lord's

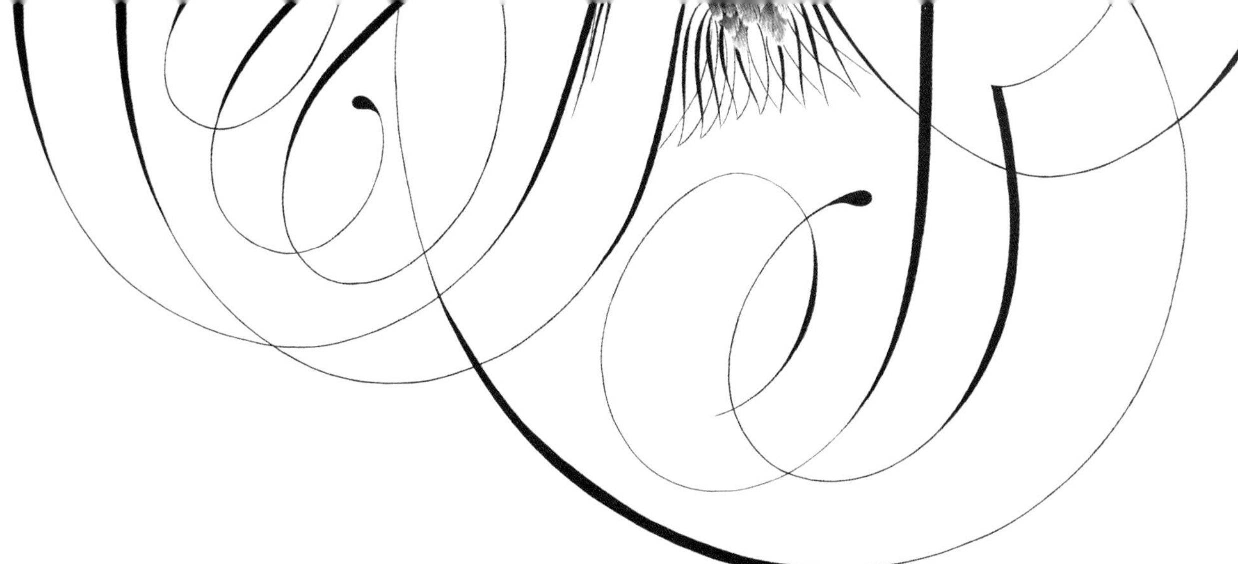

presence. I have sensed Him lend His creativity to mine and, like an osprey whose wings catch an updraft, I have been the one lifted up. Again, I cannot explain it. And I certainly can't take credit for it. But I long for this transcendence all the same. I pray that you do as well. For our God does not stand aside but draws close to us as we draw near to Him (James 4:8). So as you create, be sure to welcome your Creator's inspiring and uplifting presence. Do not be surprised if He joins you.

My hope for transcendence is thus about *encounter* and not *escape*. In fact, it's about seeking more of God and His goodness in the here and now. After all, didn't God look at all He had created and proclaim it *very good* (Genesis 1:31)? So then, when you create, let your pursuit of God make you *more* rather than *less* present to the glories of His creation. As C. S. Lewis beckoned in *The Last Battle*, "Come further up, come further in!"[2] Delve into the depths of God's goodness as you attend to each small and exquisite detail. For my part, I practice this hope each time I flourish a peacock's plumage or trace a swan's wing tips with my brush. Even though I did not yet know it, I did the same when I first sketched that humble parrot in Mrs. K.'s classroom, doing all I could to faithfully represent each detail of that gracious gift from God.

Of course, I had no idea what awaited me when I first chose to pick up that pencil. Never could I have imagined that such an apparently insignificant act would change my life in such remarkable ways. But what started as little more than an expression of childhood pain became, through God's goodness, an unexpected source of hope: my calling as an artist.

And so begins my story as an artist. These are the opening melodies of my song. God has given you your own. Your creativity may look different from mine, but you are still formed in the image of the same Creator. And just as He saw me, He sees you. Just as He worked within me, He works within you—making a *new* creation. If you feel like hope is in short supply, I want you to know, from the very depths of my heart, that He has not, and will never, turn His face from you. The many fires of this life might turn so much of what you treasure into ash, but He has the power to bring hope out of the depths of despair. And when such hope is alive in you, stand assured that others will take notice. As it says in 1 Peter 3:15, "Always [be] prepared to make a defense to anyone who asks you for a reason for the hope that is in you; yet do it with gentleness and respect." For me, art is the perfect medium for just such a ready defense. Art is not hope itself but the proclamation thereof that resonates throughout hills and valleys and even unto heaven.

fig 04 DETAIL OF WORK

Fidelity Bound, 2017. Oil on canvas, 66 x 96 inches. Swans, known for their fierce fidelity, are positioned here in their protective stance at one another's back. In Weidmann's widely recognized and acclaimed style, his largest oil painting to date displays two trumpeter swans bound to one another in their flourishes.

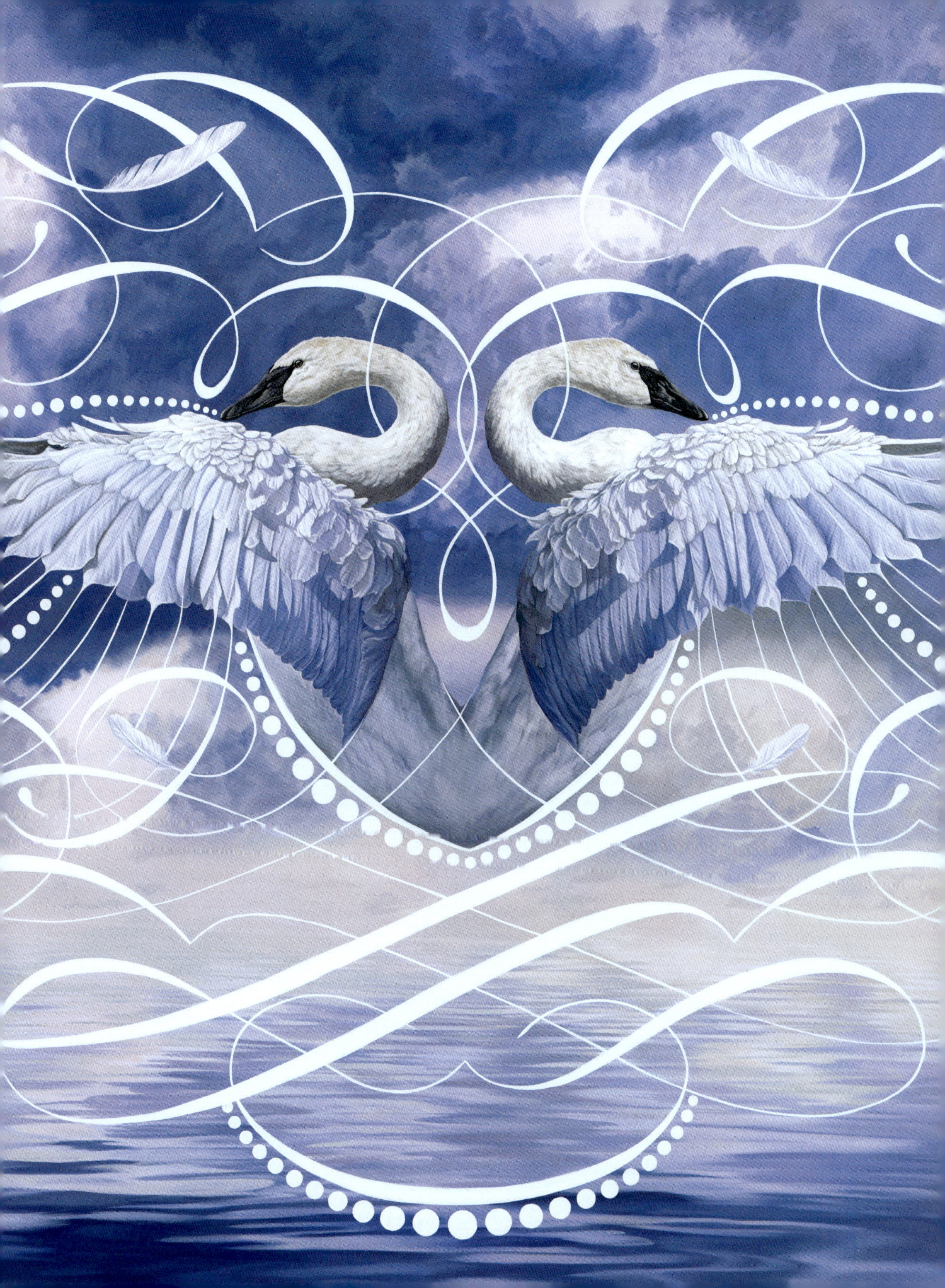

CHAPTER TWO

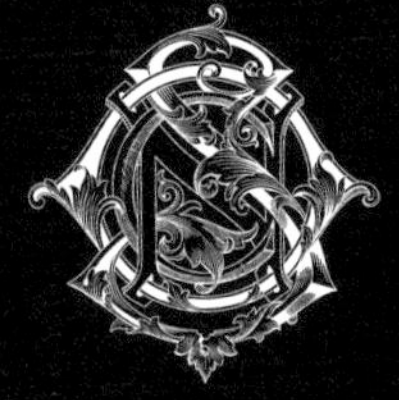

JOYFUL *Perseverance*

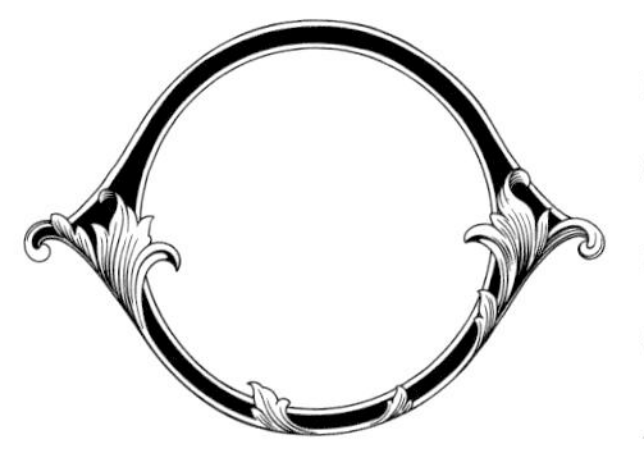ne might think my sense of calling as an artist would have only increased in the years following Mrs. K.'s validation. And in some respects, it did. As I grew from childhood into young adulthood, art continued to play an important role in my life. Despite not taking formal classes, I continued to challenge myself with increasingly difficult subjects, which required progressively higher levels of proficiency. In fact, by the time I got to high school, I had received many scholastic awards and had gained a reputation as one of the best artists in school.

On one occasion while I was in geometry class, a student walked in with a note and handed it to the teacher, who called my name with a grave look on her face. "I have no idea what you did," she said sternly, "but this comes straight from the top. You have to go see the principal right away!" I was a good kid and never did anything remotely rebellious. I was also the nervous sort, so I figured there must be some indiscretion I could not recall but was most assuredly guilty of. So I made my way to the office in a flurry of anxiety and confusion.

The secretary informed me that the principal was waiting. Trembling, I walked into Mr. Booth's office, headquartered in the center of the sprawling public school. His walls were neatly decorated with framed pictures featuring him alongside old students, photos of faculty hung salon-style around his desk, Arapahoe Warrior pennants, and other memorabilia. Mr. Booth stood from behind his stately desk and came toward me with a big smile on his face and his hand outstretched. He shook my hand firmly and apologized for pulling me out of class. I was a bit confused by his candor. I did not let myself feel relief quite yet, as I was still waiting for the hammer to fall. He then explained he was working on a book and wondered if I would illustrate it for him. *This can't be real!* I thought. We talked about the details of the book and the terms of the commission through the rest of that period and into the next—not as student and principal but as artist and patron. He then wrote me a note excusing my tardiness for the next class and thanked me for my time.

I don't know if Mr. Booth ever did end up publishing his book, but we worked back and forth on the cover design for several weeks and he paid me for my time. He continued to champion my work for the rest of my years in high school and beyond.

Now, you might well imagine the favor and accolades I received would have only confirmed in me what everyone else—including Mr. Booth—could see. But it didn't. I just couldn't, or wouldn't, be convinced. Sure, I recognized that my work brought me hope, blessed others, and drew me closer to God, but I simply couldn't believe that I could ever be a "real artist." Art, according to the limits of my understanding, would always have to remain something on the side. A passion? Yes. A vocation? Hardly.

And that's partly why, following graduation, I pursued a bachelor's degree in psychology at Biola. "Clinical psychologist" simply sounded more serious on paper than "artist." And in any case, I've always been fascinated by people, the inner workings of the brain, the dynamics of emotion, and interpersonal relationships. That doesn't mean I was completely immune to scratching my artistic itch. At one point I did explore the idea of taking a semester abroad in Florence; it just didn't come to pass.

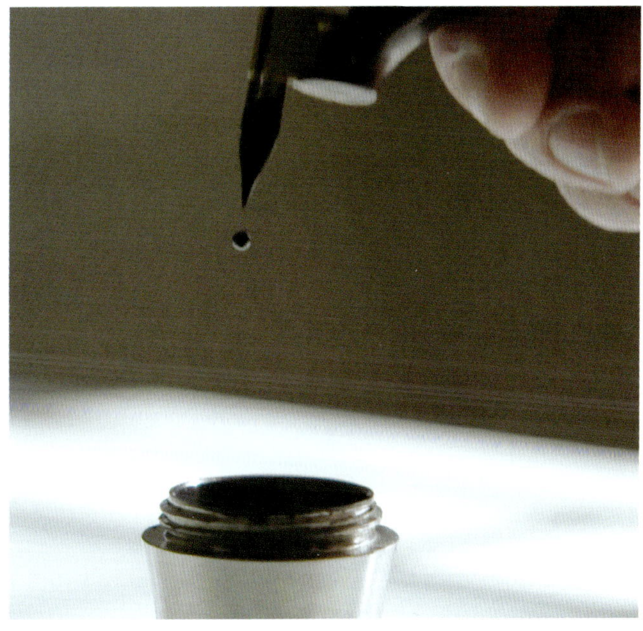

Still, the itch didn't go away. As my studies in psychology progressed, I came across the discipline of art therapy. Here, I thought, was a way to feed both passions. Even better, art therapy graduate programs require an art degree. It was as if I could have my cake and eat it too. I could make art and still not be "an artist." And so I assembled a portfolio of my best work, compiled a list of awards I had accumulated over the years, and set up an appointment with the chair of the art department. Who knows what formal training would add to this self-taught artist? I could scarcely imagine, but I couldn't wait to find out.

The day of the interview arrived at last. I strode across the Biola campus in the California sunshine with the sweet scent of tropical flowers filling the air, my portfolio under my arm and a pep in my step. I arrived a respectful five minutes early. At length, the door adjacent to the reception desk opened and the professor welcomed me inside. As I entered his office, I introduced myself and looked for a spot on his cluttered desk to set down my portfolio.

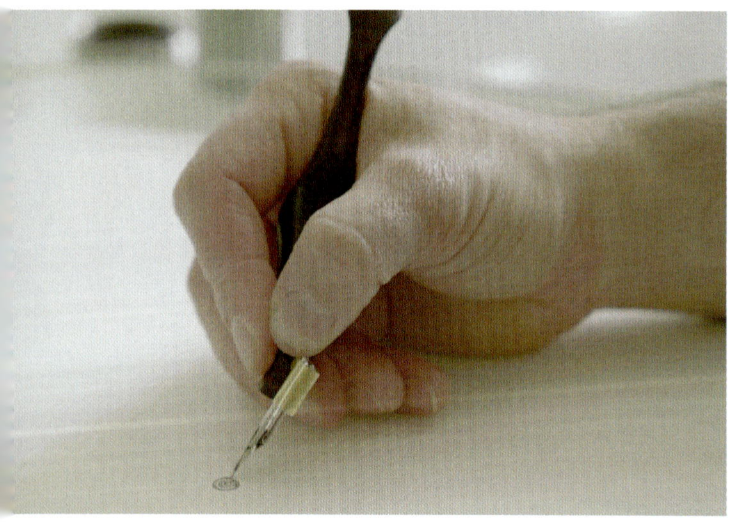

The office smelled a bit musty. Worn-edged bookshelves along the wall were cluttered with binders, old art supplies, and some of the professor's art in the assemblage style. One piece was a broken baby doll from the 1950s, secured to a scrap of barnwood with wildly wrapped red yarn, the whole thing drizzled in candle wax. Not my cup of tea, but to each his own. The professor took my portfolio and dropped it unceremoniously atop a precariously stacked pile of manila folders. I sat in the

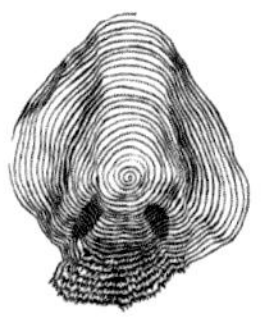

fig 05 DETAIL OF WORK

Drawing sequence of **Suffering Servant in a Single Stroke**, pen and ink. In this masterpiece, the portrait begins on the nose and gradually spirals around itself 175 times. See page 33 for final work.

tired old chair opposite and began to present both my interest in the art program and my lifelong love for art. The professor listened. Or I assumed he did, because he didn't look up. He was busy perusing my portfolio, which he had picked up once I started talking. I tried to discern his reaction and failed. I felt as though I was rambling—treading the air of awkward silence with a strained monologue.

With still some pages to go, he abruptly closed my portfolio, placed it on the tallest pile of documents stacked Jenga-style on the corner of his desk, and cut my speech short. "I'm sorry, but I just think you are wrong for our program." My heart sank. I choked out some parting words, which felt lodged in my throat. "O-okay. Thank you for your time." It was all I could say. I removed my Jenga block from his tower and walked out the door.

The rejection sent me into a spiral of dark thoughts and uncomfortable questions. Maybe I wasn't actually that good of an artist? Maybe all the praise I'd received up to that point was just a bunch of overblown niceties from people who meant well but couldn't be honest with me? All my

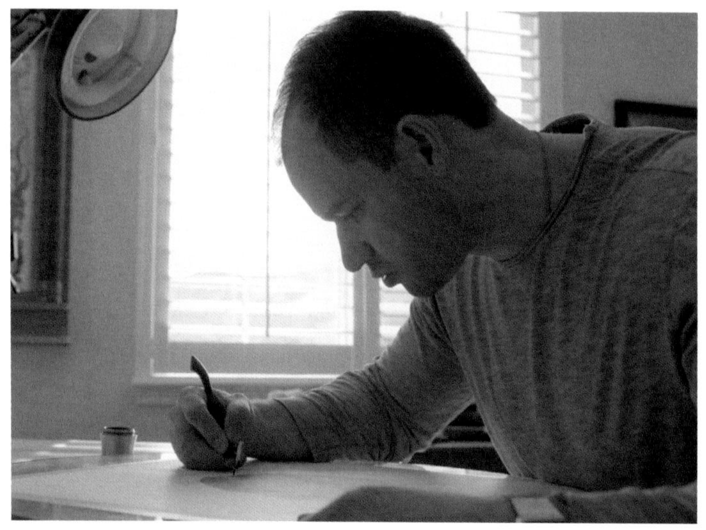

prior doubts now had solid footing and his words only confirmed those suspicions. *I knew art was a dead end. I knew I could never make it as a real artist. Who am I kidding? I'm such a fool. It's time to grow up and put this stupid, childish thing away for good.*

Do any of these questions or accusations sound familiar? Have you heard them spoken before, albeit with slightly different words? Maybe you have spoken them to yourself. Rejection is difficult with respect to anything in our lives, but when it comes to what we love, what we hold so close to *who we are*, it can bring us to our knees, as if we're collapsing from the inside out. I share this story not so you will pity me but to show you that I've been there. As I hope you can see, my journey hasn't consisted only of doting parents, encouraging teachers, and various accolades. There have been times, like right there in that office, when I really, sincerely wanted to give up. But here's the truth—when you have something that's important to you, something you feel God has placed on your heart, the pain of that rejection should tell you at least one thing: *Your calling is real.* Hold on.

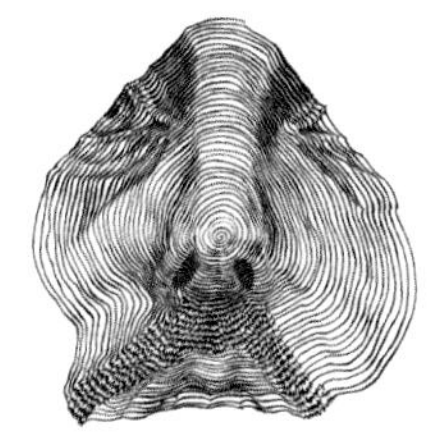

It is worth fighting for. And by all means, persevere. Who can take away the calling God has put on your life (Romans 11:29)?

Sober-minded, if still a little stung, I stayed the course on my psychology degree. And all the while I continued to receive art commissions. Only, in this season, they felt like manna in the wilderness. I found work for some clothing companies around LA and even carved some moose antler necklaces for an eccentric boutique in West Hollywood. My art career was far from glamorous, but I enjoyed the challenge of making something that would be suitable for sale. In some ways each project felt like validation in the wake of my rejection. It even felt more serious than student work. I spoke to some of my friends who *did* get into the art therapy program, and they were bewildered with some of the strange assignments their professors were giving them. *Painting in applesauce . . . really?* I could not fully grasp it then, but I had a sneaking suspicion that the rejection had in fact been God's protection. He was still working, still creating in me.

And then another commission arose, this time from a professor in another department, with whom I had met and shared my work. He asked me to carve two family crests from his mother's and father's lineage into a full-size set of moose antlers and align the meaning of their heraldic symbols with the Old and New Testaments of the Bible. The job was as crazy as it sounds, and my reaction was probably similar to what yours is now. But he promised to pay me handsomely—more than what I would have

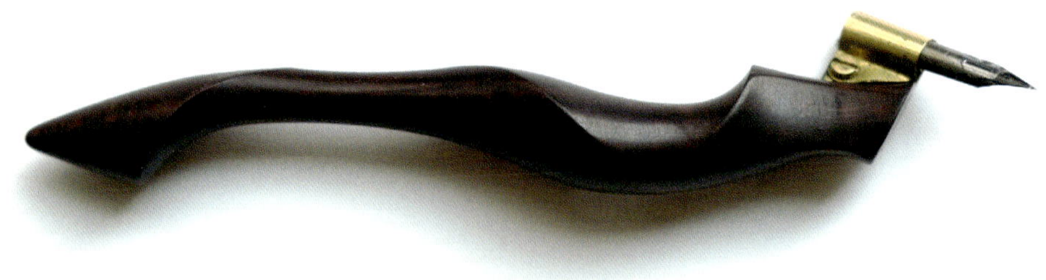

NECESSITY HELD ME TO THE GRINDSTONE WHEN THE GRINDSTONE WAS EXACTLY WHERE I WANTED TO BE.

dreamed to ask for at the time—so of course I agreed.

For an entire semester, I spent nearly all my free time carving moose antlers on the common patio of my on-campus apartment. Talk about perseverance. Moose antler is the hardest bone in the world and requires slow carving with carbide steel burs. For months on end my Dremel tool screeched as I carved away beneath the hot California sun, wearing a respirator to keep the dust out of my lungs. When you carve antler in this way it creates a particularly foul smell—not unlike burning hair. I would often give a friendly wave to the fellow occupants of the apartment building as they passed by, but most held their noses and quickened their pace. Other than the smell, the project was a good one, an opportunity to grow. And miserable as it may sound, I had an absolute blast! But it still felt like a flash in the pan; best to carry on with the psychology degree. And so I closed the chapter on higher education without a lick of formal art training.

Perhaps you know what it's like to be fresh out of college with a head full of books and not a penny in your pocket. I certainly do! Did I mention the economic

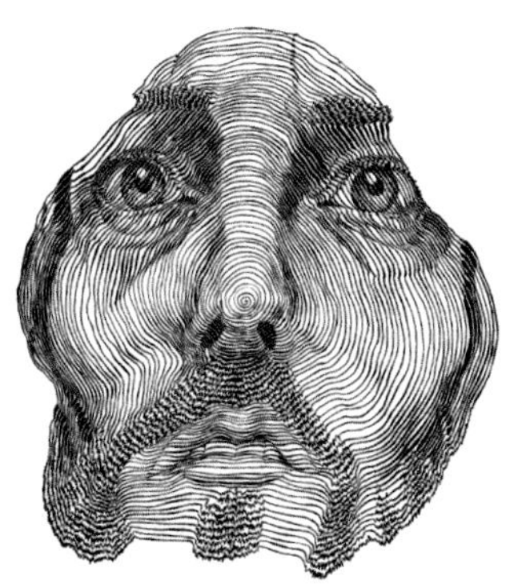

recession? I tried but couldn't find a place to live, so—to my deep and abiding shame—I went back to live with Mom and Dad. I also couldn't find a real "grown-up" job with a salary and benefits, which I was assured my degree would get me. But the art commissions continued, and these helped make ends meet. It was almost as if God was trying to tell me something. But how long would it be before I listened?

I set up shop in the far corner of my parents' basement on a small drafting table I'd had since I was a kid and said yes to everything that came my way. No matter how small or how far outside my skill set, if someone was willing to pay me to create something and I didn't know how, I would just bluff and tell them I could, and then figure it out along the way. This wasn't a very profitable (or particularly honest) approach, given how much time it took me to learn whatever it was I was supposed to execute, be it a mural or a wedding invitation. But what I lost in time and money, I gained in experience and skill. I also found I loved the furious pace of creation regardless of the medium. Necessity held me to the grindstone when the grindstone was exactly where I wanted to be.

As I look back at this season, I can see God's creative work within me. Although I had all but given up on art as a vocation following my rejection, God used these commissions to build my perseverance. In a sense, I didn't have a choice. I really didn't have anything else to turn to. And so I kept pushing and kept growing. I continued to say an enthusiastic yes even when my tired eyes and heavy hands would

AND SO I LAID DOWN THE FORGIVING PENCIL AND PICKED UP THE EVERLASTING PEN.

have easily accepted no. However, it was not a grim perseverance; it was filled with joy—*His* joy.

How could this be? you might wonder. Because I sought God in my work. And so I grew to depend on Him more and more. As hectic and hard as it was for me to meet one deadline after the next, to learn ever more complicated disciplines, He was there with me, surrounding me, and encouraging me to continue. And I felt His joy until it became my own. In fact, the harder the project, the better; the greater the trial, the greater the reward. I rejoiced with my Father at every victory. We were doing this together.

How many stop dead in their tracks when they cannot see the way? How many give up when the odds seem insurmountable and their dreams seem to vanish into thin air? But for the grace of God that would have been me. During that season, as I invited my Creator into my creativity, He prepared me to fulfill His calling. I learned to persevere. I learned to face hardship for the joy set before me. I grew to seek His presence in everything I did—even and especially in the hardest moments, in the times of great suffering.

There is one drawing that best exemplifies this formative time of my life: *Suffering Servant in a Single Stroke*. It was inspired by a print of an

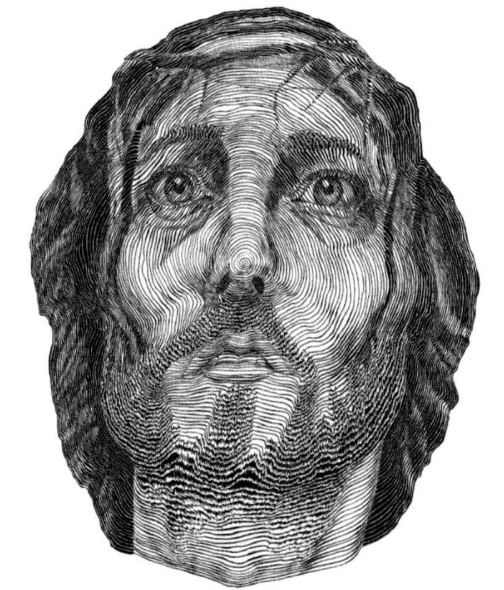

engraving I found in an old book, wherein Christ's face had been drawn in a single continuous line. That image, hundreds of years old, captured my imagination.

Almost immediately, I began deconstructing the process in my head, imagining how I might execute it with my calligraphy pen. I took some time to do preliminary sketches to determine the position and expression I was searching for. But preparation can only take you so far; eventually the hard work must begin.

And so I laid down the forgiving pencil and picked up the everlasting pen. From the initial plunge of the nib into the inkwell, I could feel my senses sharpen. The creative stakes had been raised. Placing my nib in the center of the page, I began making a light spiral with the pen in my right hand while slowly and incrementally turning the paper with my left. I had drawn a light sketch of Jesus' face, so I knew where one feature ended and another began along my spiraling journey. While contouring the face in a singular concentric spiral, I had to be mindful of the shadowing and highlights that were created not just by the pressure of the pen but by the ratio of the line width to the corresponding negative space at any given area of the portrait. Each element had to be kept in mind simultaneously. It was like humming three different songs at once.

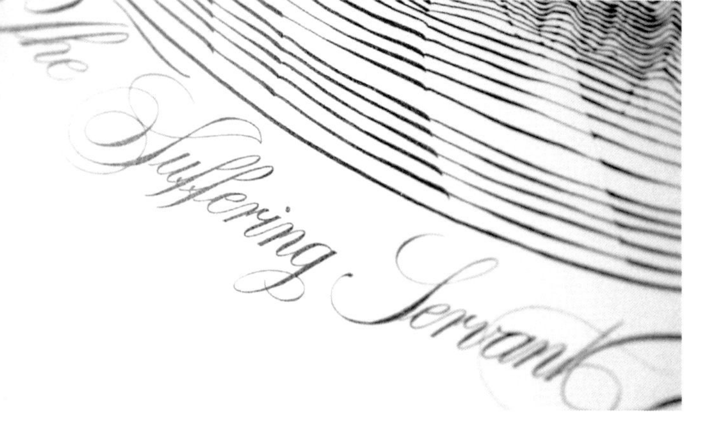

About a quarter of the way through, however, I began to wonder if I had messed up the entire thing. It was difficult to gain proper perspective. The face, partially drawn from the center outward in the middle of the page, looked odd and distorted. It was like a person emerging nose-first through the surface of a vat of milk, revealing only the center of His face out to the cheekbones, and from the eyes to the mouth. I thought about abandoning the project, but then chose to continue—that is, to persevere—if only to learn from my mistakes. But as I soldiered on, my fears gave way to joy—a combination of peace and pleasure. Joy has the uncanny ability to sustain and grow when the situation is difficult or painful. Out of the opaque, milky whiteness of the page, there emerged the face of Christ.

My momentary angst proved trivial and could easily have turned tragic had I given myself over to my anxieties and torn up that perfectly good start. Yet all was brought into its proper proportion when seen in the context of the whole. It was an important reminder: When it comes to following God's call on our lives, we often don't get to see the full picture. I wonder if we would learn even half as much on the journey if we did. His work in us, after all, is more than simply getting us from

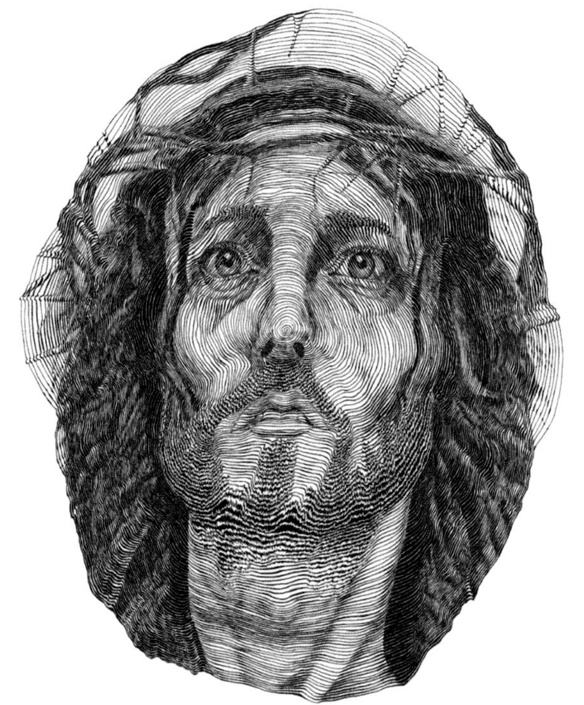

point A to point B. Our paths wind and may even seem to spiral. They may involve suffering; they will need joy. This has been the case with all my creations, but I remember it especially with this one. It remains one of my seminal works. Though it was created in the recesses of my parents' basement during one of the most trying times of my life, it is a testament to God's creative work within me. And the face of Christ remains—the one who "for the joy that was set before him endured the cross" (Hebrews 12:2).

The portrait was completed, but its story had just begun. Through a miraculous set of circumstances and relationships, I found myself in a meeting with yet another man who seemed poised to decide my fate. He was a friend of a friend who owned a financial planning firm and knew a thing or two about getting a business off the ground. This was no principal's or professor's office but a grand conference room, where I sat on one side of a fourteen-foot polished table and he on the other. I had been told he might be able to get my art career rolling, or at least get me out of my parents' basement. I can't tell you what it meant to me for this serious man to take me seriously. So I gave him my humble folio-style cardboard box, with the icon of Christ inside. He opened the flaps but didn't say a word. It didn't matter; his look of elation and wonderment spoke everything my soul longed to hear. Then he leaned in across the table, grasped my forearm, and looked straight into my eyes: "You have a profound gift, young man!" He was my first patron, and still one of my most faithful collectors, along with becoming a spiritual father figure who has been with me every step of my career since that joy-filled day.

I did not persevere without purpose. God blessed me with joy along the way. Although I could not see it or believe it, He directed my paths even as they wound and spiraled in ways that had me grasping for answers, unable to see the full picture until it was finished. Where would I have been had I entered the art therapy program? Working with applesauce?! Where would I have been without those long, smelly, bone-scraping days at college? What would I have learned without those countless hours toiling away in my parents' basement? God only knows. But this I do know for certain: He was with me each step of the way, creating in me as I created, working His artistry, turning my sorrow and suffering into joy.

Dear friend, please do not read this chapter as a story of my triumph. This is a testament to God's goodness, not only in my life but in yours. Following God's call can be difficult and confusing, but, by all means, *persevere*. Don't run from what is difficult or even painful. Trust Him to use it all for your good. He will see you through. And when you find you cannot do it in your own strength, look to His Son. May His face be revealed to you as it was revealed to me—the face of One who endured the cross for the joy set before Him.

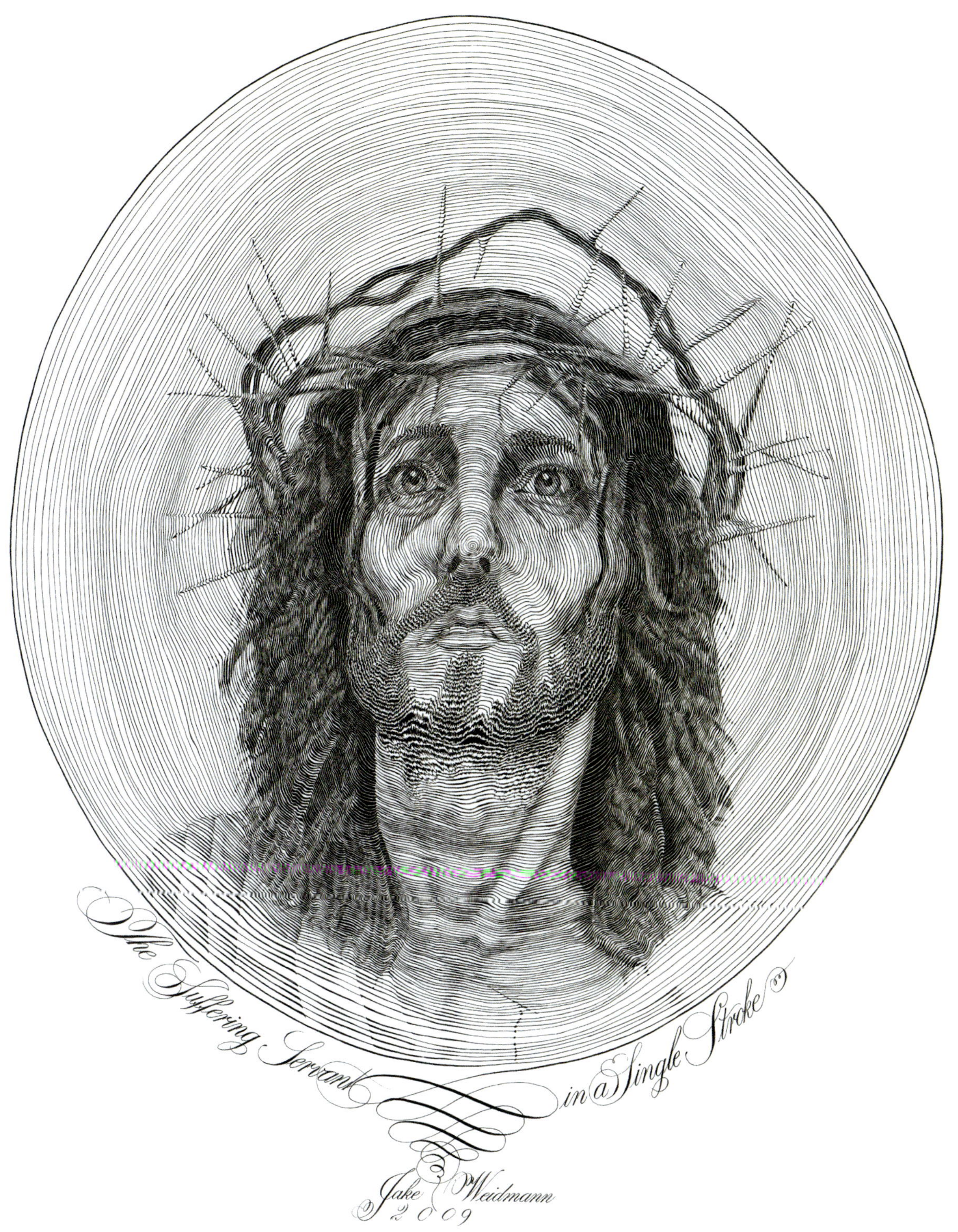
The Suffering Servant in a Single Stroke
Jake Weidmann
2009

CHAPTER THREE

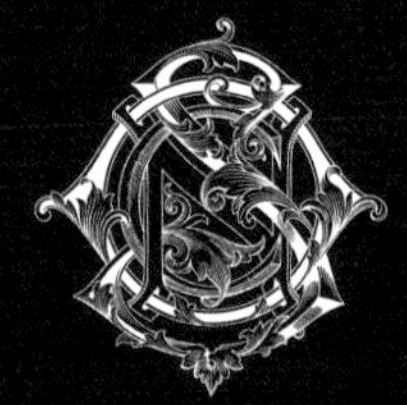

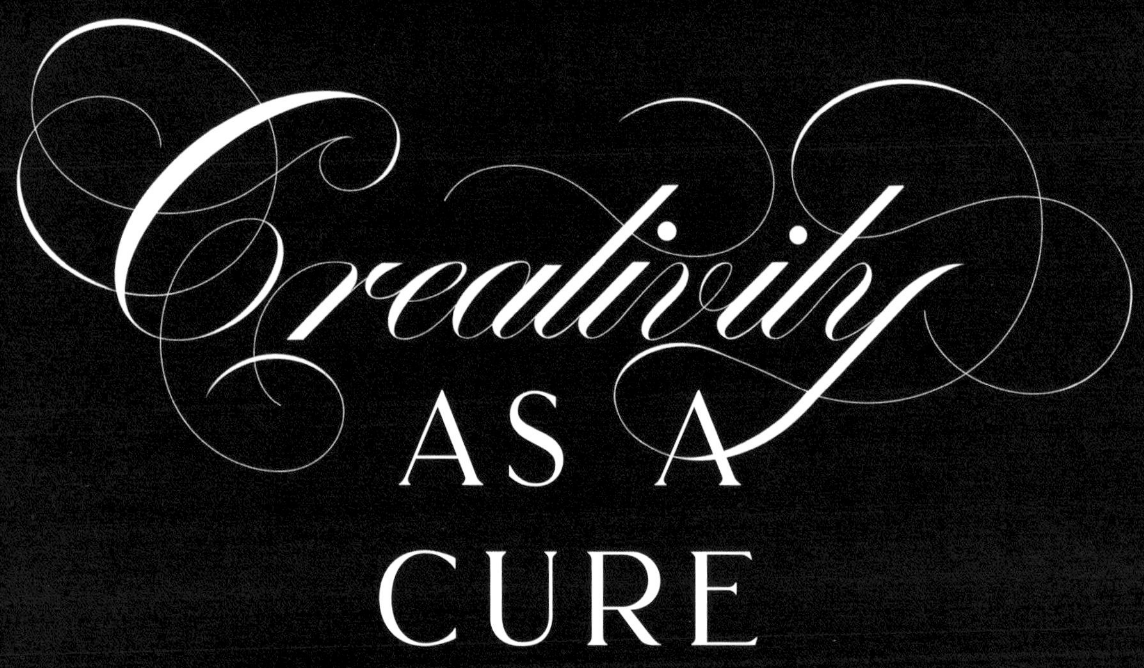

Creativity AS A CURE

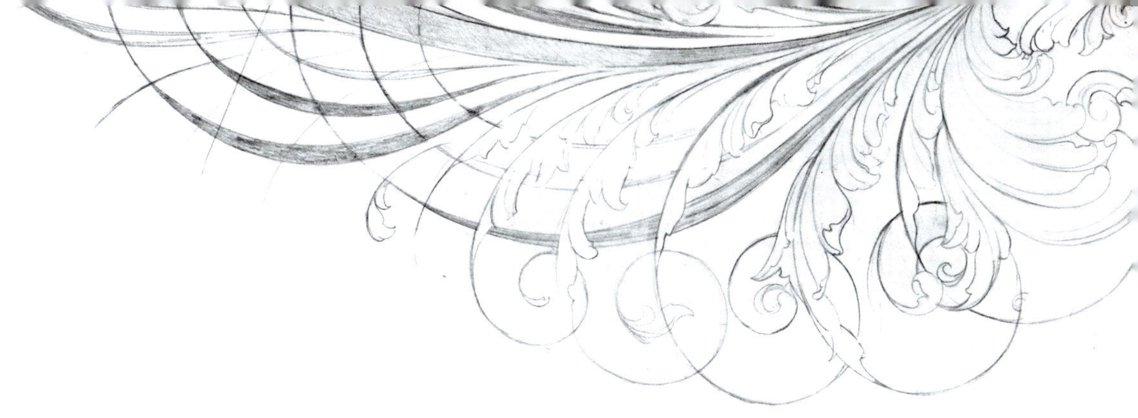

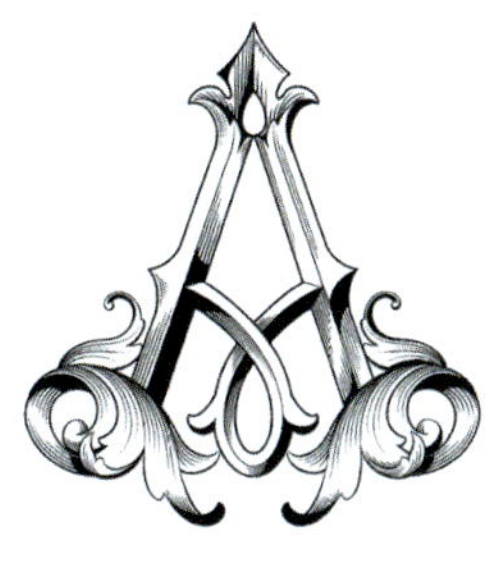

s I write this book, I have been making art professionally for more than a decade. It feels as if that fateful meeting in the conference room happened just yesterday and also a lifetime ago. I admit, however, that it has taken some time to grow into my painter's smock. Beyond the cultivation of my skill as an artist, there are the many challenges that any entrepreneur faces: What do I charge for my work? How can I become profitable? What are my vision and mission statements? How do I read a profit and loss statement? Should I register as an LLC or an S Corp? These are hardly the questions a creative usually asks themselves. Creating the infrastructure of my business, while also contending with the unique challenges of making a living from art, has been like traversing a mountain of treadmills while wearing roller skates. (It's as difficult to accomplish as it is to imagine!)

But a burden of a different kind is the array of stereotypes and stigmas that are often attached to artists by the general public—all of which I have fought to overcome. One stereotype is the "starving artist." Unfortunately, this contains more than a grain of truth. An artist's love for what they do often means they lose track of the time, labor, and skill involved. And an artist's fear of rejection often leads them to underprice their work so it won't seem inaccessible to potential buyers.

I FEEL IT IS PART AND PARCEL OF MY CALLING AS AN ARTIST TO RESTORE ART TO ITS RIGHTFUL PLACE—NAMELY, AS WORSHIP TO GOD AND COMMUNICATION TO OTHERS.

I know this love and fear all too well. On the other hand, another example is much less romantic: Artists can be arrogant. Again, unhappily, this stigma is partly justified. To guard our often-fragile egos—we are a tender sort—an artist can become condescending, perhaps making a viewer feel stupid if they don't understand or appreciate their work. This apparent lack of comprehension about an artist's merits can quickly devolve into a cynical opportunity. For example, an artist might sell blank canvases, bananas taped to walls, or golden urinals to an otherwise befuddled audience. (Yes, these are all *real* examples from the marketplace of modern art.) Any self-respecting individual is right to reject such narcissistic gamesmanship, such naked attempts to build a brand. But even a few outlandish displays are enough to shape popular opinion.

Following my calling as an artist has involved contending with these stereotypes and stigmas, along with many others besides. I feel it is part and parcel of my calling as an artist to restore art to its rightful place—namely, as worship to God and communication to others. I know that God has called me to more than the quest

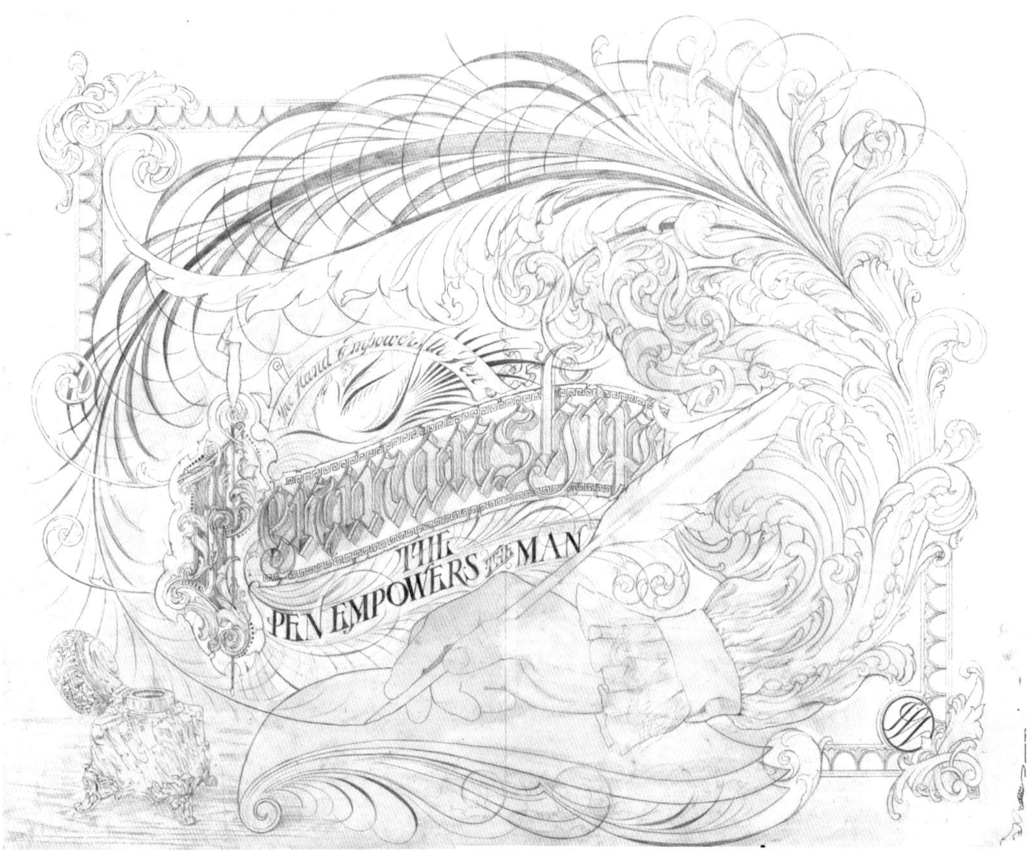

for fame or financial viability. Like He has for anyone else with any other calling, God has made me for so much more than the glorification of my own ego. But what should this vocation look like in practice? How might I create most fully in the image of my Creator? How could I be part of the cure and not contribute to the cause of all these creative ills?

I may not have answers to all these questions, but here is what I have learned so far: Embrace all that is before you, from the tiniest brushstroke to the endless spreadsheets—even the things you learned along the way that might otherwise seem incidental—and do all for His glory and purposes. Then, when receiving it back from His hand, invite the inspiration and guidance of His Spirit to help you onward. This is how I have learned to be a *Christian* artist. And what has God done with what

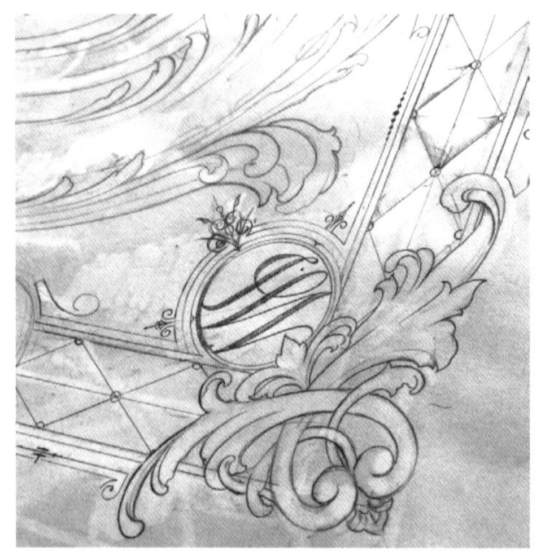

I have given? He has taken my loaves and fishes and created an almost unimaginable feast. And nowhere has this been more evident than in my handwriting.

I have always loved penmanship. Even before I could read it for myself, I admired my mom's beautiful cursive handwriting. I marveled at the way it gently leaned and danced across the page, one letter flowing gracefully into the next, as the rhythmic movement of her hand and the wave of her pen turned precious words into timeless beauty.

As I learned to write, it became a passion that always waxed and never waned. When I received my first cursive handwriting book in school, I completed a week's worth of assignments in a single evening. And so I continued to improve, mimicking whatever handwriting styles and computer fonts I encountered along the way. By the time I entered college, my cursive was ornamental in the extreme. This did, however, have the unfortunate consequence that I was always last to finish my in-class essay

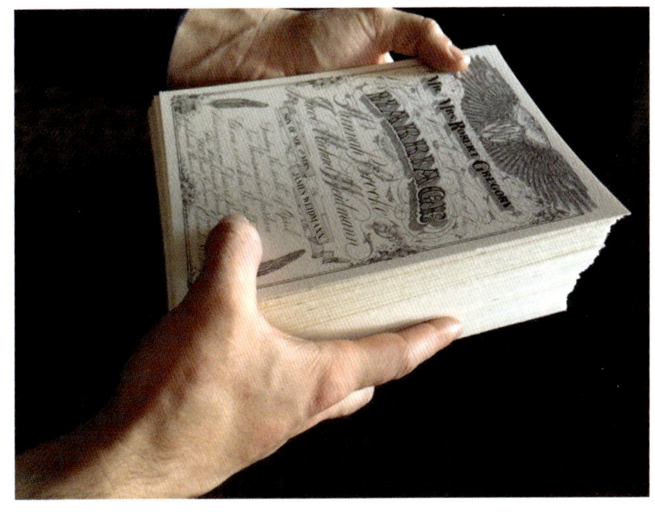

tests. It wasn't that I didn't understand the material (I promise); I was simply taking the time to write properly. On one occasion my professor asked if he could keep my essay booklet after grading it because it looked so beautiful. I should have asked for bonus points in return!

As it turned out, my penmanship was to be employed for other purposes than just class notes and exams. One day, a student sitting beside me asked if I would design her wedding invitations. She explained how she had gone through a slew of samples from wedding calligraphers, but none compared to my class notes—which she'd been surreptitiously observing all semester long. Apologetically, I told her I was not a calligrapher and only wrote with a ballpoint pen. Perhaps my reluctance was again getting the best of me. But she wouldn't take no for an answer, so I told her that I would do a bit of research and see if I could mimic some formal style.

That evening, I went back to my dorm room and scoured the internet for key calligraphy terms. I eventually stumbled upon a video of a Master Penman named John DeCollibus, who demonstrated several script styles with a dip pen.[3] I couldn't believe my eyes; it was like watching ballet on paper. My eyes began to gloss, and it would be the most useful. Surely the world could use more counselors rather than more artists? Whether or not you read that question rhetorically, it calls to mind a quote from John Eldredge's *Wild at Heart*: "Don't ask yourself what the world needs. Ask yourself what makes you come alive . . . because what the world needs is people who have come alive."[5] I was interested in psychology for lots of good reasons, but it didn't make me come alive like my art did, and certainly not like my penmanship—but that doesn't mean it was without purpose. When you surrender everything to God, He will use it all, and often in unexpected ways.

Perhaps the most important thing He salvaged from my studies was my ability to listen. There is immense power in listening well. And with the multitude of distractions that clamor for our attention these days, it is no easy task. In fact, active listening has become an art unto itself. It requires care, cultivation, and no small amount of patience. I have found it to be invaluable when working on commissions. Emotional cues are often interwoven through the words my clients use when they tell their story. Such cues can point to important values or major touchstones in their lives. So, as I listen, I carefully attend to what they say, using these cues to formulate an art piece in real time. I have come to refer to this as *artistic* listening. My clients and patrons provide all I need to create a piece that is profoundly meaningful to them; it's just a matter of having the ears to hear it.

fig 07 DETAIL OF WORK

Master Penman Certificate, 2011. Illumination on calfskin vellum set inside a hand-carved wooden frame, 29 x 45 inches. Weidmann completed his certificate in 2011 as the final test in order to become a Master Penman.

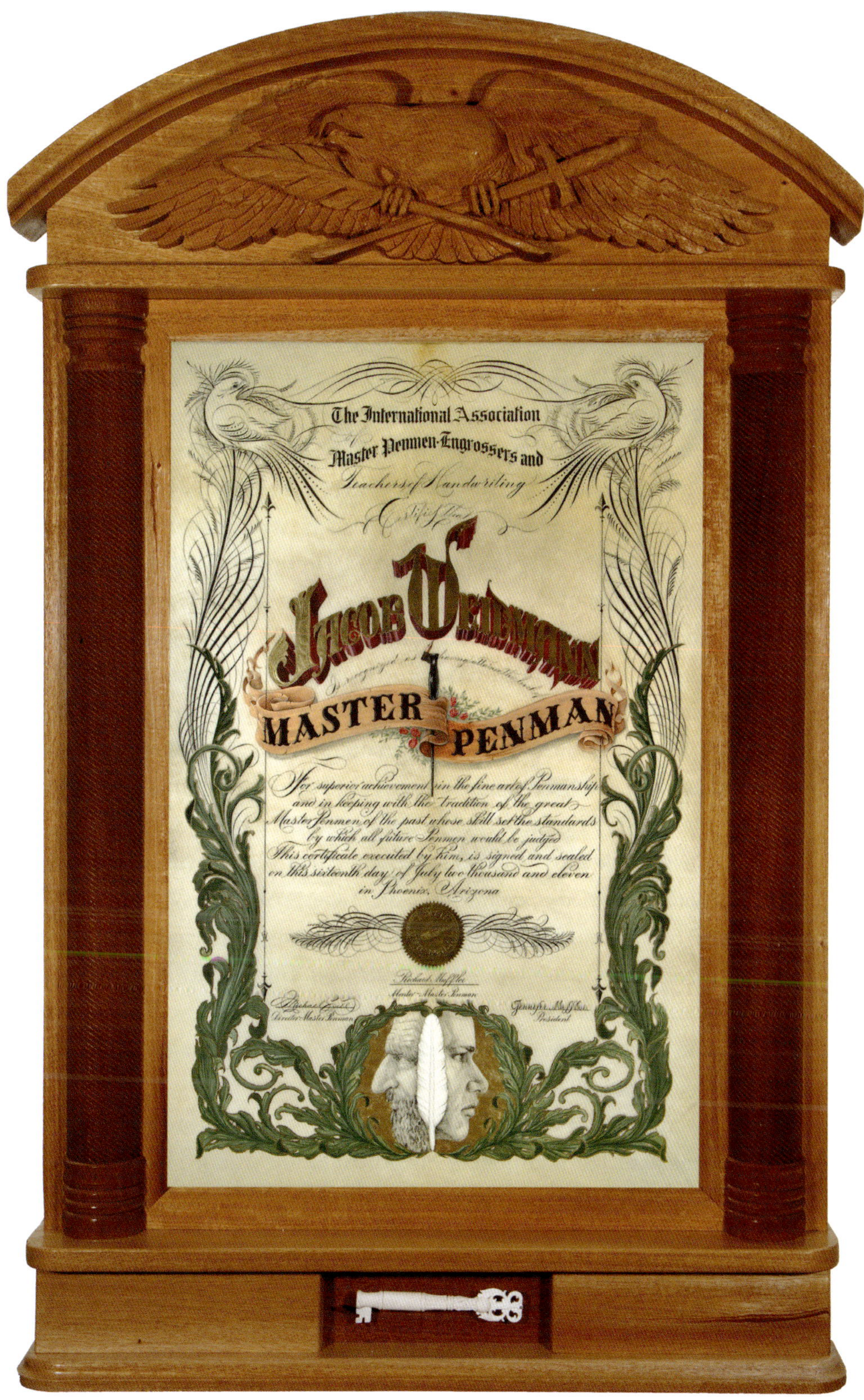
The International Association
Master Penmen-Engrossers and
Teachers of Handwriting
Jacob Weidmann
MASTER PENMAN
For superior achievement in the fine art of Penmanship
and in keeping with the tradition of the great
Master Penmen of the past whose skill set the standards
by which all future Penmen would be judged
This certificate executed by him, is signed and sealed
on this sixteenth day of July two thousand and eleven
in Phoenix, Arizona
Master Master Penman
Director Master Penman
President

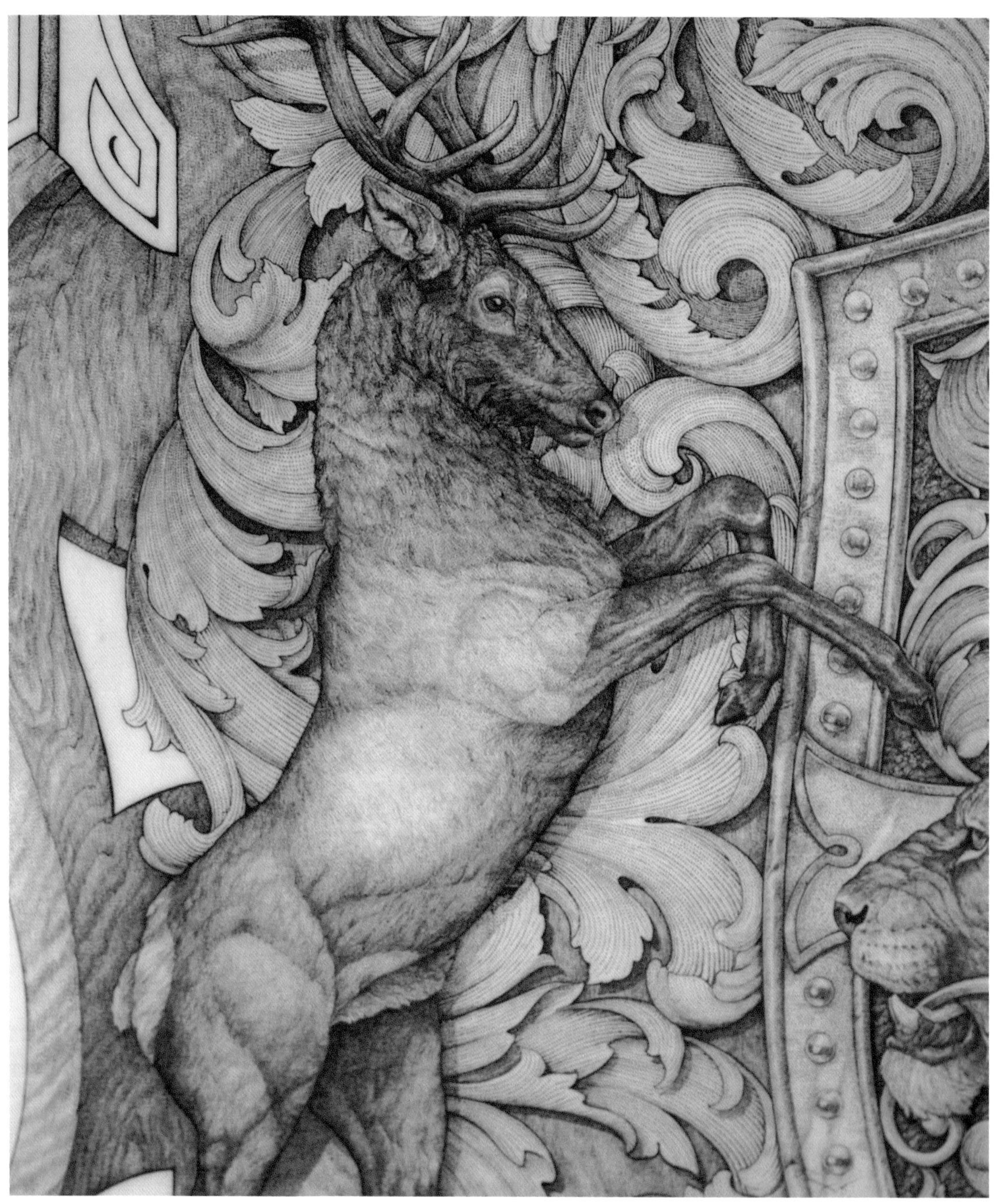

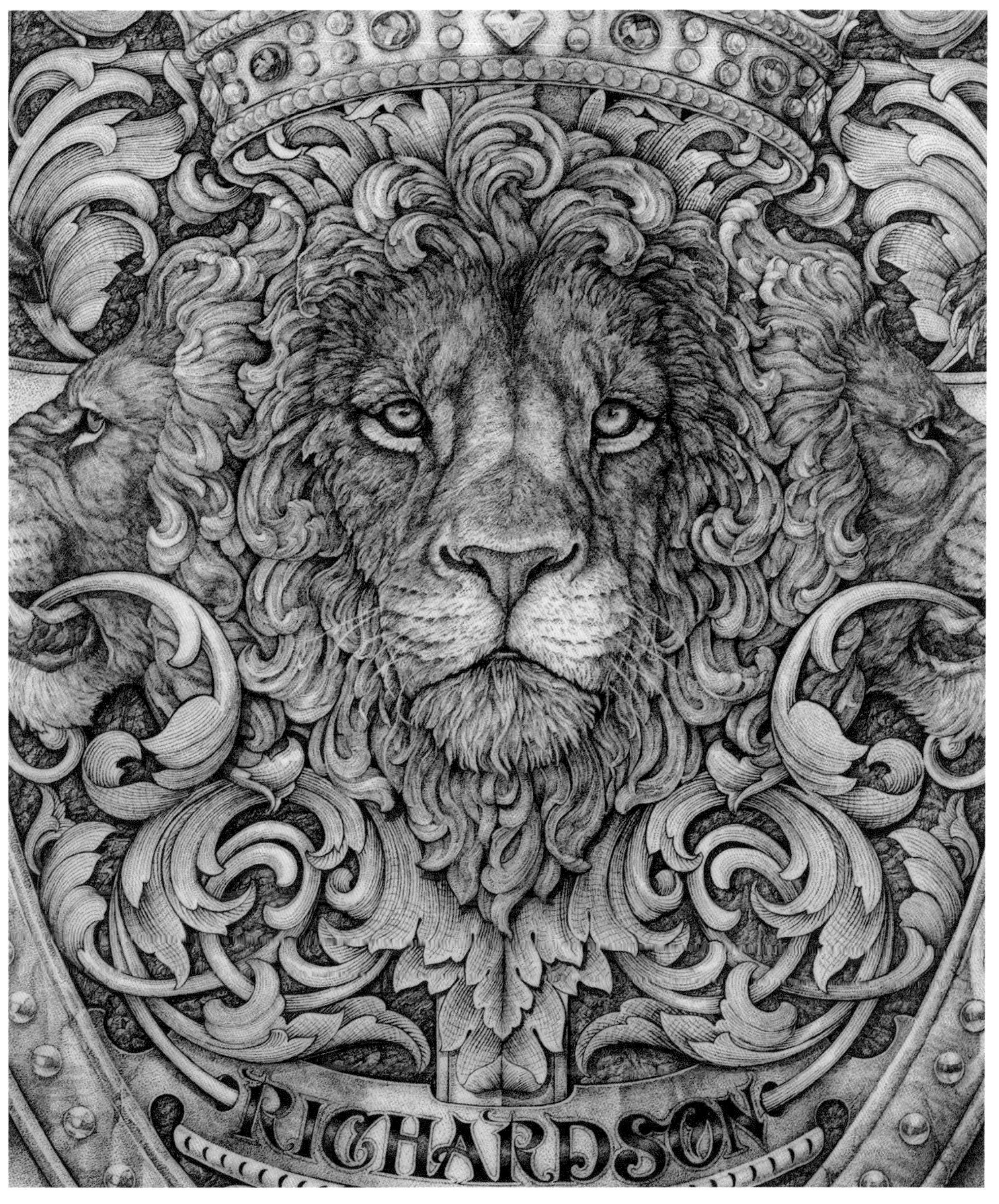

Fig 08 DETAIL OF WORK

Close-up details of **Richardson Family Crest**, pen and ink on calfskin vellum. See final piece on page 53.

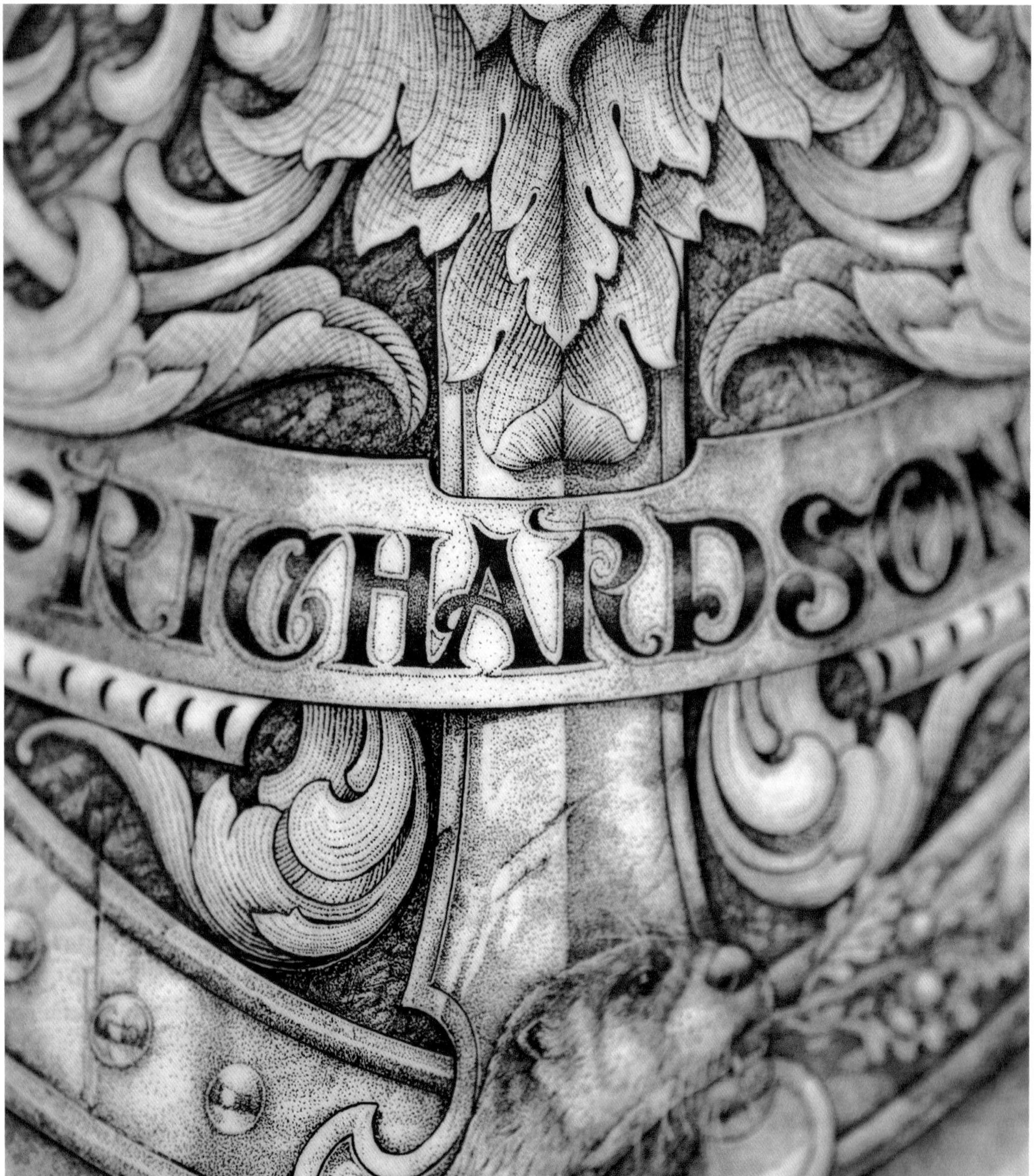

attributes, and life achievements. It hasn't all been hard work, however. The preparatory research has been really enjoyable (and even a little nerdy!). I have loved learning the history of heraldry and coming to understand its language.

I HAVE LOVED LEARNING THE HISTORY OF HERALDRY AND COMING TO UNDERSTAND ITS LANGUAGE.

When having the first conversation about the creation of the family crest, I felt as if I were walking onto holy ground. Over the course of an evening, each member of the family expressed their deepest values, traditions, personal histories, and life verses—laying them before me like sacred heirlooms. I listened as well as I could, wishing to serve them in all humility. But even though I was prepared and attentive, I could not help feeling inadequate before something so precious. These dear people were my patrons but have since become like family. Blurring the lines between the personal and professional may go against conventional business practices, but it is absolutely necessary, indescribably wonderful, and eminently possible when the Spirit of God is invited into our creativity.

I then began to transpose the family's legacy into heraldic legend. Matching each of their closely held values and beliefs to their corresponding icons, the crest began to take shape. I spent a great deal of time on the concept sketch, which involved fixing all the elements in their respective places of prominence. I would erase, redraw, shift, and massage the elements into a dynamic balance. While there are about sixteen

ELATION AND TREPIDATION MAKE FOR AN INTERESTING EMOTIONAL COCKTAIL, AND BOTH STRUCK IN THAT VERY MOMENT.

individual elements to the entire achievement, they must all look cohesive and natural within the ensemble. I spent dozens of hours drawing alone before sharing the concept art with the family. Their legacy needed to be accurately and dynamically represented, of course, so the full scope of the project would include a detailed ink drawing of the crest on vellum *and* a large-scale high relief carving of the same to be hung in their family home. This singular work will occupy the next few years of my life.

We met again. With eagerness laced with a bit of trepidation, I unveiled the sketch and walked them through the entire piece, symbol by symbol. I anticipated some pushback and was prepared to welcome any input they might have. It was their crest after all, and if it did not ring true, I would return to the drawing board to ensure that it did. My role was to serve. I welcomed any critique. This can be a sensitive area for artists, who can get understandably defensive about such matters, but I knew the husband and wife to be skilled artists in their own right—she, a greatly skilled portrait artist and painter; he, an accomplished sculptor. I respected and trusted their judgment. But as I explained the sketch, they intently listened, and not a word of criticism was offered. There were only gasps and a few glistening tears. And when I finished, the family patriarch simply but effectively offered the following command: “Get to carving!”

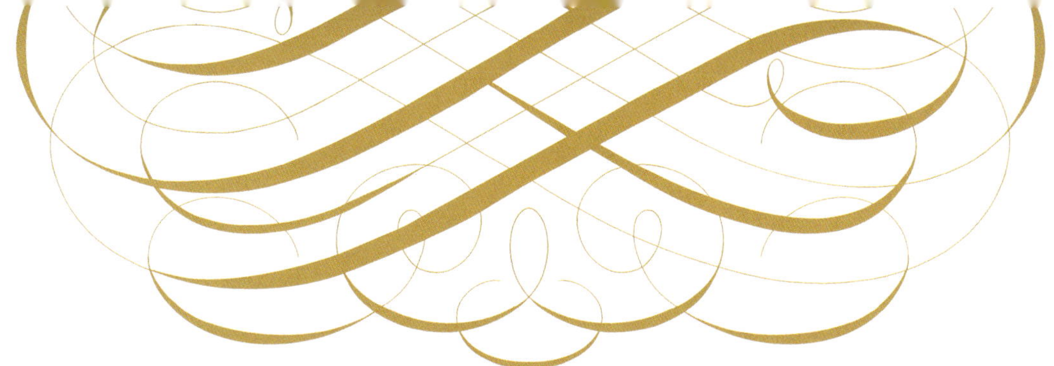

Elation and trepidation make for an interesting emotional cocktail, and both struck in that very moment. On the one hand, it is a dream to have your proposed sketch so wonderfully and graciously received; yet, on the other, it is quite another thing to turn that sketch into reality. God grant me strength!

I am now only halfway through the first phase of the pen and ink drawing on vellum. To attain the highest level of detail and shading, I have chosen to use a technique called "stippling," which means that nearly the entire drawing is made of individual dots from the tip of my dip pen. The process is extremely time intensive, the work painfully slow and monotonous. Certain critical details have even been performed under a stereomicroscope to ensure the precise placement and spacing of individual dots. But each dot serves a purpose, reminding the viewer that a legacy is not made quickly or easily but is composed of great multitudes of wise decisions, faithful actions, fervent prayers, and loving words.

The culmination of all that God has instilled in me over the course of my life has been brought to bear on this piece. I have given Him my all, and He is using it for His good purposes. He has taken my love for penmanship and calligraphy and taught me patience—a patience I employ dot by dot by dot, even under the watchful eye of a microscope. He has taken my interest in psychology and shown me how to listen well, to attend carefully to the words of those longing to be heard. He has taken my heart, with its fear of rejection and tendency to self-promote, and trained it to serve Him and His children in humility. This, my friend, is how creativity can be a cure.

So, what is it that makes you come alive? What is it that so moves you that you'd pursue it for all the days of your life? Whatever it may be, may I offer a suggestion? Place it, and everything else that you bring with you, into the hands of your Creator. He will use your offering in unimaginable ways. Let your relationship with God permeate through every nook and cranny of your life. And when you do, you will discover a greater sense of purpose in all you put your hands to. How could I have known that He would bring together my penmanship, my studies in psychology, and even my years as a barista to live out my calling as an artist? Who knows what He will do with your gifts, your experiences, and—yes—your creativity? Why not trust Him and find out?

WHAT IS IT THAT MAKES YOU COME ALIVE?

fig 9 DETAIL OF WORK

Richardson Family Crest, 2023. Pen and ink on genuine vellum, 26 x 30 inches. Composed of traditional heraldic symbolism, the piece represents the central values, virtues, faith, and legacy of the Richardson family.

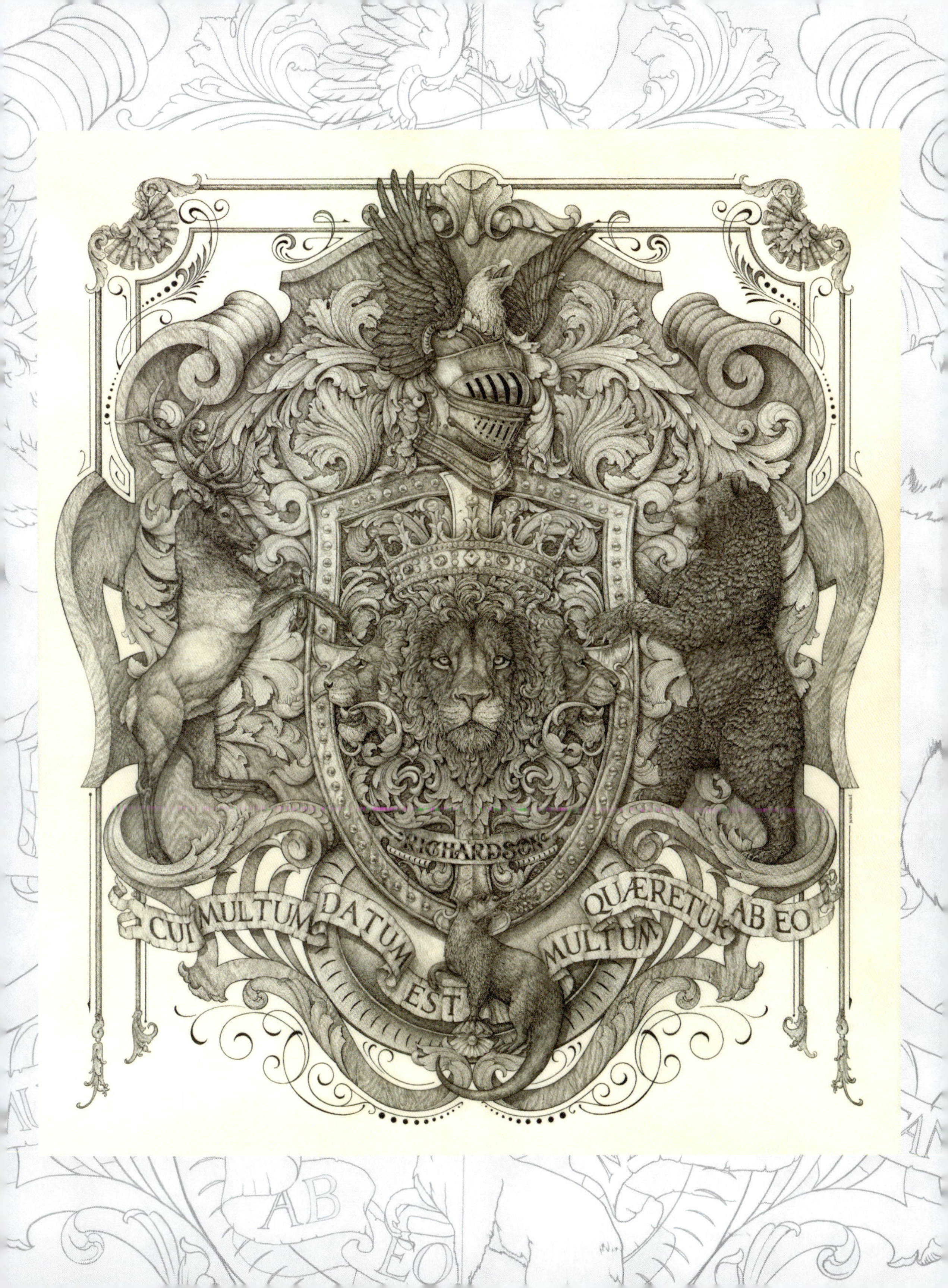
RICHARDSON
CUI MULTUM DATUM EST MULTUM QUÆRETUR AB EO

CHAPTER FOUR

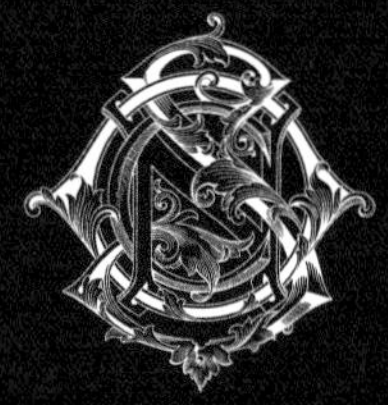

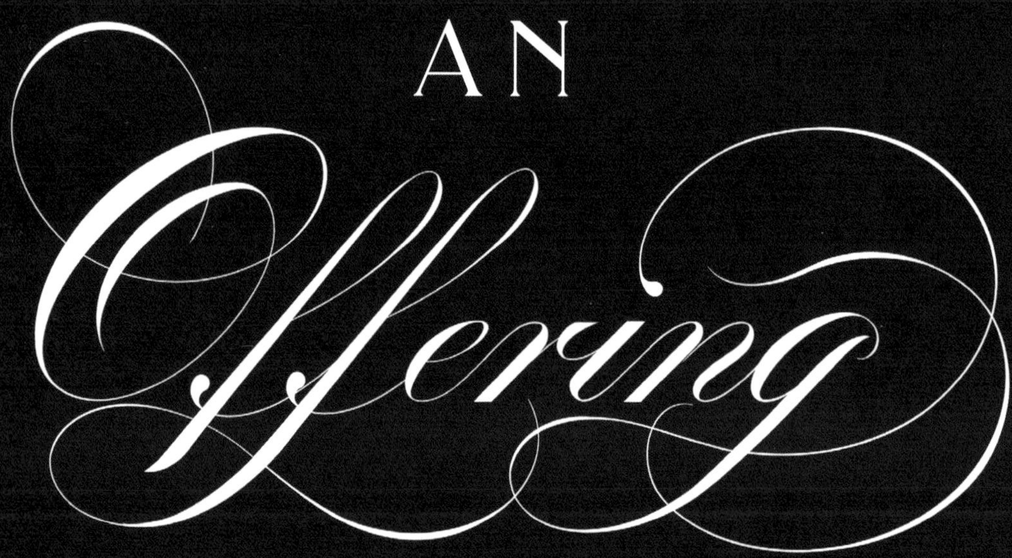

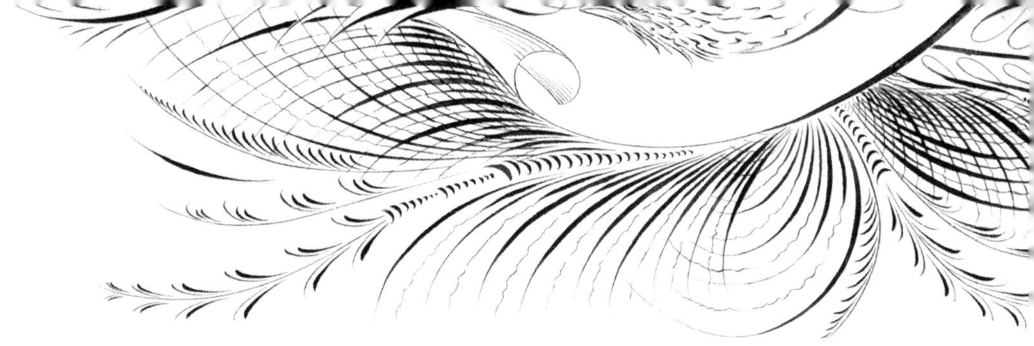

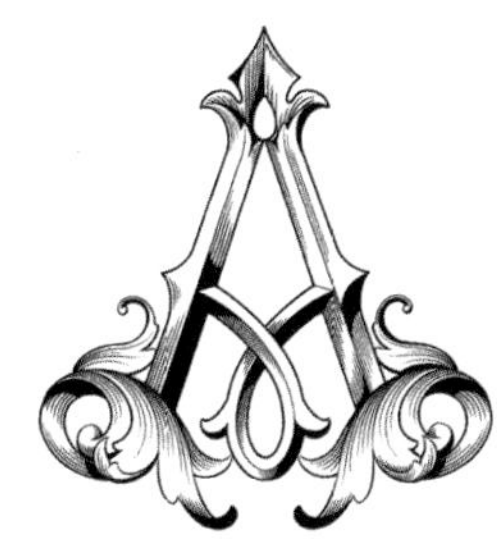

rt is an offering in at least two senses of the word. On one hand, it is an offering to the Lord. When I create in His image, my easel, drafting table, and workbench become like altars upon which I surrender the firstfruits of my talent. On the other hand, it is an offering of myself. Pouring my heart, skill, and energy into a creative work and then presenting it before another is an intensely vulnerable act. It requires courage and involves no small measure of trepidation. This is what I do, time and time again. Yet even this vulnerability pales in comparison to when I first offered myself to my wife.

It probably comes as no surprise that I am a hopeless romantic. For as long as I can remember, I have prayed for the one I hoped to marry. As it turns out, the story of how Hannah and I fell in love has all the trappings of a Victorian romance. We may not have been Mr. Darcy and Elizabeth, but we had our fair share of surprising twists, comical scenarios, insurmountable odds, and lighthearted whimsy.

It all began when I started dating her sister. Yes, you read that correctly—*her sister.* In fairness, it didn't last long. We were friends and we tried seeing each other for a short period. The romance never took off, however, so one evening we met to have the dreaded DTR (define the relationship) talk. These are typically uncomfortable affairs, especially

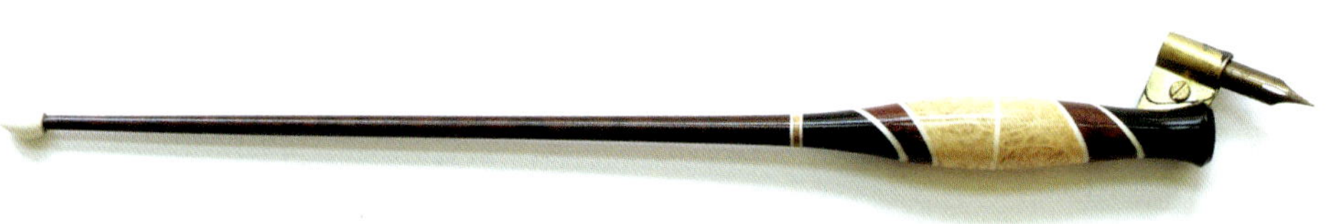

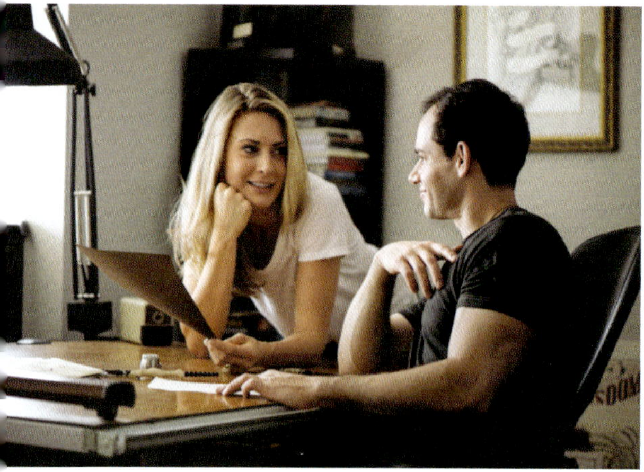

when your date turns to you and says, "I feel like you should be dating my sister." I had received my share of brush-offs, but this was something else.

Dear reader, I did not take it well.

A couple of weeks later, Hannah and I met for the first time. It was a chance encounter, but then again, in God's world, what ever really happens by chance? We talked for only a few minutes, but it felt like seconds. Simply put, I was captivated by her beauty and hung on her every word. One might say I was (ahem) "actively" listening. Our shared interests, the depth of her faith, the richness of her insights, and the sound of her laugh—she *must* be the one I had been praying for. But there wasn't time to tell her. Anyway, I had dated her sister. She went one way; I went another.

Resigned to this misfortune, I poured myself into my art over the next few months. I had a debut art show in Denver coming up and the preparations proved to be a helpful distraction. When the evening of the show came, I was delighted by the turnout. And so I found myself speaking from a small stage in the gallery to some three hundred faces. As I looked out across the crowd, however, I chanced to see a single radiant face. *Her* face. It was as if my audience dissolved at once into a single person. I tried to stay focused—I truly did—but I would be surprised if anyone understood a word I said thereafter.

I finished my short address and left the multitude to mingle over the art, wine, and hors d'oeuvres. A gentleman came up immediately after I got offstage and we

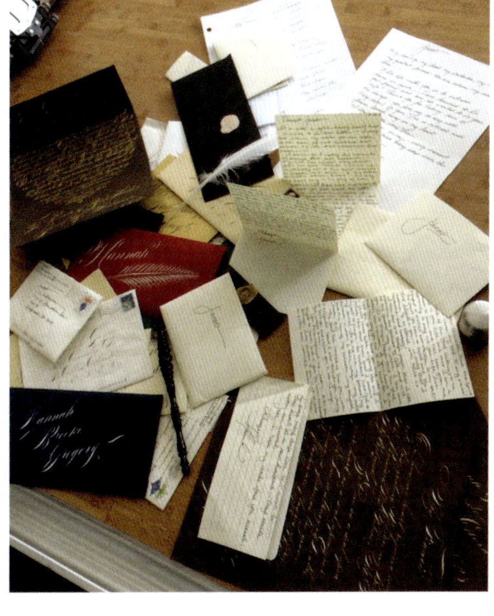

began to talk. Only, there she was again, approaching slowly with her parents by her side, looking at my art as she came toward me. Just as my conversation ended with the gentleman, she arrived. I turned and greeted her. And yes, my friend, it was a perfect moment, our two worlds coming together. So perfect, in fact, that I managed to blurt out, "Hi! You look so gorgeous!" *Smooth, Jake. Very smooth.*

The embarrassment did not end there, however. As I awkwardly talked to Hannah and her parents, the air around me grew uncomfortably warm. Beads of sweat began to gather on my forehead, glistening indiscreetly under the hot gallery lights. I tried my best to save face in more ways than one. "You know what—it's a little warm in here, so I'm going to talk to the staff about turning up the AC. Excuse me!" I beelined for the punch bowl and started chewing on ice. Having collected myself, I tried to make my way back but kept getting diverted by well-wishers. The rest of the evening continued in this way—looking over the shoulders of everyone I talked to, hoping to see her again. The show was a great success. I had offered up my work to an audience and it had been well received. Yet how quickly it paled when at once I had a far greater goal in mind. Hannah had stolen the show . . . at least for me. From that moment on I would have her steal

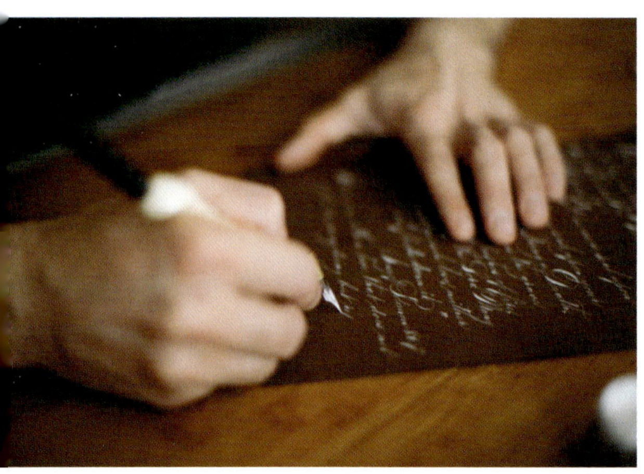

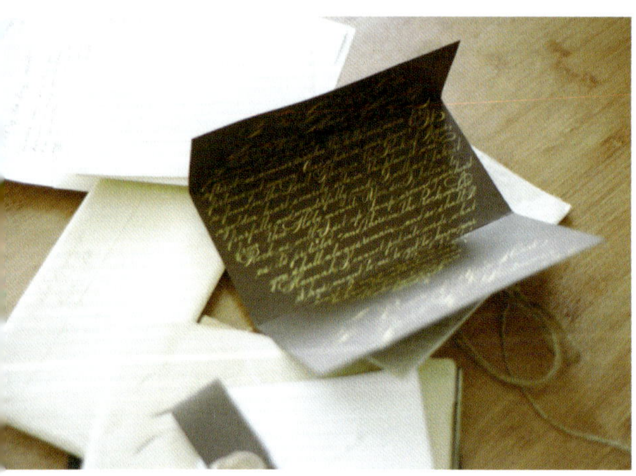

CHANCE IS A FINE THING, AND I WOULD NOT MISS MINE A SECOND TIME.

my heart. If only I could catch her eye one last time.

Hannah, as you might imagine, recalls that evening a little differently. Yes, she remembers our brief exchange and my sweaty escape. She also remembers waiting for me for a while before assuming I'd gotten caught up in the crowd and so went home with her parents. But all was not lost—at least for my sake. As she walked out through the gallery doors, she declared to her mom almost absentmindedly, "I'm going to marry that man." *Really?* When Hannah realized what she said, she tried to walk it back. Only now the die was cast. What was said in private would prove prophetic. The Spirit had spoken. I called her as soon as the last guest departed and the gallery doors were locked. Chance is a fine thing, and I would not miss mine a second time.

My first offering to Hannah came in the form of love letters. She lived only an hour away and we communicated, nearly moment by moment, via phone and text. Yet we found that some words were deserving of greater

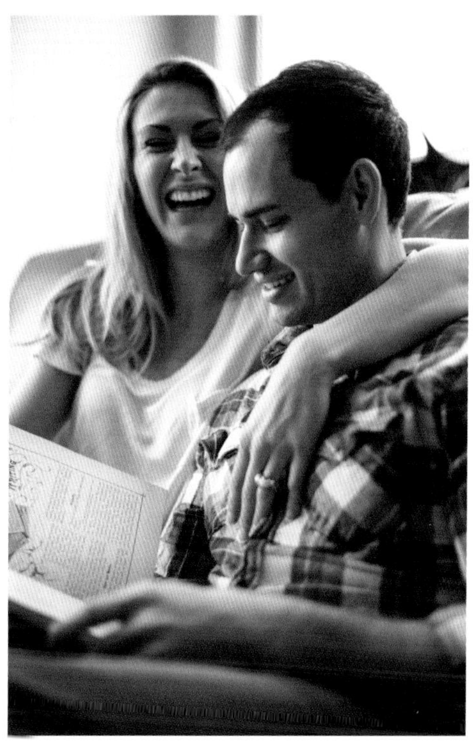

substance and permanence. The art of letter writing served that higher end. Week after week, letters arrived in her mailbox and mine. Together we chronicled every step of our love story within wax-sealed envelopes and perfumed pages. Spencerian script danced upon fine stationery as we reveled in our growing infatuation and earliest expressions of love. This correspondence is now kept in a specially made letterbox in our room. But it is not complete. We still add letters to it all the time. Our loving correspondences mark every birthday and holiday, plus the occasional extra when sentiment or circumstance inspires.

The letterbox contains some of the greatest examples of my calligraphy and perhaps the largest collection of my original words. For weeks and weeks on end, I honed my craft while scribing these letters to Hannah. In every letterform and flourish, I offered her my heart on gilded page.

When it came time to propose to Hannah, instead of ring shopping, we decided to go ring *sketching*. I booked us a table at the little Italian restaurant where we'd had our first date. We even had the same waiter! Over glasses of wine and charcuterie, I sketched our ideas for an engagement ring on the pages of my Moleskine notebook.

I asked for her hand; in exchange, I offered her mine and all the skill that was in it. With our hands and creativities thus joined, we sought a design that would best exemplify our covenantal union. Above all else, we wanted to represent God's central place within our marriage. The union was not only of two but three. Furthermore, we wanted our marriage to shine the light of Christ to the world. As husband and wife, we were inspired by Paul's teaching in Ephesians 5 to become living symbols of that deeper mystery in which Jesus Christ is the Bridegroom and the church is His bride. It was so fun to work with Hannah in this way and it opened a door into a new dimension of our relationship. As it turns out, this collaboration would be the first of thousands.

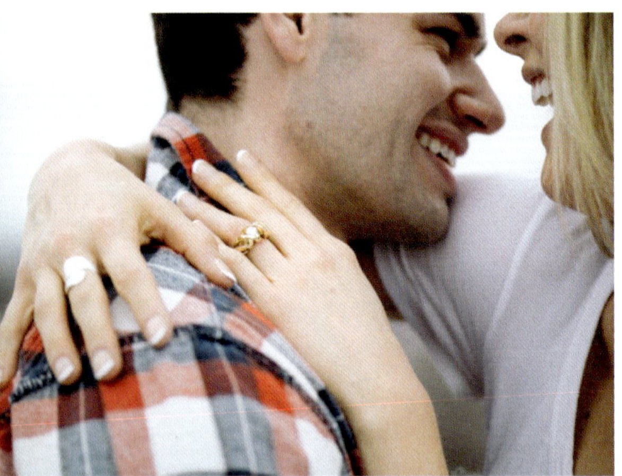

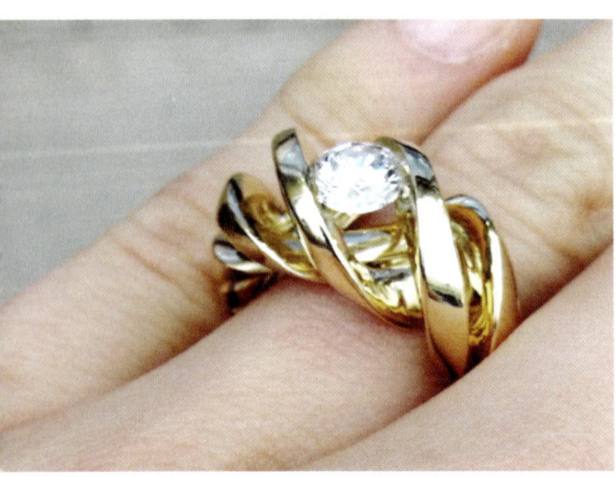

Having been inspired by Ecclesiastes 4:12—"A cord of three strands is not easily broken" (CSB)—we decided the band should be solid on the underside but split apart into a triple helix over the top, where, between the three strands of gold, we would set a single diamond to represent both the light and purity of Christ and the unperishable bond of marriage. Before dessert had arrived, the design was done and decided upon. We toasted our successful collaboration with clinking glasses and a celebratory kiss.

That same week I took our little drawing to some professional jewelers who were good friends of mine. They insisted they try and build it for me through CAD (computer-aided design) and have it 3D-printed, because the design was too difficult to carve by hand.

> WHETHER YOU OFFER A HEART IN LOVE OR A WORK OF PASSION, BOTH INVOLVE DEEP VULNERABILITY.

Two weeks later, it turned out the software wasn't up to the task, and I was on my own. I took the drawing back home and got to work straightaway. I carved the overall shape of the ring out of a kind of hard, green casting wax. I then mapped out the placement of the diamond. With a small metal scribe, I etched in each of the spiraling strands, marking them as I went with my dividers to ensure their uniform thickness. Then came the hard part. I carved between the inscribed strands, slowly excavating the hard green wax from all sides until I broke through to open air in the middle. Little by little I removed the wax from the inside, refining each of the twisting strands as I went. Within two days the carving was done. I returned to the jewelers, ready to have it cast in gold.

At sunset, in late October on my favorite beach in Laguna, I went down on bended knee and offered Hannah this sacred symbol of our love, affection, and collaboration. As you may have guessed by now, she said *yes*.

Not everyone has romantic stories of love and courtship, flush with letters, ring designs, and, yes, sweaty foreheads. I share this story with you, not that you would compare it with your own, but rather to help you reflect on what it means to offer your work, and yourself, to another. Whether you offer a heart in love or a work of passion, both involve deep vulnerability. For some, that may be too much to bear. And if you are one of those, I know how you feel. There is real fear of having someone reject your offering. But I urge you: Do not give in to that fear. While I may not

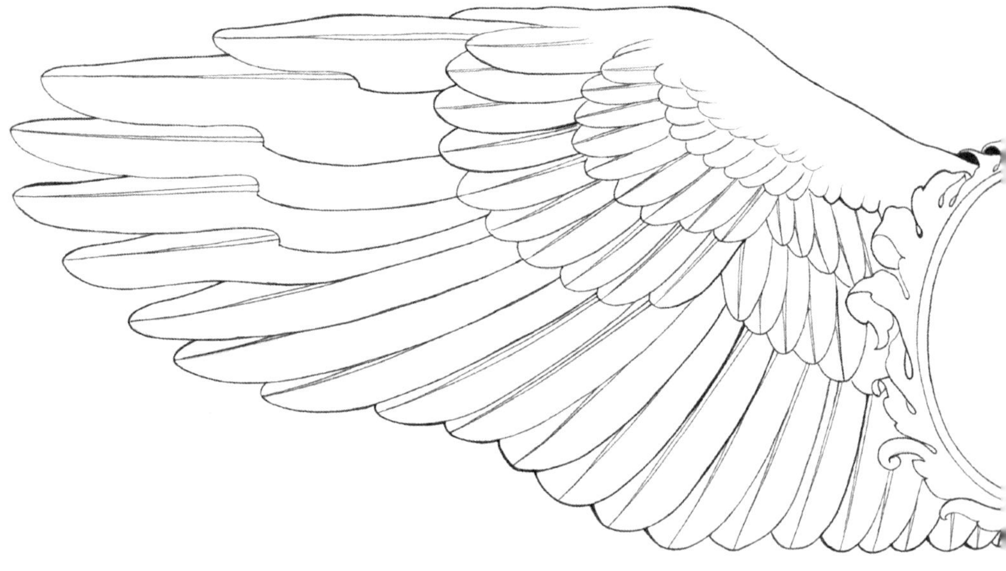

know you personally, I truly believe you have much to offer. Why not start by offering your creation, your service, your heart, and—yes—even your life to the One who created that desire within you?

Once engaged, we set our wedding date. In the ensuing months, I looked for more artistic opportunities to love my wife-to-be. I also wanted to do the unexpected. As I thought about the big day, my mind fixed upon the chuppah, a canopy under which a bride and groom are married in a Jewish ceremony, but whose tradition appears to reach back to the time of ancient Israel. I have always loved its symbolism; its covering represents the presence of God over the betrothed not only at the moment of marriage but also in the home they will make together.

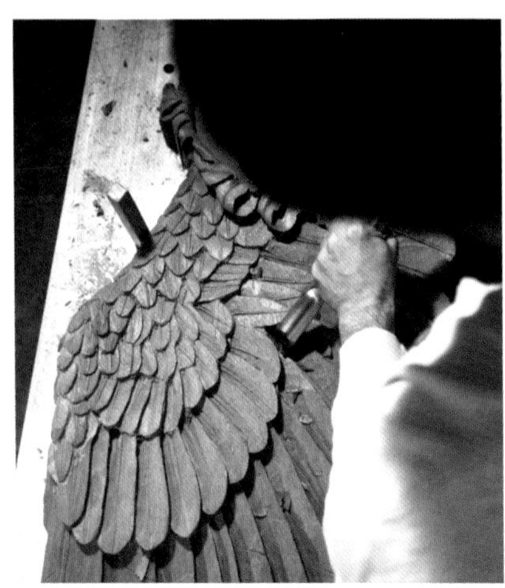

Yet it is also more than a canopy; it is a wedding altar—a holy place where two lives are joined before God and offered in union to Him. So if the altar is where the covenant and sacrifice is made, the canopy tells us who the sacrifice is for.

I decided to make this idea a reality by

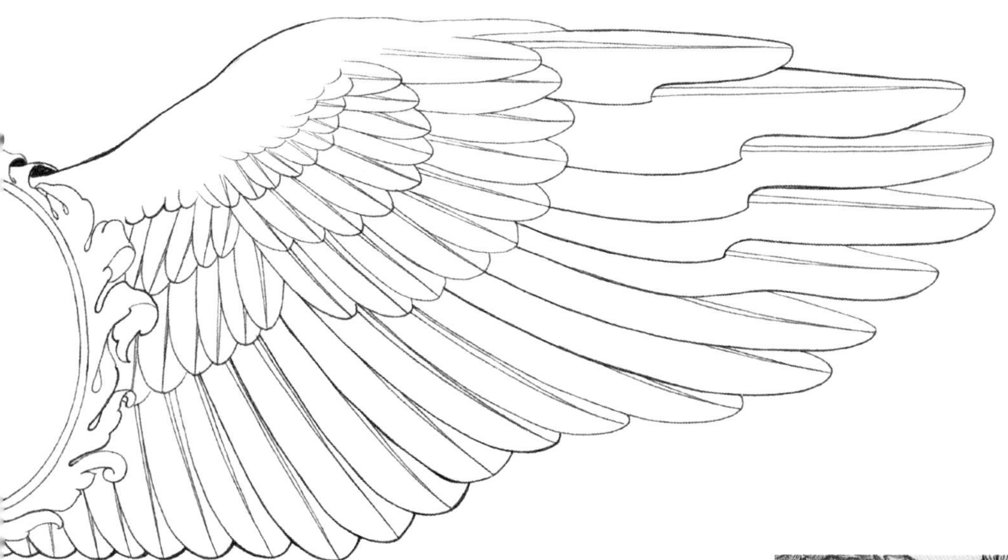

carving outspread wings from wood, taking my inspiration from Psalm 17: "Hide me in the shadow of your wings" (v. 8), one of our favorite psalms. The piece would also hearken back to our first date, when I asked Hannah if there were any particular symbols that spoke to her. "Birds and trees," she replied. Wooden wings were close enough!

Once again, I hadn't chosen the easiest artistic path. Finding a piece of wood large enough was extremely difficult. I assumed I would have to laminate several pieces together before I could begin carving. I went to my local lumber supplier where I get most of my wood for my art pieces. When I inquired of my choice of wood—Honduran mahogany in twelve-quarter (three inches thick)—the clerk told me they had very little of that in stock. Still, I asked him to have the dock loader bring that pallet out of their storehouse. From a distance, things didn't look promising. This pallet's contents looked measly when compared to the others. Yet as they brought it closer my heart leapt. Right on top of the pile was a piece that might just be good enough. As a matter of fact, it turned out to be perfect. I couldn't have

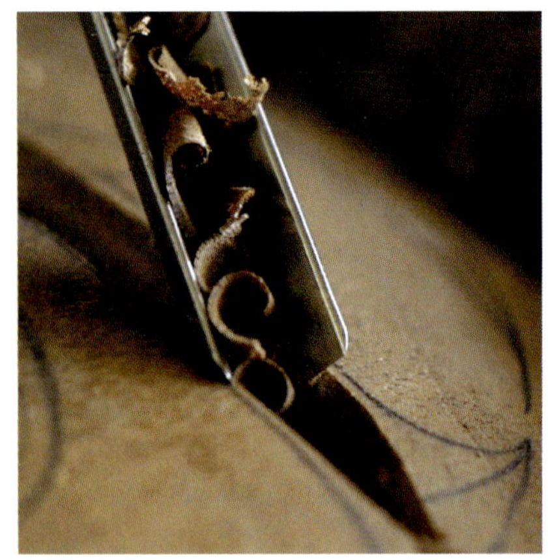

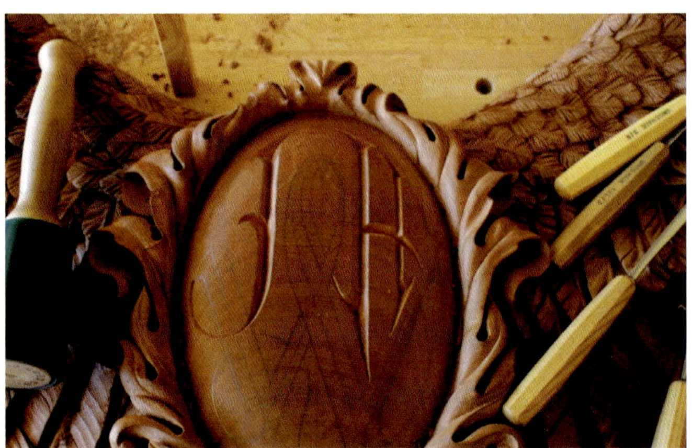

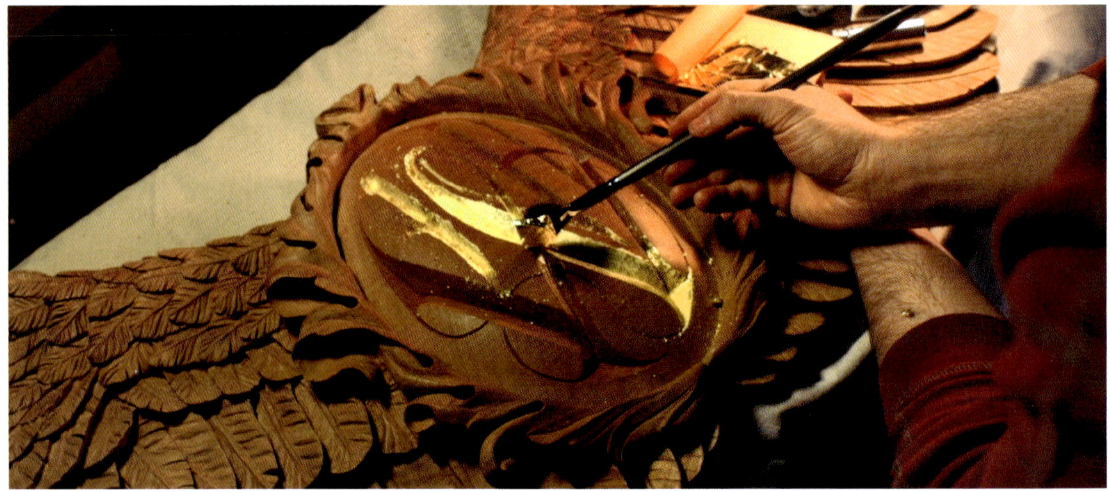

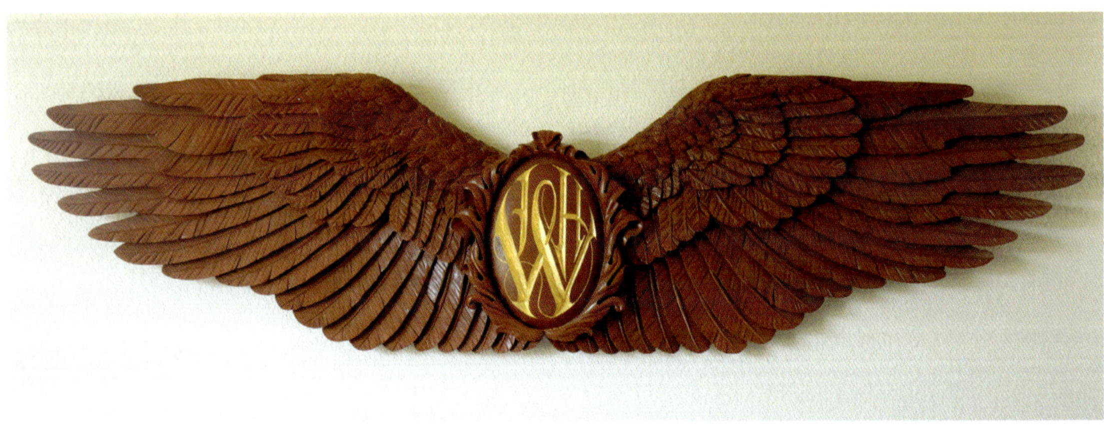

asked for better had I milled it from a tree myself. I loaded the board in the back of my truck and away I went.

I got to work immediately. Not long afterward, I met with a close friend for breakfast. I shared how excited I was about the project and the miraculous discovery of the wood—only he didn't return my enthusiasm. In fact, he began to lecture me: *My focus was in the wrong place; my wedding and marriage should take the priority; I shouldn't be so prideful.*

I stared down at my untouched plate of eggs Benedict in confusion. I tried to marshal a defense, but I never expected the betrayal. Maybe he thought he was being helpful. Maybe he thought it was just a bit of friendly advice. But his words stung. And I simply couldn't convince him, so I quit trying. In my silence, the questions continued within. *What is so wrong about carving an altar for my wedding? How could this friend criticize this visual acknowledgment of God's presence over us? How could something I had such clarity and passion for be completely misunderstood, if not ridiculed, by someone I love?*

I felt wounded. And sometimes that's the cost of vulnerability. After all, the Latin root of the word *vulnerable* is *vulnus*, which means "wound." We offer our gifts and ourselves and sometimes we get hurt. Perhaps you have also been wounded in this way. I wonder if you carry your hurt the way I have carried mine. Sometimes it takes a long time to heal, especially when the pain has been caused by someone close. I pray that if you do have those wounds, God would bring healing. I pray that in His grace He would give you opportunities to offer yourself again without fear of being hurt.

After my disappointing breakfast, I went straight home to my woodshop. In my left hand I grabbed my largest chisel; in my right, my heaviest mallet. I pounded away on the giant piece of timber till my palms were blistered and bloody. Percussive blows sent woodchips through the air like shrapnel. I brought my anger and hurt to the altar. All of my pain, all of my sadness—I emptied it then and there. Such furious work would hardly look like prayer to an outsider, but I was pouring my heart out to God. And even as the anger subsided, I continued to meet God there to pray. I prayed for our marriage. I prayed for God's protection. I prayed that I would always fight passionately for what God had brought together. And as I prayed, I worked. And from the piece of mahogany emerged a panoply of pinions arrayed in outstretched wings. I placed a monogram of our initials in the middle—gilded in 23 karat gold leaf.

All the while, I had kept their making a secret from Hannah. She knew I was working on our altar but had not seen a thing since my initial concept sketch. Then, on the eve of our wedding day, I presented it—my wedding gift to her. Her reaction was everything I could have hoped for. She kissed and embraced me in my vulnerability. Then she studied the carving. As her fingertips traced wing tips, she noted every gilded letter and glossed feather. We sat on the floor and prayed for what would be the first of many times beneath those wings. Then we brought the holy moment to a close by reading aloud the psalm that helped inspire it all.

Those wings would be to us an Ebenezer (1 Samuel 7)—a signpost of not only what God had done to bring Hannah and me together, but all that He would do through us and for us in our marriage. They also taught me about the vulnerability involved in offering myself as an artist and a husband. Had I chosen to protect myself at all costs, I never would have shared my work or fallen in love. I had to sacrifice my ego on the altar. But this itself is what it means to create in the Artist's image. The very act of creation assumes a sacrifice: a Lamb slain at the foundation of the world (Revelation 13:8); a life given for the ransom of many (Mark 10:45).

You might think to yourself, *Jake, with all due respect, all this doesn't sound like much of a sacrifice. After all, you got the girl in the end and it all shapes up to a pretty neat and tidy romance story of happily-ever-after and all that.* By and large I would agree with you. In hindsight, everything feels pretty safe because I have been given far more than I sacrificed—which gives away the punch line. But

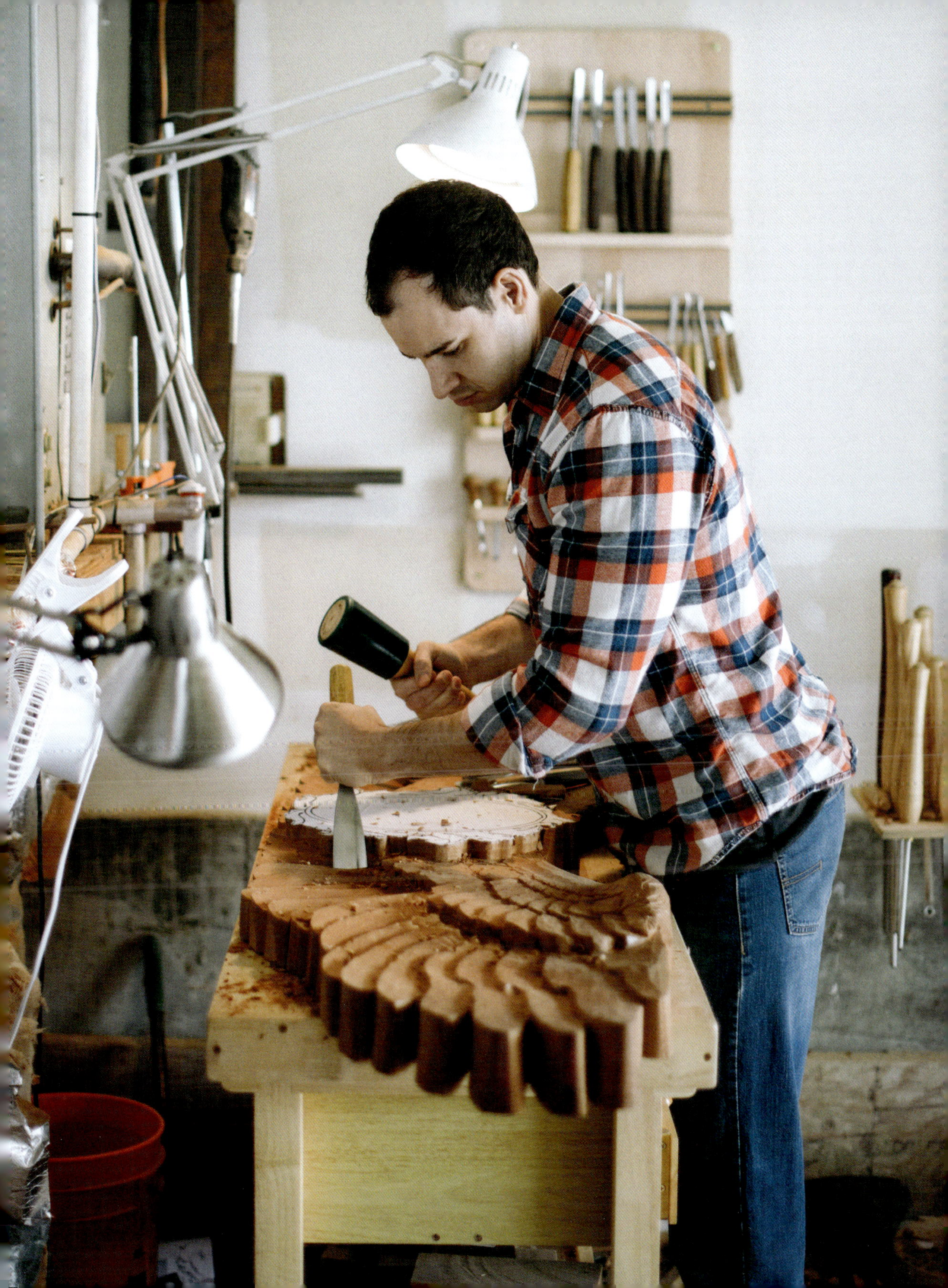

Sacrifice comes when we are asked to surrender what we hold most dear.

what I know now I did not know then. Just as Abraham did not know God would stop his hand right before he was going to sacrifice Isaac and then provide a ram in the thicket as a substitutionary sacrifice, neither did I know what lay for me on the other side of my obedience—small in comparison as it may be. Sacrifice comes when we are asked to surrender what we hold most dear. It's easy to become grabby with our God-given gifts—they were *given to us* after all. I know very well that my time and the art pieces I can produce with it are finite. Sure, I could have produced an illuminated manuscript of untold value with the time and energy I had poured into the letters written to Hannah. I could have created a massive public art piece instead of the wings that hang in the privacy of our bedroom. But I have seen real-life examples of what happens to those who build altars to their gifts rather than put their gifts on the altar. I have seen men consumed by their own pride and I have seen families destroyed. By God's grace that will never be me. Sacrifice is so much more than a tax exacted by God; it's an invitation into obedience—into alignment with Him. The power of a God-given gift is in the nature of it being *given* in the first place. When we give as we have been given, it perpetuates and even magnifies the power of our gifts. Sacrifice to the Lord never returns void. In my marriage to Hannah, I have committed to sacrifice my time, my ego, and all of myself to see her flourish. I put her worth above my work. It is a sacrifice that is easy to make because of the power of love in Christ between the two of us. Together, we are a new creation. I will forever be indebted to her, that she would deign to say yes to my offering—sweat and all.

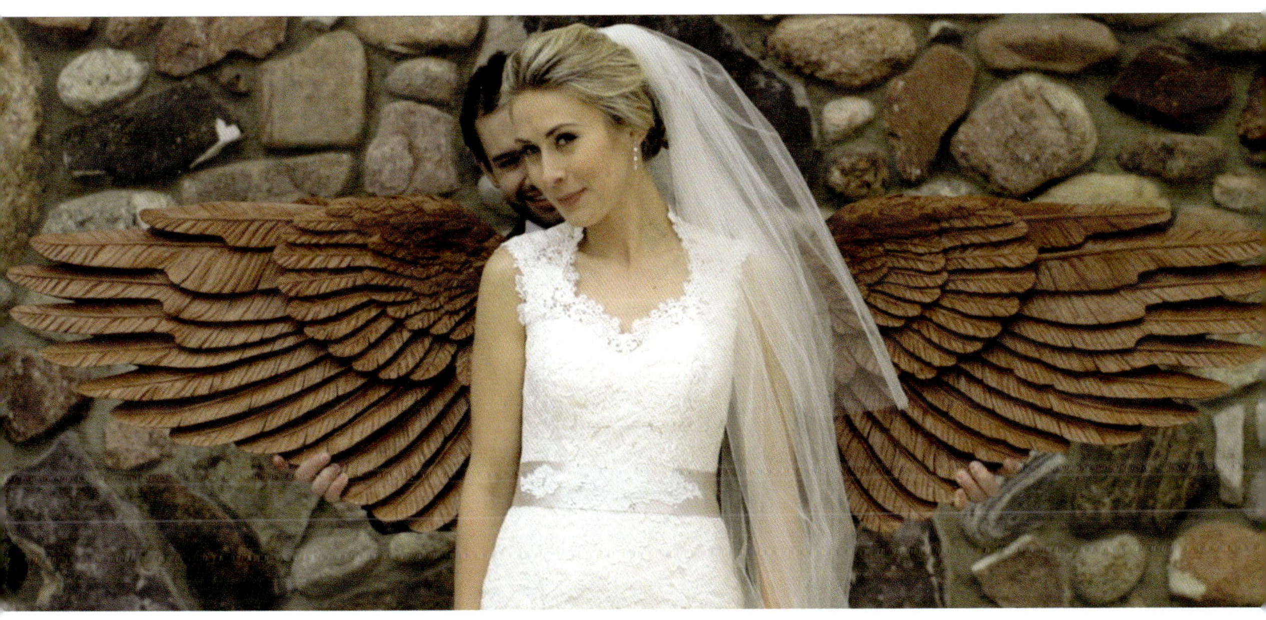

fig 10 DETAIL OF WORK

Weidmann Wings, 2014. Hand-carved sculpture in wood, made from Honduran mahogany, 3 x 21 x 72 inches. This wooden altar was created by Weidmann for his wedding ceremony as a gift to Hannah, his bride.

CHAPTER FIVE

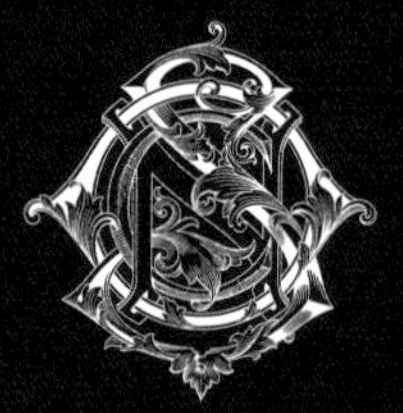

LIKE A *Swan*

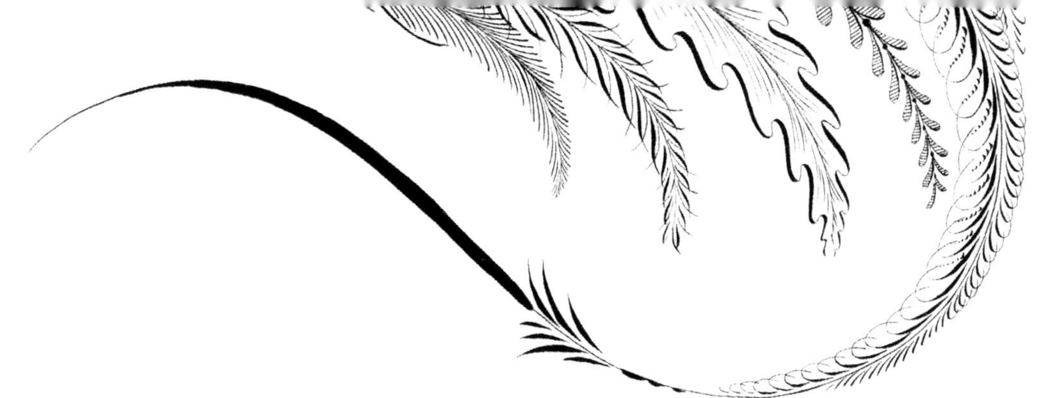

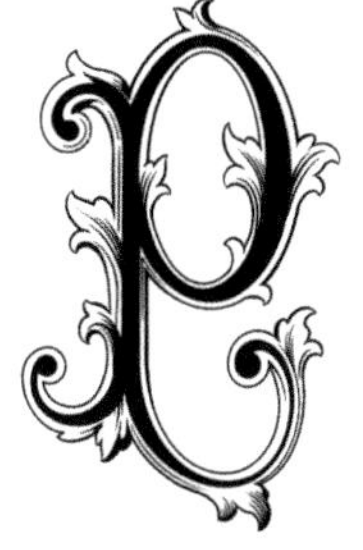

icture a mother swan swimming on a glassy lake, her cygnets nestled between her back-turned wings. Above the water all appears tranquil, a model of grace. Beneath the water, however, strong webbed feet churn the water in a torrent of constant motion. Peace and chaos together, the very picture of parenthood.

Ask any ornithologist (and I have!): The swan is an excellent example of a family bird. They mate for life and are fiercely loyal to their partners and offspring. Should a predator threaten a male swan's mate or young, he will display a defensive behavior known as *busking*, in which he raises himself up, draws up his wings, and cocks his head back like a viper, ready to strike.

As a parent, I can relate. Fatherhood can be a majestic, beautiful calling. Yet chaos is ever-present. For all my apparent graciousness, I may perhaps be provoked to busk in my own way, whether on behalf of my children or, sometimes, because of them. And like that mother swan, I feel the weight of my own precious cygnets, who depend on me to carry them through the rough waters of life until they are ready to leave the nest. How fitting then that our baby's first cradle was modeled after a swan in water.

As I shared in the previous chapter, after falling in love and marrying Hannah, I was no longer an artist unto myself

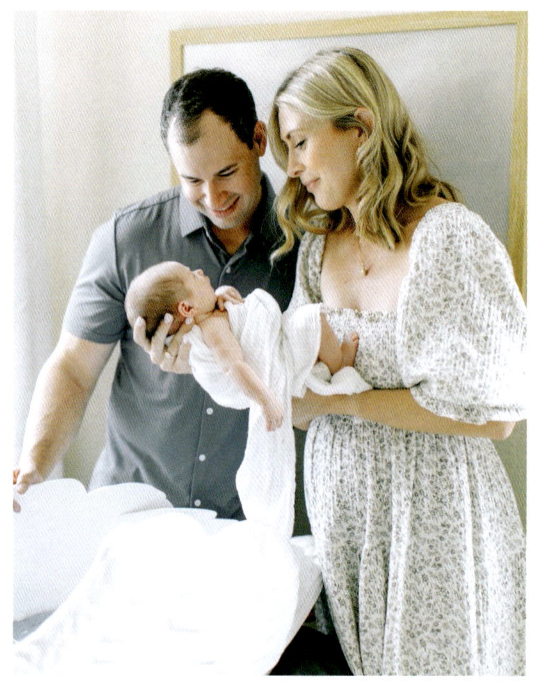

but had entered into a lifelong collaboration. This had implications for my art and my calling, which can be seen most clearly in the winged altar. When it came time to start a family, further changes were on the horizon.

The most obvious of these was a deeper awareness of my need to provide. For most, art is a luxury, but to me and my growing family, it has become a necessity. There is a lot more weight riding on my pen these days given the lives that depend on it. But this weight is not so much a burden as it is a gift. It is profoundly affirming to have gone for so many years believing I could never make a living from art to now being able to support and sustain the ones I love.

Beyond the higher purpose my family has given to my creativity, it has also enriched it as my daily muse. Fatherhood has been a blessed season in this respect, at once sweet and fleeting, yet bursting with inspiration.

Some days feel as if I have taken an extended holiday in fairyland. Small figures flit about on pointed toes, filling the air with unending laughter. A faun in the shape of my son transforms the mundane into the magical whenever it falls under the spell of his imagination. Gentle coos of will-o'-the-wisp call to me through baby monitors, leading me to my fate—and oh, what a fate!

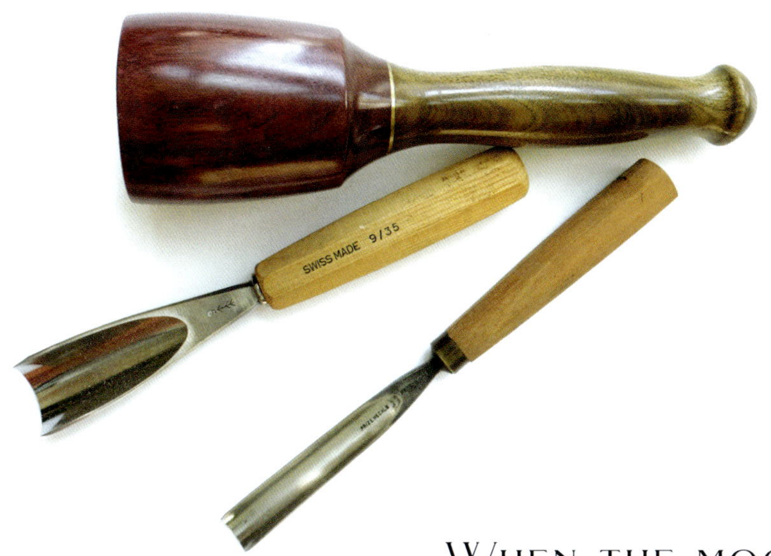

WHEN THE MOON RISES IN THE STAR-STUDDED SKY AND THE HEADS OF FAIRIES, FAWNS, AND WISPS ALL BEGIN TO NOD TOWARD BED, MY HEART MELTS WITHIN.

But my children are not the only magical creatures here. I, too, have been granted great power in this land. As a lofty oracle, I answer innumerable questions and curiosities. As a great wizard, I cure ills or curses with a kiss and need only whisper a prayer to banish nightmares into oblivion. And like a towering castle with battlements and a surrounding moat, my arms offer protection and refuge. But for all that power and strength, when the moon rises in the star-studded sky and the heads of fairies, fawns, and wisps all begin to nod toward bed, my heart melts within. With tears in my eyes and a daughter in my arms, the nightingale (singing sweetly within the Sonos speaker on the dresser) sends us to sleep with the sweetness of his song.

You might think my artist's sentiment has run away with me, and that may be so. Still, it speaks to a deeper yet very real magic that my children have worked in me. What an incredible time and place to be a creator.

But all is not always well in fairyland. Some days, chaos reigns. Hannah and I love our kids endlessly, but they are still just that—kids. They get tired, cranky,

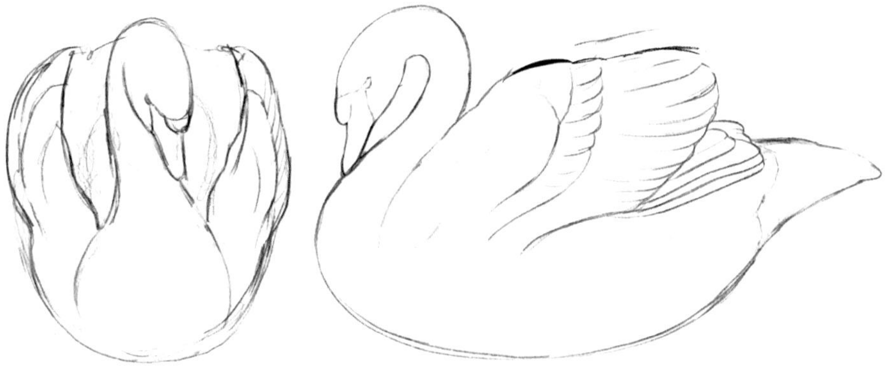

rambunctious, disobedient, quarrelsome, and destructive. And to make matters especially complicated, Mom and Dad work from home. We are thus constantly reminded of the vivaciousness of our children, which, on the one hand, can fuel our creative flow and, on the other, stop it dead in its tracks. But we know well where our priorities lie. Cultivating a joyful, peaceful, loving, and God-centered environment within our home is not only incumbent upon me as a parent, it is foundational to my effectiveness as an artist. So long as I keep first things first, second things flourish.

Before I had kids, I remember being able to get into a creative flow and remain there uninterrupted for hours on end. Before marrying Hannah, I could work into the odd hours of the night—as late as inspiration would carry me. But those days are long gone and I have needed to adapt. At first I would get frustrated when interrupted by a crying child or a call to dinner. But over time I have grown in my ability to move in and out of flow and to do so with less exasperation.

Some see this as finding balance, but I prefer the term *harmony*. Consider that image of the swan. Yes, it is balanced on the surface, but there is a deeper harmony between the stately peace above and the chaotic eddies below. And rather than a kind of stasis, which balance seems to imply, harmony suggests a sense of movement, even propulsion, as the swan glides across the water, cygnets between its wings.

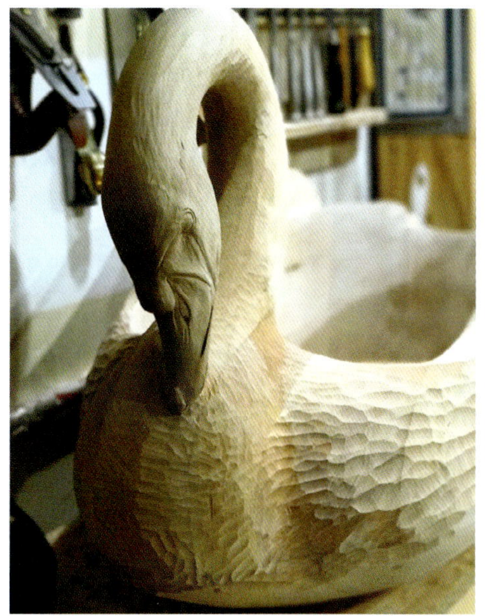

But harmony also requires a measure of order. Melodies without restraint produce cacophony. I am so grateful to Hannah for helping set up crucial boundaries, which ensure that when it's time to work, I can work. And when it's time to play, I can—and must—play. So, as young as they are, my kids have come to understand those times when Daddy must be left alone.

The studio door is an important boundary even when it's not closed; I never want them to feel as if they are in competition with what takes place within. Often I'll invite them to sit with me while I draw, paint, or lay gold leaf on an illumination. It is such a joy to see them so enamored by the process. They ask the best questions. I believe this proximity to my work has grown their respect and appreciation for it, but it also touches on that deeper mystery we have been talking about—creating in the Artist's image. While they don't literally contribute to these pieces (or, at least, not yet!), in seeing me at work they are learning what it means to be an artist. Sure, they're already bursting with creativity, but by participating in Daddy's stillness, quietness, and attentiveness, they have come to recognize the importance of each when it relates to producing work of lasting value.

True, it feels more difficult than ever to find harmony in our lives. Stress and anxiety often overwhelm. We each have our responsibilities and obligations. And

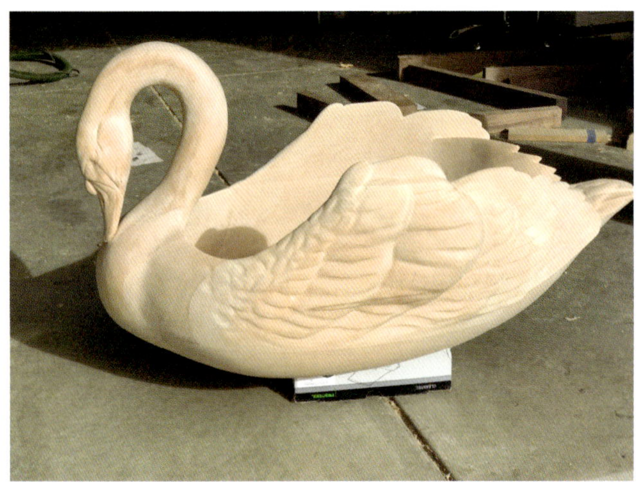

I understand that creating healthy boundaries is easier said than done. Sometimes we simply find ourselves in seasons where chaos reigns and peace is in short supply. When I find myself in those circumstances and seasons, I find it even more important to keep Christ at the center. I encourage you to do the same. Bring your voice into harmony with His. And as for all we can't control, as the author of Ecclesiastes suggested, take each season in its turn (3:1–8). As you do, listen for the grace notes of God's creativity—whether that be in those brief glimpses of peace in the margins or in the very midst of the storm—that still small voice that says, *Yes, I am still working here; behold, I am making something new.*

So, this has been my story in the fullness of family life—swanlike. But once upon a time, we were expecting our first. And I will never forget that moment: Hannah, coming up to me with a radiant smile on her face and a positive pregnancy test in her hand. I was excited, but entirely unprepared for what was to come—both for good and for ill.

The ill came first. Morning sickness hit Hannah hard and fast. We ought to have taken things slowly, but we had already scheduled a trip to Europe and

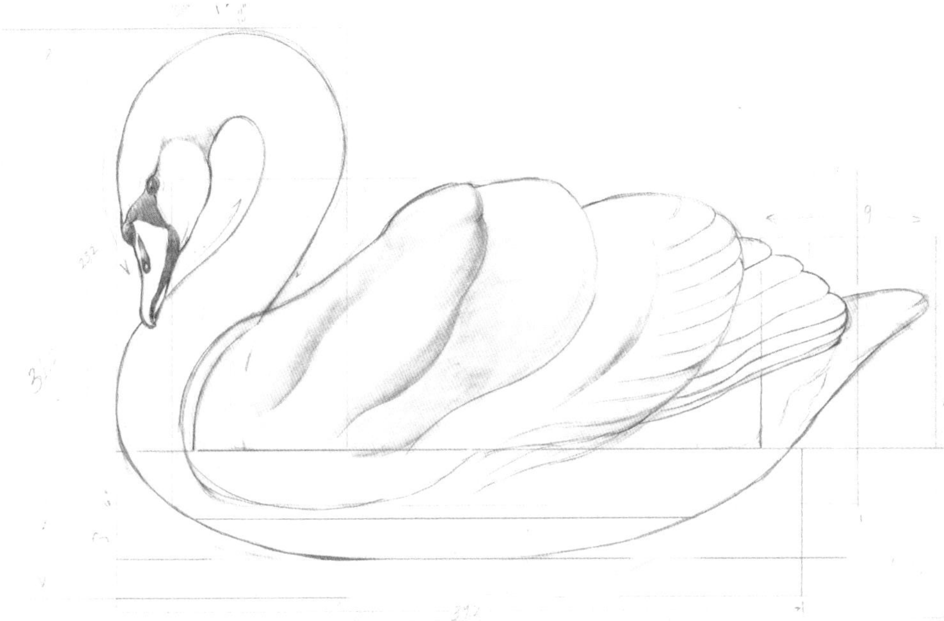

thought—however naïvely—that everything could continue as planned. But tiniest Emma, hidden in her mother's womb, made herself known every step of that feverish trip. Strange smells, unfamiliar foods, crowded trains, and narrow, winding roads proved a recipe for disaster. When we returned home from our not-so-grand tour, Hannah was often bedridden. I did all I could to care for her while running our business, but it could hardly be described as harmonious living.

Mercifully, Hannah's morning sickness abated after the first trimester. She was picking up more and more of her usual work duties and I finally got reacquainted with my pillow. I had some margin back in my life. Yet the melancholy air that hung about us during that first hard season had bothered me and I wanted to change the spirit in which we would welcome our first baby into the world. I was going to put up the bunting the best way I knew how.

With Emma well on her way, I decided to carve her a cradle. Following the theme of the altar, I sketched out the model of a swan in which this precious baby girl would lie, nestled sweetly between its back-folded wings. But rather than remain simply in balance, this would move in harmony—gliding back and forth, as if on water. It was

It was again time to pray with chisel in hand.

again time to pray with chisel in hand; there was another Ebenezer to create.

I'm sure many fathers can relate to the helpless (and dare I say guilty) feeling I wrestled with during this season. The contribution we make to the creation and growth of children pales in comparison to that of their mothers. The imbalance is only compounded as we witness the many trials and tribulations our women must endure. It's enough to make even the most supportive husband feel like a putz. So, even as I made the cradle in a spirit of celebration, it also became another altar. Rather than dwell in my feelings of guilt, fear, angst, and inadequacy, I placed them there, and then put them to work.

As is often the case with my art, there is only so much planning you can do ahead of time. Some queries of execution are only answered along the way, and such was the case with the swan. I began by cutting and gluing several pieces of wood to build the shape of the cradle. At this point it looked more like a LEGO version of a swan and nothing like the sleek, graceful creature I wanted to portray. So, once the glue cured, I grabbed my largest draw knife, which has a twelve-inch-wide, inward-facing blade with handles on either side. The tool is designed to be pulled toward the carver to remove long, large shavings of wood. Think of it like a giant razor-sharp cheese slicer.

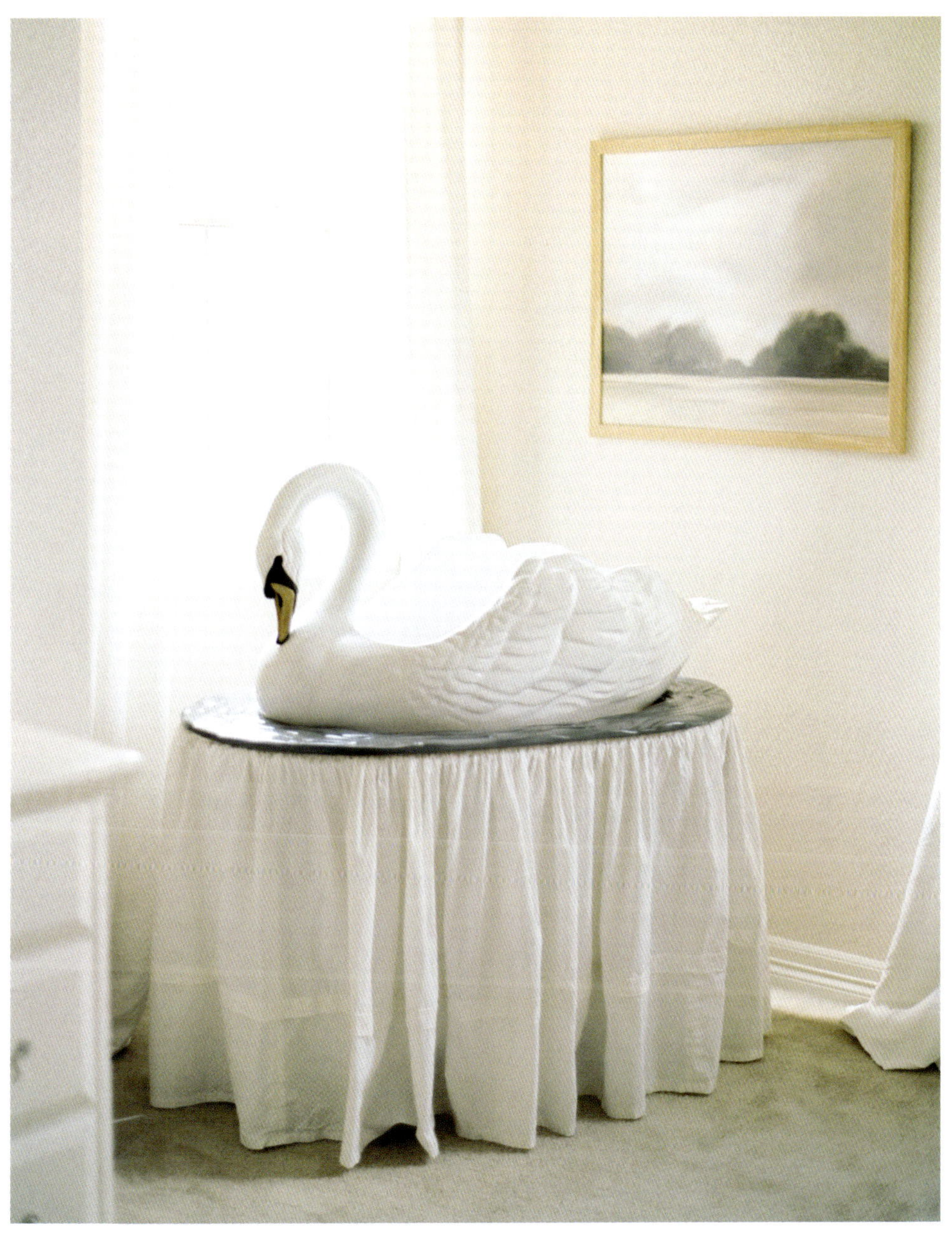

fig 11 DETAIL OF WORK

Swan Cradle, 2017. Hand-carved and hand-painted wood bassinet made from basswood, walnut, and lignum vitae, with magnetic rocking mechanism.

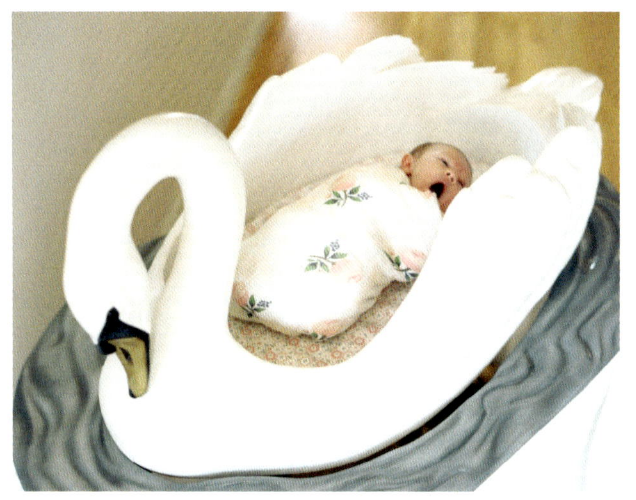

I secured the awkward mass of laminated wood to my workbench and began to aggressively shave down the bulky corners and flat surfaces. After hours of chaotic carving, wood shavings large and small covered the woodshop floor and myself. Still, the wooden mass was far from any semblance of a bird, let alone a cradle, but at least we were getting somewhere.

Even as I worked, our precious baby girl grew within Hannah, fearfully and wonderfully made by the very hand of God. We followed each stage of creation through an app on Hannah's phone. One week Emma's heartbeat was perceivable; another week, her toenails and fingernails began to grow. I still recall Hannah's first ultrasound, when Emma was but the size of a peanut. The sound of her heartbeat brought me to tears. And as I gazed at the grainy black-and-white image of her on the monitor, I felt as if I were peering into the keyhole of God's holy workshop. It filled me with overwhelming joy.

The formation of my cradle, by contrast, was far less impressive. But even for the great divide that exists between my wood carving and His soul crafting, I was grateful for the opportunity to mirror His handiwork with my own, however

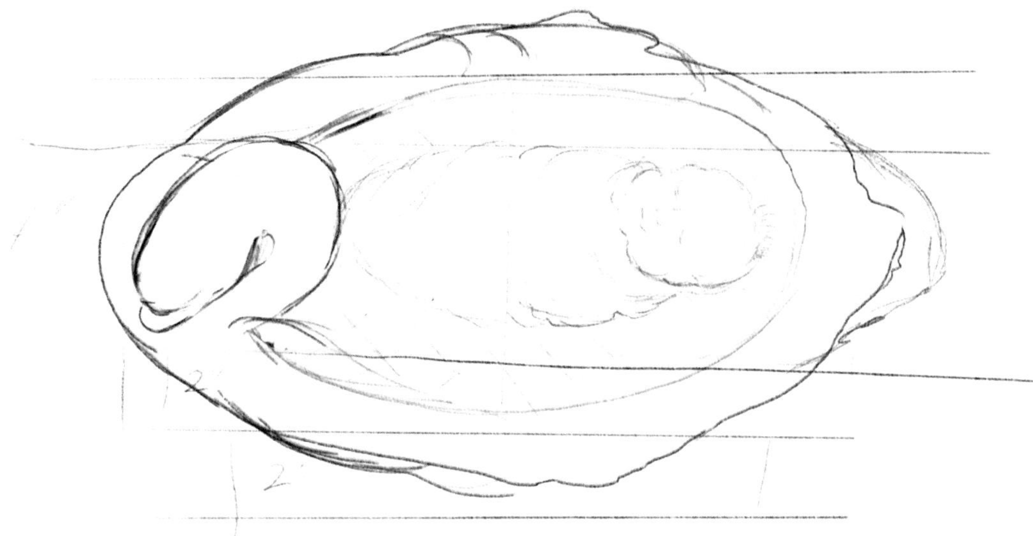

incompletely. In the prayer closet of my woodshop, He met me daily, drawing me to deeper mindfulness and praise.

And sure enough, out of the layers of wood shavings, the wings and neck of the swan finally emerged. With the carving now done, it was time to sand. And so I spent countless hours removing the chisel marks. I preened the wooden feathers with nothing more than scraps of sandpaper between my fingertips. Then it was time for the finishing touches. I stained the swan with whitewash to allow some of the wood grain to show through and gilded her beak with 23 karat shell gold so it would glisten as she swayed upon the carved water surface of her black walnut base.

Stephen Goebel, a good friend of mine and brilliant engineer, helped me design the cradle's magnetic rocking mechanism. The swan glides on two dowels front and back, which I turned on a lathe from a wood called *lignum vitae*, which is Latin for "tree of life." This dense, oily wood's self-lubricating properties are ideal for mechanical applications. The rocking motion itself is driven by a strong magnet, which is imbedded in a sickle-shaped pendulum attached to the bottom of the swan. The crook of the sickle passes through another electromagnet on the base that gives a short pulse every time it senses

> EVEN AS I CREATE, HIS CREATION IS GREATER STILL.

the other magnet passing through. All the while, two large brass clock weights hang below the cradle to counter the weight of the swan above and the babe within. Once the baby is placed in the cradle, all one needs to do to start it rocking is pull gently on one side and the magnets below perpetuate the motion and sustain its harmony. Like a real swan swimming on a lake, the power of its propulsion is veiled beneath the surface—in this case by a white skirt lovingly sewn by my mother-in-law.

From start to finish, the project took five months. Hannah's, of course, took nine. And even as I look fondly on the work of my hands, it only reminds me of the greater work that was done in and through Hannah, culminating in the miraculous gift of our little girl. Even as I create, His creation is greater still. Yet He lovingly chooses to work within and among us.

As I reflect now upon my time in the woodshop, working as our child grew within Hannah, I am reminded of a carpenter, long ago, who witnessed the miracle of God's creation firsthand. I wonder if Joseph shared the same feelings of helplessness, angst, fear, and inadequacy when faced with a pregnancy over which he had so little control. And as he spent his days carving and building, did he also find himself imagining what was being formed within his young wife? I wonder, too, at the birth, whether he chose the manger. Perhaps he even refashioned it to receive his son more gracefully. I imagine him clearing out the old hay, half-chewed by the resident animals, and replacing it with fresh straw. Did he restabilize the legs? Check to make sure the lashing was tight? What thoughts and emotions must have churned beneath the surface, even as he may have presented calm in the face of so many strange and unexpected visitors, all come to worship his little boy—his son, his Savior.

The swan's peaceful appearance is not a pretense. And it is certainly not an illustration of the need to keep calm and carry on. Men, especially, have an unhealthy habit of keeping our struggles beneath the surface. And it is often the case that what is hidden is not healthy. We all—men and women alike—must acknowledge the chaos in our lives. But even more, we must invite God into that chaos. This is the Lord, after all, who calms the storm (Mark 4:35–41). And in any case, is He not already right there with us? He knows what we are going through. We need not endure it alone.

At long last, following eighteen hours of harrowing labor, we welcomed our precious Emma Jane into the world. I was overwhelmed with love for my daughter and her beautiful mother, who had endured so much for so long. When we arrived home, I placed Emma in her new cradle—eager to see my work completed. As I looked upon my sleeping daughter, rocking gently within the wings of the swan, I reflected upon the many times I had imagined her there, and how they paled in comparison to the incandescent reality. This divine masterpiece, lovingly bundled and swaying sweetly, now sheltered within the work of my own hands: my creation made meaningful and wonderful by His.

In light of those earlier forays into fairyland, you are probably aware that our brood has since grown. Indeed, two further cygnets—Henry and Eloise—have been held within the shelter of that same swan's wings. I pray they never go a day of their beautiful lives without knowing the love we have for them all.

And so, what originally began as a cradle for my daughter has now become an image of parenthood. Swanlike, Hannah and I remain committed to each other, keeping our children near as we move ever forward through the waters of this life. In the person of Christ, we seek to take both the peace and the chaos and bring them into harmony, trusting that He will find us to be willing parents and partners in His creative work.

A Prayer of a Father

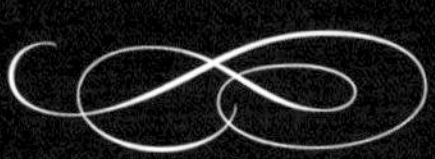

Abba God, my Father,

A father and creator am I, for the two are one and the same. A call to be a father is a call to go further toward the likeness of the imago Dei. Thou hast invited me into Thy making where souls and sinew are formed. I with Thee and wife makes three to merge and make and breathe. Collaboration marks Thy method to mimic holy Trinity. Our union imparts a life that starts in the sacred and unseen. From heart's first beat to babe's first breath, a miraculous process unfolds. Oh, what joy overtakes come the arrival of beloved, begotten souls. For what glory is Thine is shared as mine—to be held and to behold. But the creative alliance between us has not yet reached its end. For the crafting of character remains, and Thy Great Commission begins. So, God, make me skilled in my making as truth and love I instill. Thy Word and Thy Spirit shall guide me as I implore them to walk in Thy will. Lord, teach me well to remember that my first mission field is my kin. The souls Thou hast bid me watch after shall be returned to Thee in the end.

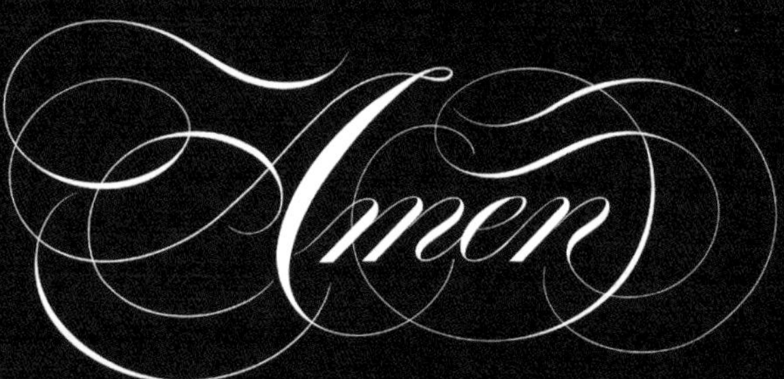

CHAPTER SIX

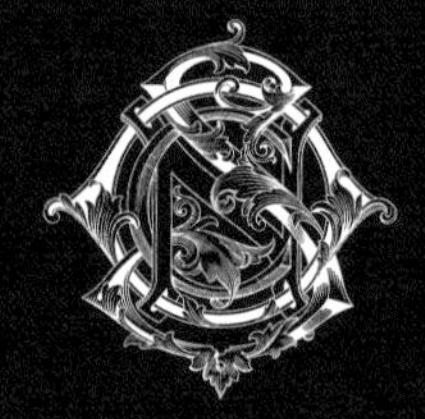

HIS EYE IS ON THE

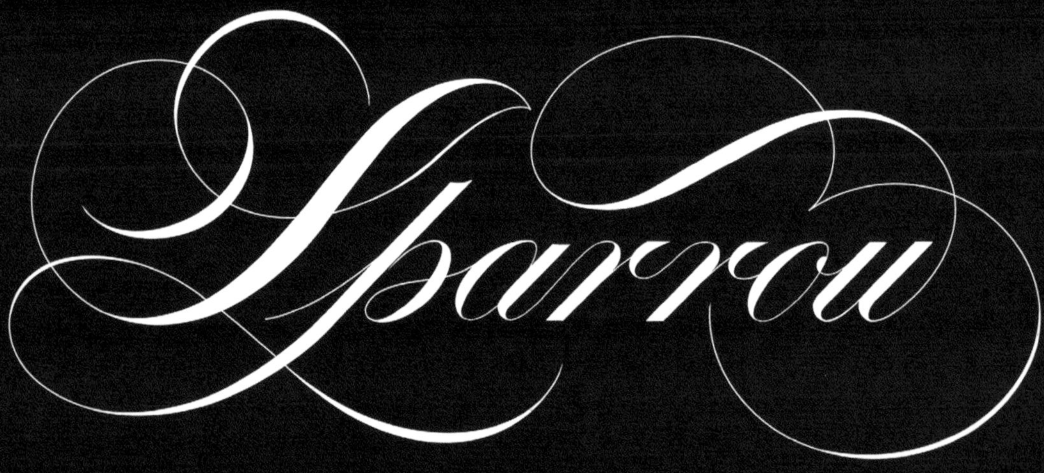

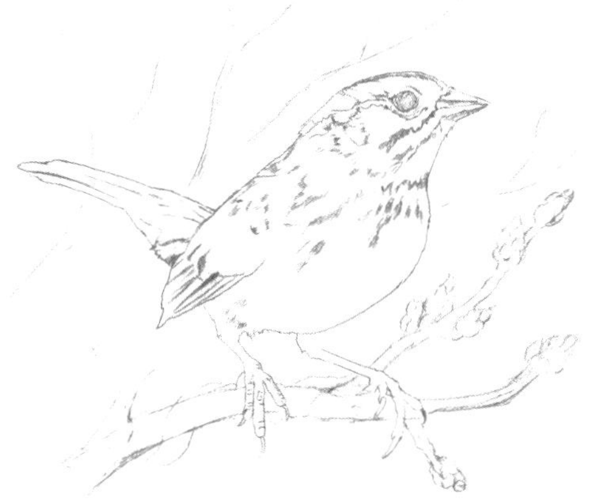

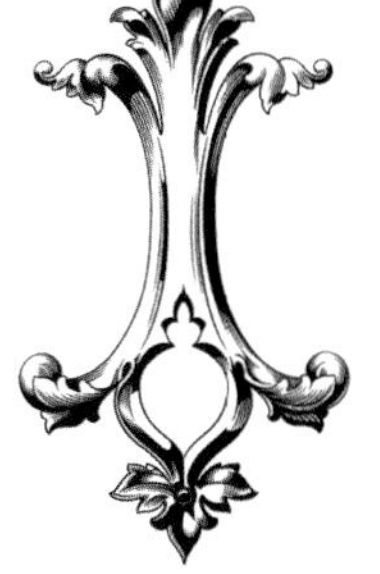

n my story thus far I have written about resonance and harmony. These are not only fitting metaphors for my calling as an artist, but they also speak to a deeper passion—a love for sacred music. Few experiences move me more than when I lend my voice to a chorus of others in the praise of our Savior. The singing of hymns, with their rich interplay of melody and poetry, moves me most of all. Many we sing today testify to the faith of generations. Some of the more recent are still more than a century old; others go back further, to a time when the faith was still young.

Behind each composition are tales of tragedy and triumph, lamentation and praise. Yet they continue to speak to, and for, so many. Some hymns may mark major life events, like marriage or the loss of a loved one. Others might strike us so powerfully they become our life's anthem, whose tune and lyric we'll carry for the rest of our days.

In the following suite of chapters, I will explore the illustrations of three hymns that have played an important role not only in my life but also in the lives of so many others: "His Eye Is on the Sparrow," "The Old Rugged Cross," and "Be Thou My Vision." And I will share, too, how I have sought to fill my voice with their melody as I follow in the steps of the many who have come before.

THE FOOTHILLS OF THE FRONT RANGE EMERGED LIKE A MIGHTY KING ENTHRONED BEHIND A GLASSY RESERVOIR, HIS ARTICULATED ROCK SHOULDERS DRAPED IN PINE TREE FORESTS, HIS HEAD CROWNED IN THE LAST LIGHT OF DAY.

in both directions. Hannah was pregnant with Henry, our second child. It was clear we needed more space—and fast. With coffee in hand, I spent each morning scanning new listings, searching for an answer to our prayers.

One listing seemed promising but turned out to be less than ideal. Its view of the Colorado Rockies, however, was transcendent. The foothills of the front range emerged like a mighty king enthroned behind a glassy reservoir, his articulated rock shoulders draped in pine tree forests, his head crowned in the last light of day. Inspired by this vision of God's creative handiwork, I looked up the neighborhood again that evening and found a listing captioned "coming soon." It did not take long to realize this was the place we were looking for.

In the meantime, the composition was coming along, but the title's background still eluded me. Nothing quite seemed to fit. Once again, the view of the foothills captured my imagination, so I brought them into the composition. I guess you could say it was an act of faith—a prayer offered up for a home I longed to be ours. And sure enough, the sale went through. We had our dream home. But as is so often the case, the material things we believed would dispel our worries only managed to create new ones. The boxes weren't even unpacked before the pressures of the new house and our growing family began to take their toll.

What is it about human beings that we continue to live like this, chasing after things we think will satisfy, only for them to bring us greater dissatisfaction? It

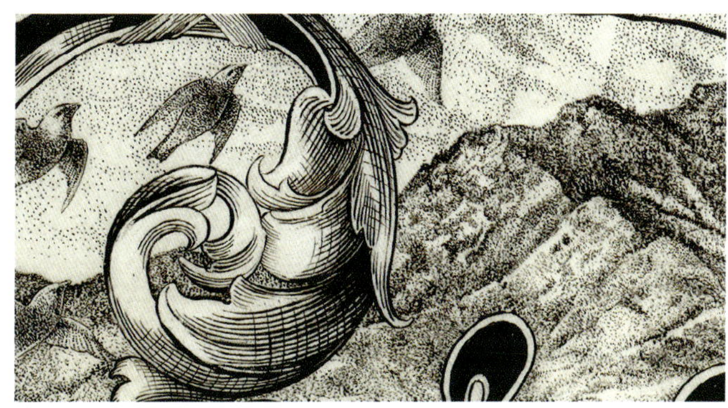

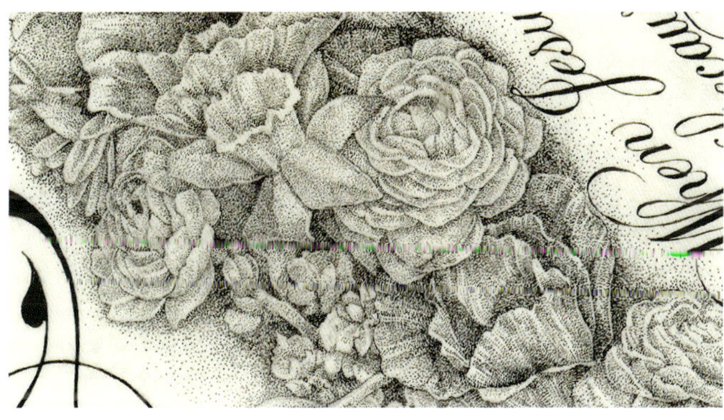

makes curses out of blessings and turns what should be a source of happiness and joy into a cause of frustration and resentment.

To make matters worse, I had no commissions lined up at the time but was still working hard on the piece. Not only was this "out of pocket" in a financial sense, but I had also chosen to execute it using some of the most tedious and time-consuming techniques. The spiraling sequence of the script took days to lay out. The drawing of the sparrow in the middle, the wreath of flowers circumventing the script spiral, and the entire background were all done with stippling—the meticulous process I described in an earlier chapter. Nevertheless, I was ecstatic about the piece and felt the Lord's blessing upon it, however "unprofitable" it might have seemed in the moment.

But try as I might, the stresses and demands of our new home were far outpacing the rhythmic tapping of my pen nib on the vellum. After a hard and hopeless conversation with Hannah one evening about the mounting bills and housework, I retreated to my studio in the back room of the house, hoping to find solace in my

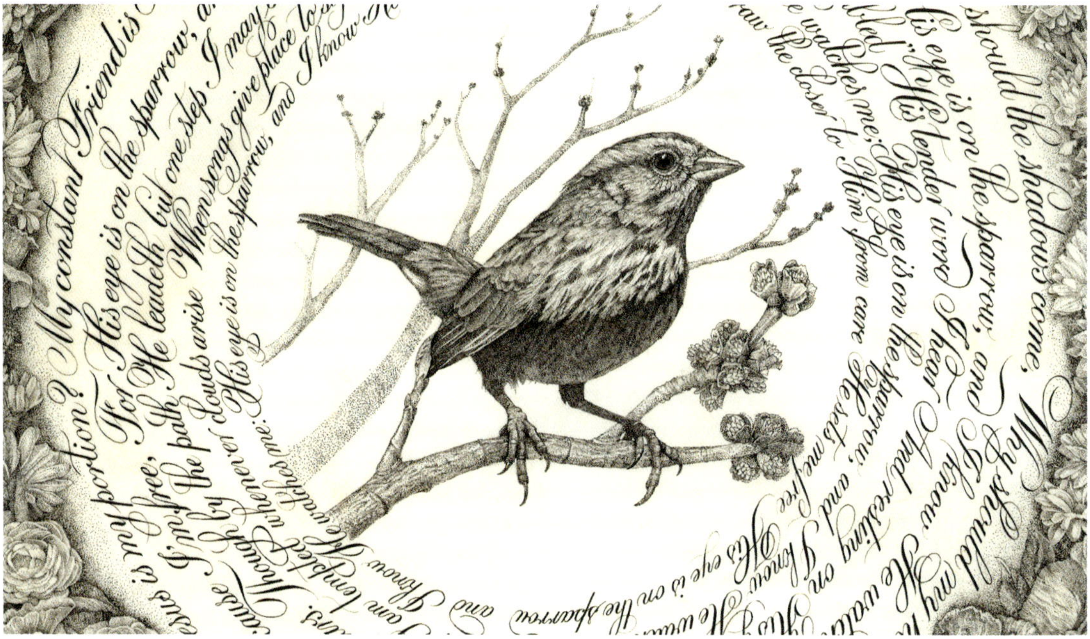

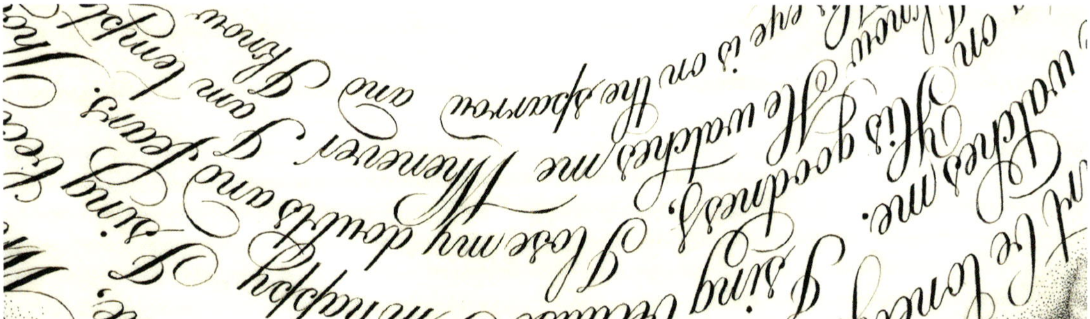

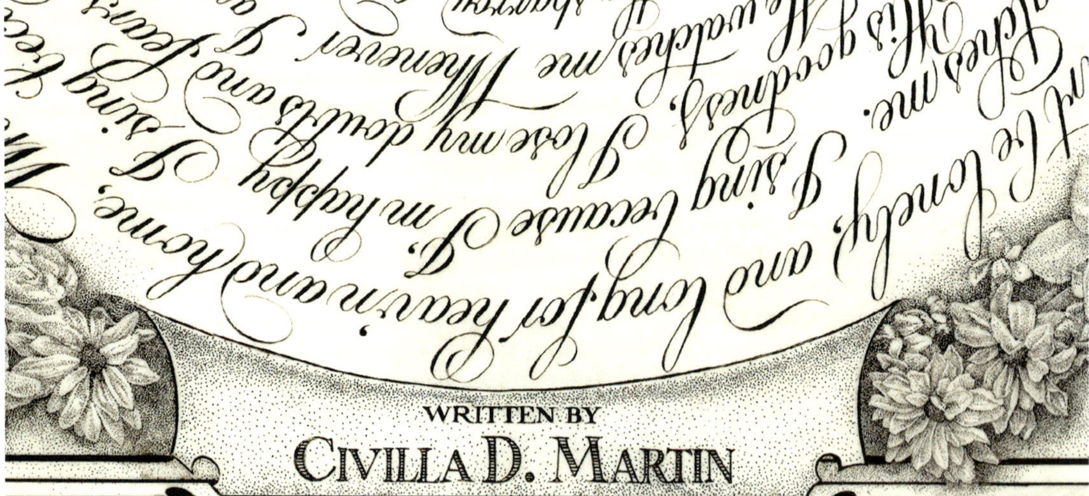
WRITTEN BY
CIVILLA D. MARTIN

I WAS ECSTATIC ABOUT THE PIECE AND FELT THE LORD'S BLESSING UPON IT.

work. There upon my drafting table lay the half-finished hymn, with a million or more dots to go. I stood for a while staring over it, unable to conjure up the motivation to proceed. It was then that I heard a still small voice. It prompted me to turn the piece over and pour out all the doubt and pain I was feeling into the Father's hands. As I penned my pain on the back of the stretched vellum, my lower eyelids felt like a dam ready to break. I could barely hold back the growing swell of tears. With my heart wrung out on the page in tight, twisted strokes of cursive script, I dated my lament "June 1, 2018," and went to bed.

But I couldn't sleep. The ceiling of our bedroom was illuminated by the moonlight pouring in through our uncovered windows. I stared wide-eyed, trying to discern answers in the paint texture above. Even as Hannah slept, her unconscious anxiety was as palpable as my own. I tried to force my eyes closed, as if to shutter the whirlwind of worries from my mind. And in one final plea, having exhausted every other prayer I could think of, I simply uttered, "Please, God."

I cannot recall how long I lay there, trying desperately to fall asleep, but at some point the still small voice returned. This time, it said, "*For years Hannah has supported you—it is time now for you to support her.*" In a matter of moments, I went from being restless with worry and depression to being restless with excitement. I thanked the Lord in silent praise. As I fell into a deep sleep, one thought remained: *I can't wait to tell Hannah!*

Never could I have imagined all that we would reap from this season of sowing humility. I can do many things as a multidisciplinary artist, but I can only do them *one at a time*. God, on the other hand, is the great multitasker, able to do exceedingly more than we could ever hope or imagine with the very little that we bring Him. What I gave of my time and my passion humbly, as the Lord directed, was repaid to me tenfold . . . and maybe more. The richest reward was seeing Hannah flourish—in her faith, in her friendships, in her calling, and in our marriage. All I did was engrave a bit of jewelry while God took care of the rest. Quicker am I now to humble myself, especially where the betterment of my beloved is concerned. Ultimately, my gifts shape me further into the likeness of Christ when they are exercised in humility. In that sense it is *good* to serve!

Though small like sparrows we all are, we do not escape His loving gaze. And though lowly we were made to be, still we all share in His glory. So let's sing this hymn amid the chorus of the faithful, as a reminder of our Creator's promise—a promise He made to all those created in His image. If His eye is on the sparrow, it is also on you. Hallelujah.

fig 12 DETAIL OF WORK

His Eye Is on the Sparrow, 2018. Pen and ink on genuine vellum, 16 x 22 inches. Weidmann brings beautiful imagery to the celebrated gospel hymn "His Eye Is On the Sparrow," originally written by Civilla D. Martin in 1905. Around the nest of lyrics, a floral wreath hails on either side, containing spring-blooming flowers. Among them are daisies, crocus, peonies, tulips, and daffodils: each one chosen for its symbolism of cheerfulness, brightness, compassion, perfect love, rebirth, faith, and everlasting life.

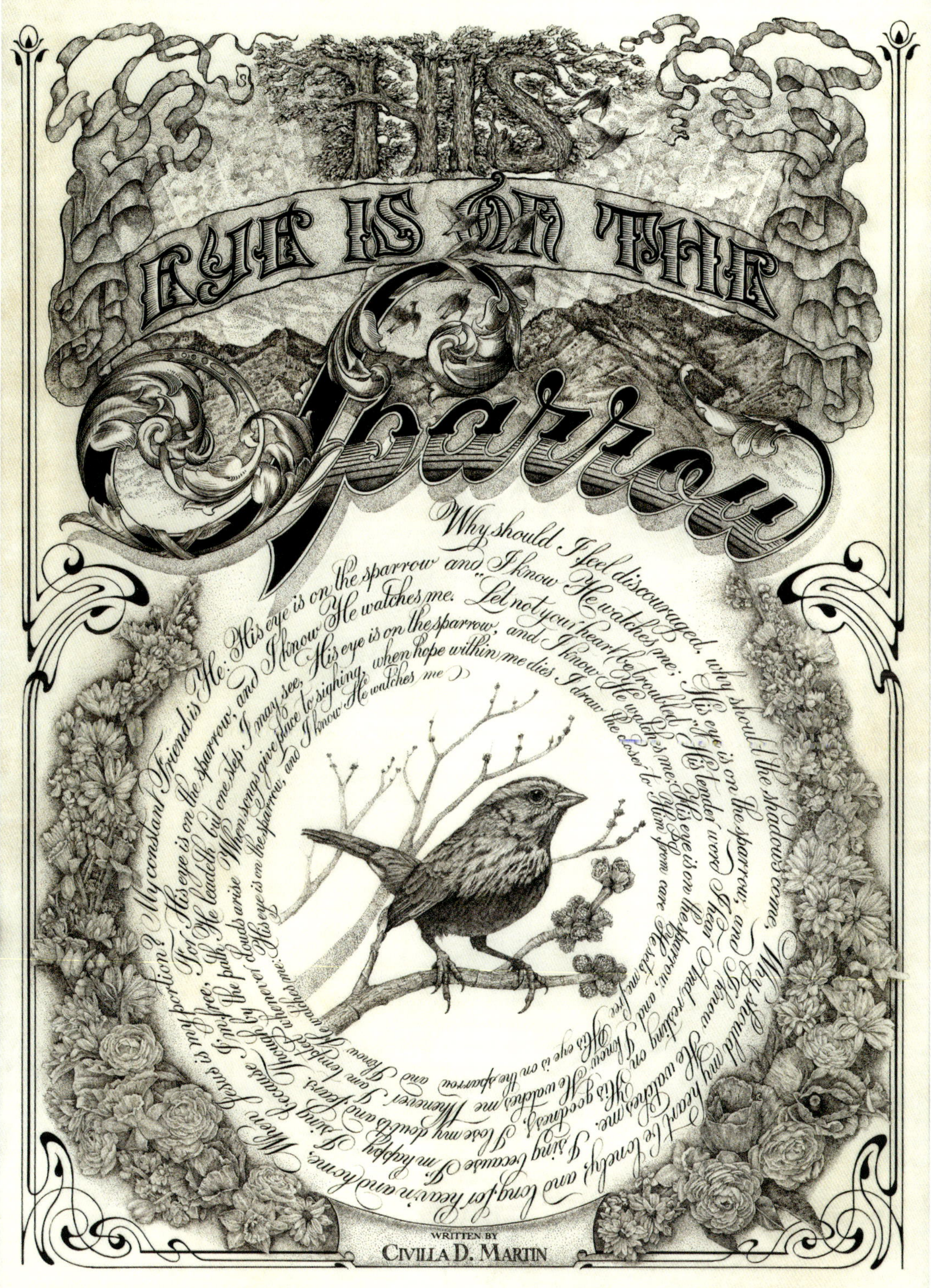
His Eye Is on the Sparrow
Why should I feel discouraged, why should the shadows come,
Why should my heart be lonely and long for heav'n and home.
When Jesus is my portion? My constant Friend is He:
His eye is on the sparrow, and I know He watches me;
His eye is on the sparrow, and I know He watches me.
I sing because I'm happy, I sing because I'm free;
For His eye is on the sparrow, and I know He watches me.
Let not your heart be troubled, His tender word I hear,
And resting on His goodness, I lose my doubts and fears;
Though by the path He leadeth, but one step I may see,
His eye is on the sparrow, and I know He watches me;
His eye is on the sparrow, and I know He watches me.
Whenever I am tempted, whenever clouds arise,
When songs give place to sighing, when hope within me dies,
I draw the closer to Him, from care He sets me free;
His eye is on the sparrow, and I know He watches me.
Written by
Civilla D. Martin

A Prayer of Smallness

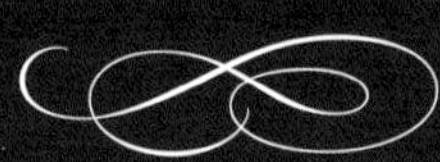

Yet who am I that Thou would take notice of me?

Yet who am I that Thou would take notice of me? Who am I that Thou would be mindful of me? I am so small and insignificant a person; Thou art so great a God. While I am weak, corrupt, and broken, Thou art enthroned in glory on high. How shall my prayers ever reach Thee? How far shall my feeble cries climb? When in the dark I am blinded and lowly, what ray of hope there shall I find? I am but one sparrow in a myriad, a nameless face in the flock. In this endless expanse I stand no chance to be anything but lost. Yet before despair overtakes me, before downtrodden I become, Thou bended low to find me and made a way for me through Thy Son. Now the apple of Thy eye Thou shalt keep me. Rescued from shame and from fame, God, teach me the power of smallness as I bask in the grandeur of Thy name. Let not pride overtake me; let humility mark my way. Forever I am found in Thy favor, for a new creation of me Thou hast made.

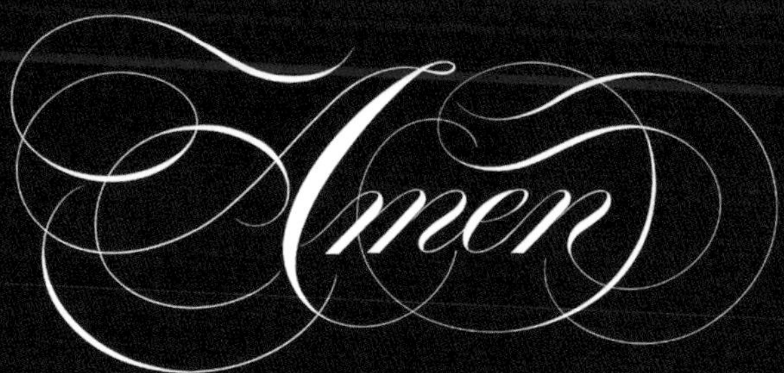

CHAPTER SEVEN

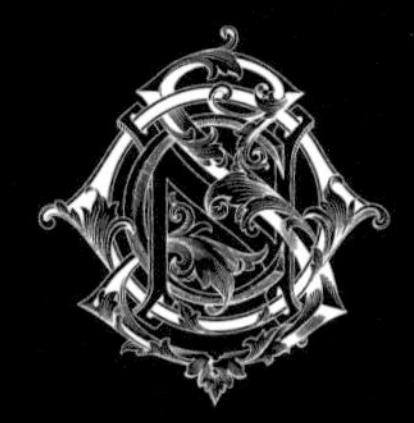

THE OLD RUGGED *Cross*

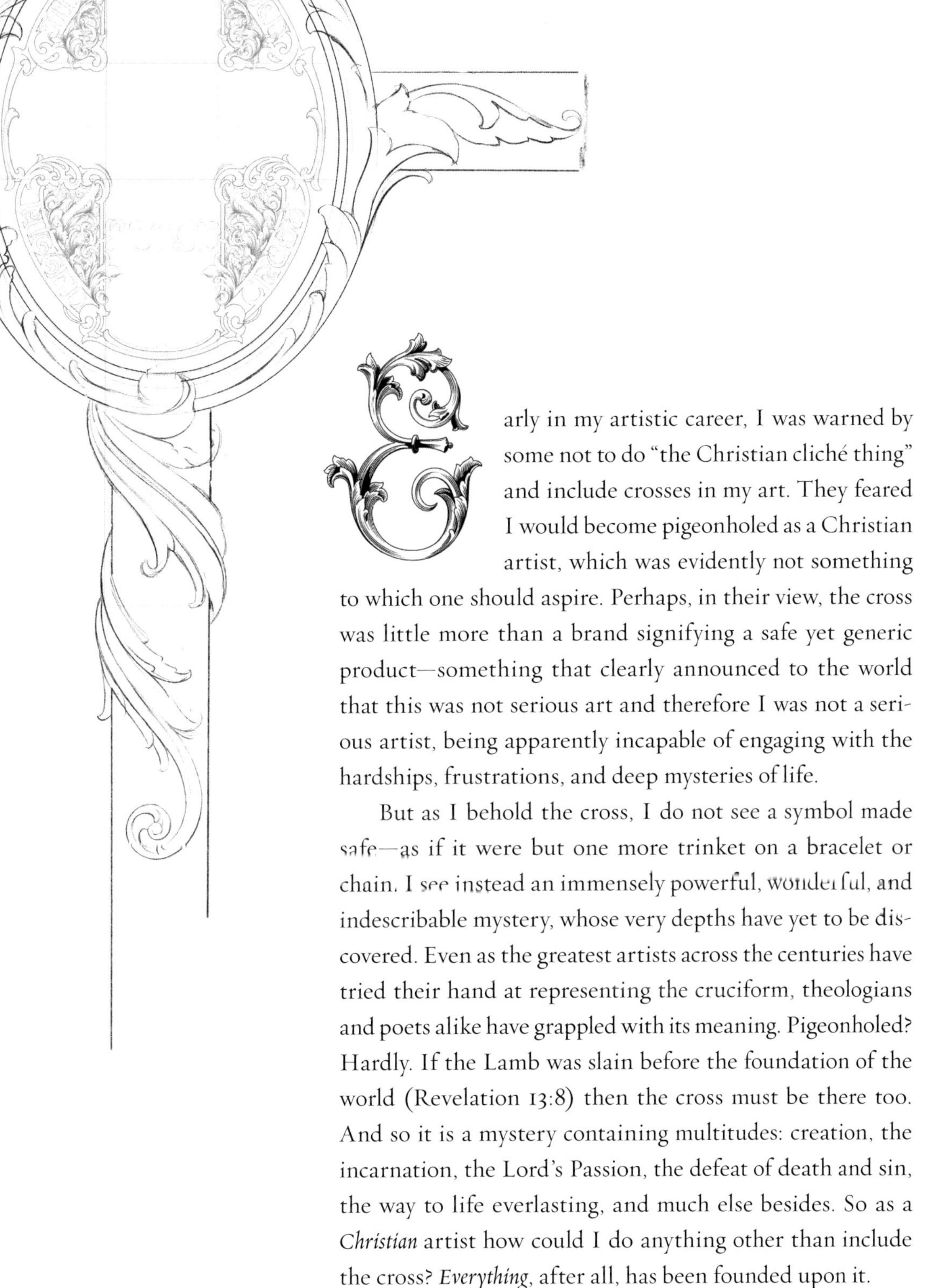

Early in my artistic career, I was warned by some not to do "the Christian cliché thing" and include crosses in my art. They feared I would become pigeonholed as a Christian artist, which was evidently not something to which one should aspire. Perhaps, in their view, the cross was little more than a brand signifying a safe yet generic product—something that clearly announced to the world that this was not serious art and therefore I was not a serious artist, being apparently incapable of engaging with the hardships, frustrations, and deep mysteries of life.

But as I behold the cross, I do not see a symbol made safe—as if it were but one more trinket on a bracelet or chain. I see instead an immensely powerful, wonderful, and indescribable mystery, whose very depths have yet to be discovered. Even as the greatest artists across the centuries have tried their hand at representing the cruciform, theologians and poets alike have grappled with its meaning. Pigeonholed? Hardly. If the Lamb was slain before the foundation of the world (Revelation 13:8) then the cross must be there too. And so it is a mystery containing multitudes: creation, the incarnation, the Lord's Passion, the defeat of death and sin, the way to life everlasting, and much else besides. So as a *Christian* artist how could I do anything other than include the cross? *Everything*, after all, has been founded upon it.

In my desire to honor His suffering, I found myself encountering the Crucified in the mystery of the cross as never before.

It was then with some trepidation that I received a commission in the spring of 2022 to produce an illustration of the hymn "The Old Rugged Cross." Little did I know that it would become the longest, most difficult project of my life to date. And yet through that immense difficulty, in my desire to honor His suffering, I found myself encountering the Crucified in the mystery of the cross as never before.

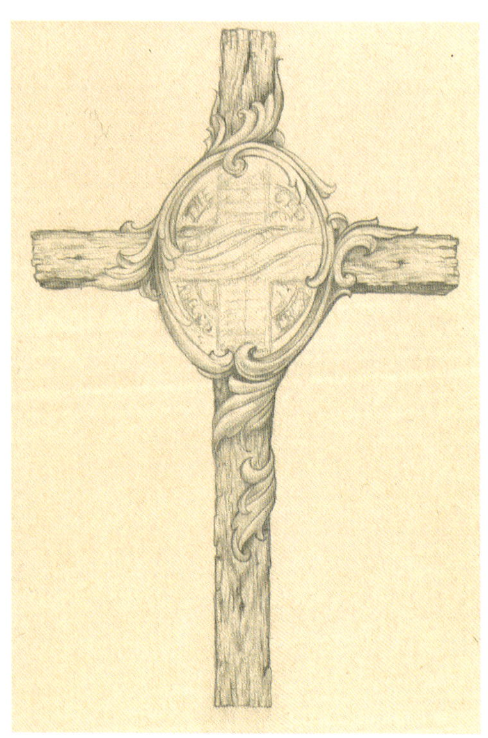

The elderly couple who commissioned me to create *The Old Rugged Cross* had grown up singing in a choir at a small, picturesque chapel. The two had met at practice and developed a lifelong love for both hymns and each other. This was one of their favorites. On the day we were scheduled to meet and discuss the commission, a wild idea popped into my head. I thought it would be amazing to not only write the hymn on vellum but to carve a frame for it as well—a frame recessed into the middle of a seven-foot-tall wooden cross.

Having sat down with the couple, I made a quick thumbnail sketch of my idea. Elated by the concept, they encouraged me to get on with the project. As it turns out, I had no idea how I was going to turn

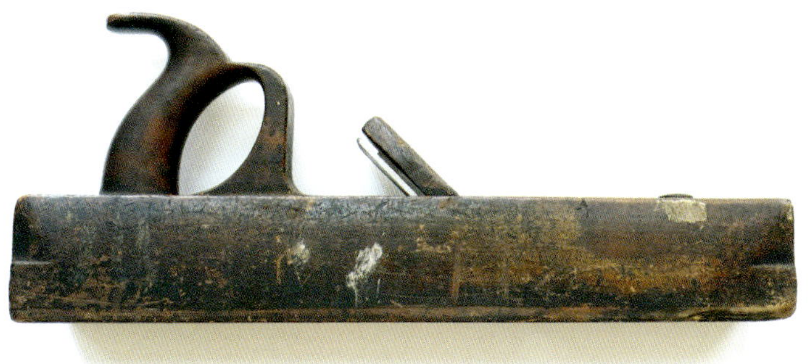

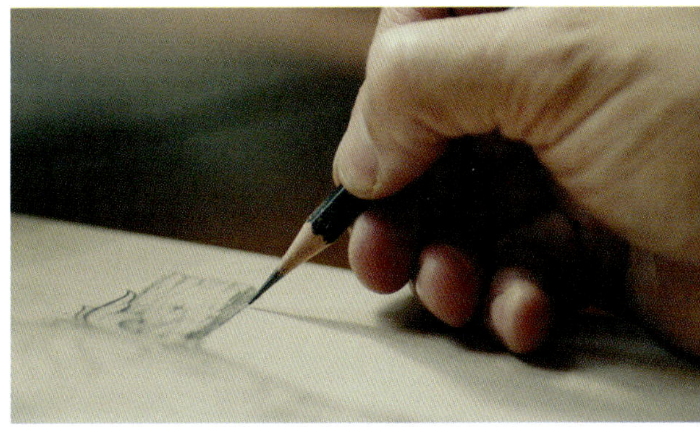

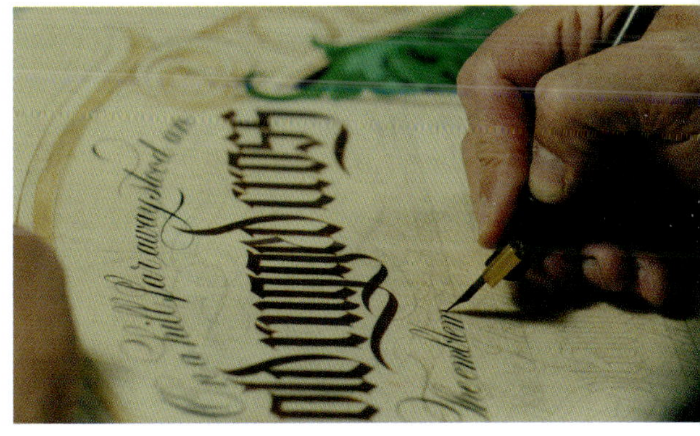

the concept into reality. The logistics of fitting a two-dimensional art piece within a three-dimensional one are complicated to say the least.

Apparently unsatisfied that the job was sufficiently difficult, I decided to use some aged, reclaimed wood to ensure we evoked the *old* and *rugged* aspects from the hymn. And so I searched for weeks, exhausting every resource I knew, to find reclaimed lumber that would serve the requisite look and feel. On Good Friday, as it happens, I brought the matter before God. Would He help me in my creation? I prayed I would not only find the right kind of wood, marked with years of age and weathering, but also that He would make it abundantly clear which pieces I should use.

In the eastern plains of Colorado, I found a lumberyard that specialized in reclaimed lumber. I wanted black walnut specifically; its dark color would contrast nicely with the creamy, light basswood that would comprise the frame and ornamental

> THE COMBINATION OF ALL THESE FACTORS . . . LED MEDIEVAL WRITERS TO INTERPRET VELLUM AS A SYMBOL OF CHRIST'S SURRENDERED LIFE—PERFECT, STRETCHED OUT, AND SACRIFICED.

leaf work. I drove through forest and farmland for a good hour until I arrived at a small lumberyard on the side of a county road. I hopped out of my truck and donned my leather work gloves, ready to sift through piles of old beams. The owner of the lumberyard emerged from his small office to meet me. I introduced myself and asked if he had any walnut timber in stock. Immediately, he turned and led me to the far end of a massive corridor bearing every kind of wood suitable for building: oak, hickory, alder, ash, heart pine, and cedar. In the far corner under a stack of odd cut-offs were two beams just barely visible. As I worked to uncover the beams and pull them from the heap, I found to my delight that they were beautifully aged and weather-worn—reclaimed from an Amish barn built in the mid-1800s.

As I heaved the largest beam onto my shoulder and began walking toward my truck, the significance of that holy day fell upon me. With my ear and cheek pressed against the worn surface of that timber beam, and beads of sweat rolling down my brow, I began to tremble—not from the weight of the beam but for the weight of what it meant to be carrying what would become a cross. I spent the drive home praising God, tears streaming down my dust-covered face.

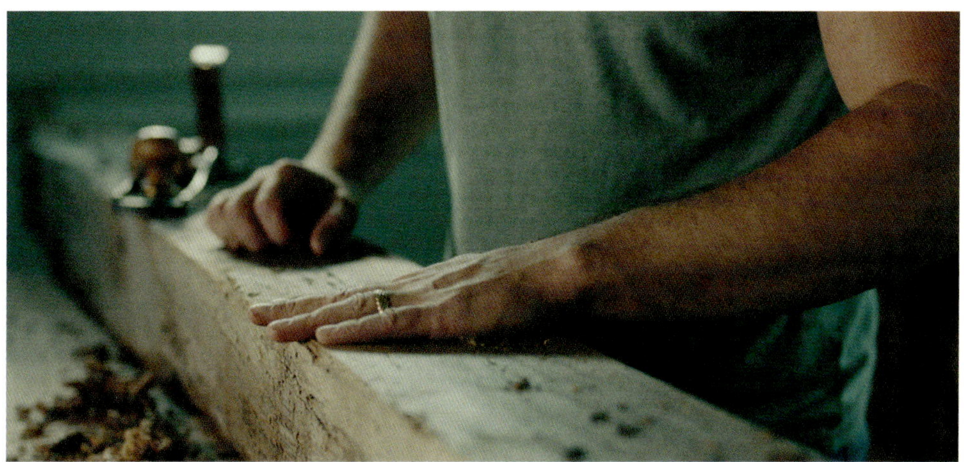

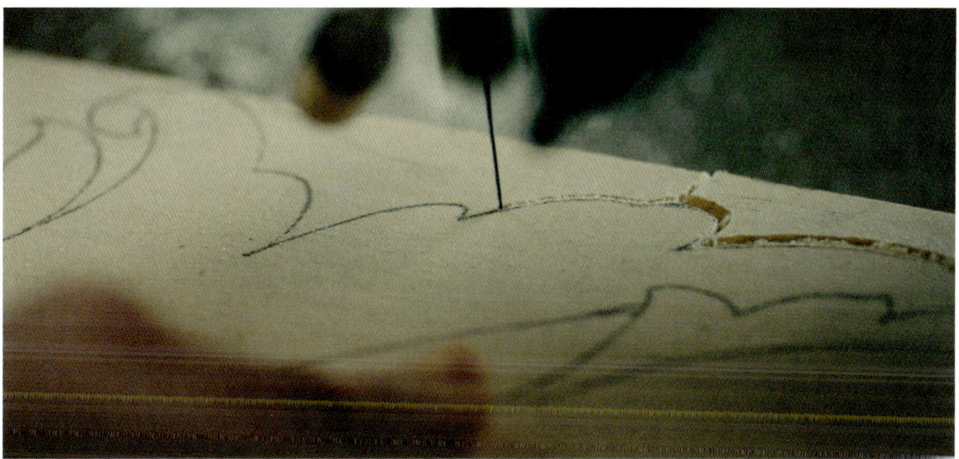

With my lumber chosen, I turned to writing the hymn itself. For this portion of the project, there was no material better suited than vellum. This rare material is produced from calfskin that has been treated, stretched, and dried. The highest quality comes from animals without spot or blemish, for a flaw of any kind would spoil the text written upon it. If given the opportunity to have some in your hands, you will find it both remarkably tactile and relatively dense, such that it feels much more substantial than a piece of paper or card. The combination of all these factors, interestingly enough, led medieval writers to interpret vellum as a symbol of Christ's surrendered life—perfect, stretched out, and sacrificed.

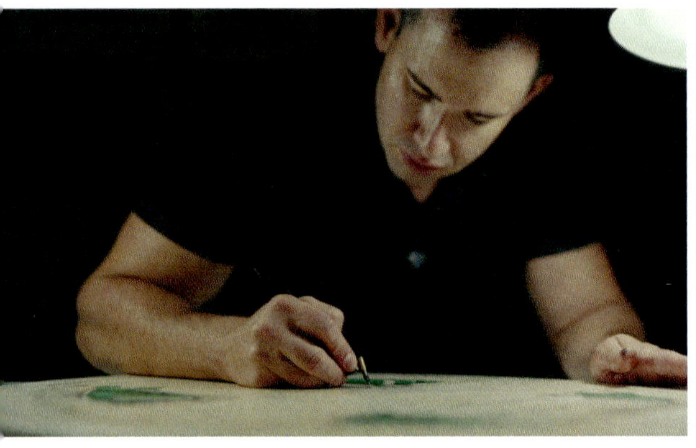

For my part, I approach vellum with a different measure of conviction than I do even the finest sheet of paper. A certain reverence marks my posture and focuses my mind. Although "The Old Rugged Cross" was composed long after vellum gave way to paper and the printing press, the material contributed the necessary substance, preciousness, and symbolism to the hymn's contents.

Carrying the lumber and handling the vellum offered ways for me to reflect more deeply on the mystery of the cross. It is important, of course, for such objects not to become ends in and of themselves, but such resources have often been used throughout the centuries to help the faithful imagine that fateful day, so they might more greatly appreciate Christ's suffering and sacrificial love. Perhaps you have something of a similar kind. It could be a piece of music, a picture, or a film—any creative work that has helped you grow deeper in your understanding of our Lord, something that's grown your passion for Him. This is what this heavy lumber did for me.

The Tragedy of the Cross

Each illustrated hymn involves a fair amount of research into its provenance. What stood out to me about George Bennard, the composer of "The Old Rugged Cross," was his devotion to the hymn's composition. Apparently, he carried a draft in his

A CERTAIN REVERENCE MARKS MY POSTURE AND FOCUSES MY MIND.

pocket for years, diligently working out each word. Occasionally he would share it with a few close friends to get their opinion. But he was in no rush; it would be ready when it was ready.

I wanted to honor that diligence by taking my time in selecting the overall layout and choosing individual lettering styles for each line of the hymn. At length, I made good progress on its written portion, having both painted the border with several layers of oil glazing and penned the script in ink. I was eager to make further headway on this marathon piece.

And then I returned home one day to find our cleaning crew packing up their equipment. About twice a month we have them come into the home studio to help us keep the chaos of three children and two businesses at bay. Everything seemed as usual when I entered my scriptorium. Then I looked to *The Old Rugged Cross* lying on my art table. To my utter shock and horror, every letter of the freshly written script had been smeared in a wash of wet rag strokes, running the full length of the piece. I caught myself on the edge of the art table as my legs gave way beneath me.

When I showed the piece to Hannah, she was also bewildered and in despair. Thinking it would help, she urged me to step away from the piece and go work on anything or nothing—whatever I needed to get my mind off this calamity. But the piece, like so many others, had a deadline, and I was already behind. I needed to salvage what I could.

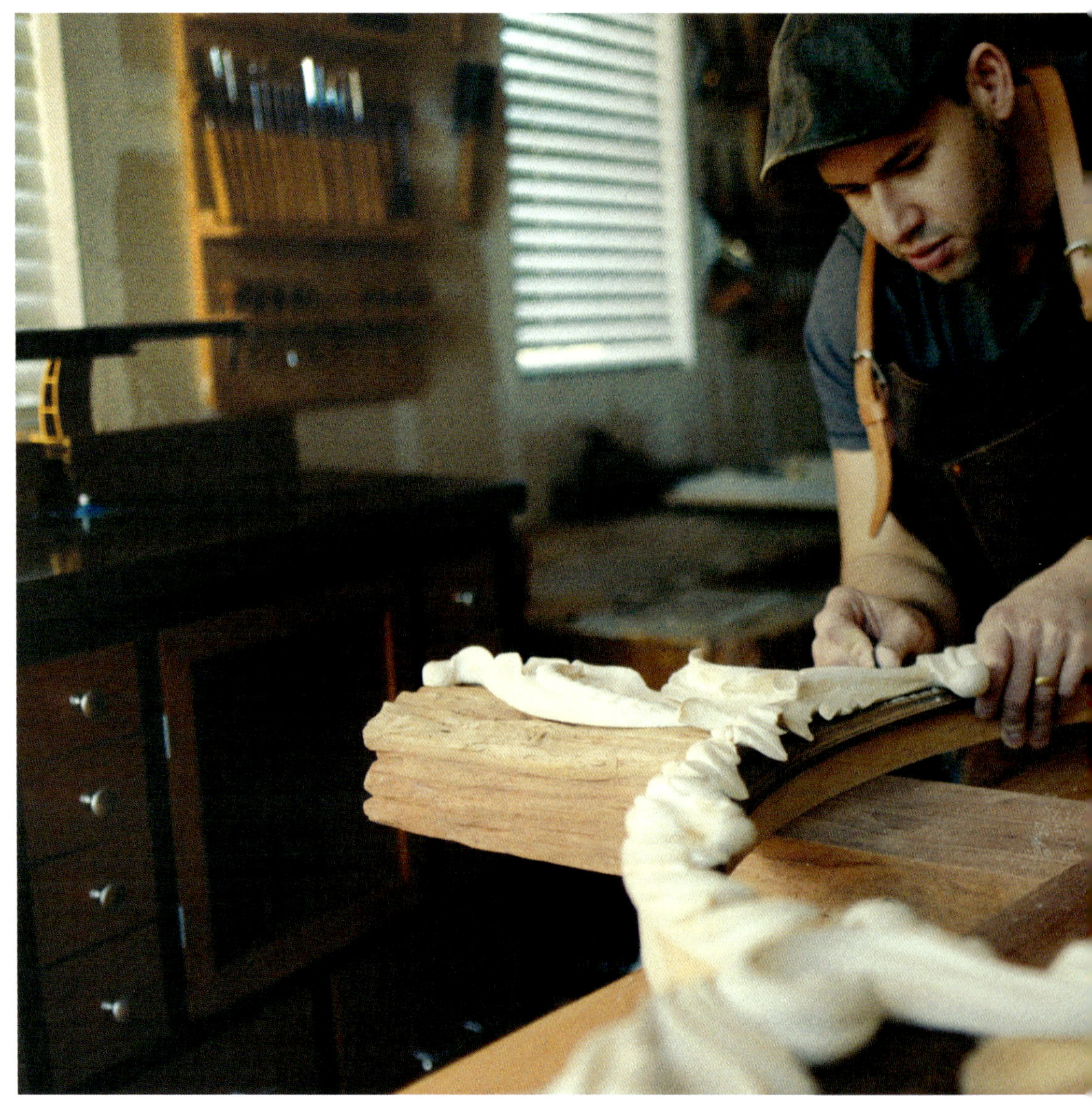

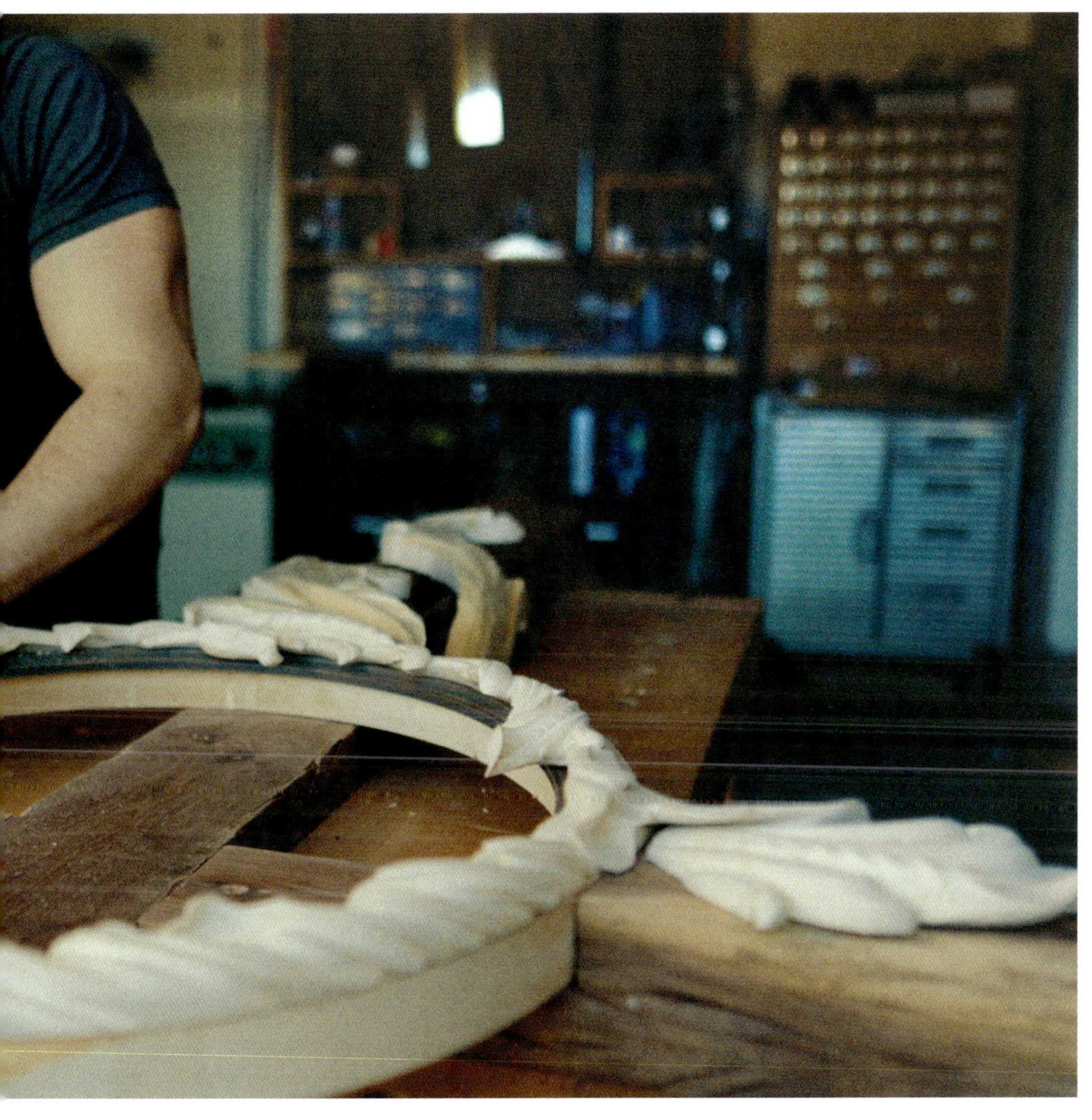

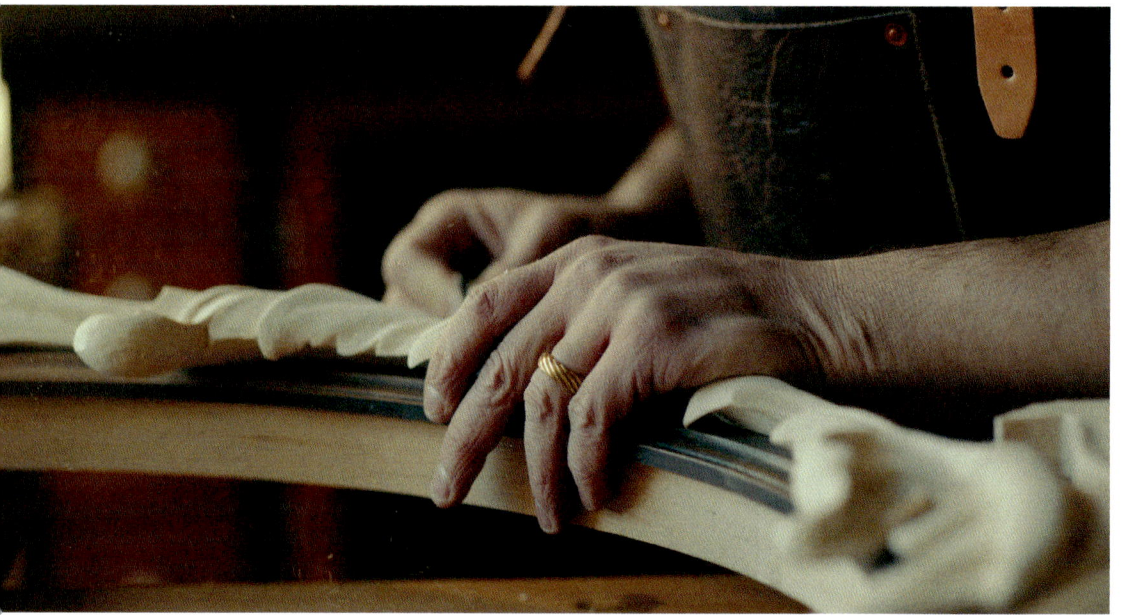

One of vellum's greatest attributes is its resilience. In the past, entire books of vellum have been "recycled" by scraping the lettering from the surface of their pages with the edge of a sharp knife. The process is painstaking but, when considering vellum's value, ultimately worthwhile. So, with knife in hand, I completed the destruction of my earlier work. Bit by bit, with a round-bladed scalpel, I carefully scraped away every letter of script and every smear of ink from the vellum's surface. Nearly all my penciled outline, which had taken several days to transfer, was lost and would have to be redrawn. The oil-painted border, however, was another matter. Rather than destroy the glazed layers I had spent weeks painting, I treated it with an art restorer's combination of Q-tips and saliva. Saliva has an enzyme in it that helps break down particular binders within pigments. This had me sucking on Q-tips for days, carefully rolling the saturated swabs over each square centimeter of the painted border. The work was tedious and gut-wrenching. All told, the restoration took three weeks.

Mine to Bear

At one point, Hannah asked me how I was able to cope. I told her I needed to do something with my pain, and putting it to work seemed the most edifying option. While it might have seemed natural to run from my suffering, that is not the way of the cross. At no point does the Lord tell us to give up when the going gets hard. Instead, as we read in Matthew 16:24, Jesus told His disciples to take up their cross and follow Him. And this view of suffering echoes across the New Testament. In James 1:2 we are told to "count it all joy" when we meet various trials, while in Romans 5:3–4 we are encouraged to "rejoice in our sufferings, knowing that suffering produces endurance, and endurance produces character, and character produces hope." Our suffering, then, when endured for the purposes of our Savior, ultimately leads not to our destruction but to new creation.

Perhaps you are suffering in this very moment—creatively or otherwise. You may be struggling with pain or brokenness, whether inflicted by the sins, shortcomings, or mishaps of others or your own. My friend, bring it all to the cross. You need not suffer in vain. Behold, He is making all things new (Revelation 21:5)! And what is more, even as you persevere, He is present in His kindness and care: "Blessed are those who mourn, for they shall be comforted" (Matthew 5:4)

You are blessed. Be comforted. Seek the cross in the midst of your suffering, God has promised to rescue and redeem you.

With the restoration complete, I embarked again upon the calligraphy piece. At every step I sought to draw attention to the mysterious work of Christ upon the cross. I set the hymn within a cruciform outline, employing different scripts for each line to emphasize their meaning. One of the more prominent is Fraktur, a calligraphic hand that originated in the monasteries of medieval Europe. Taking this hand at its literal meaning, I used it to symbolize the breaking of Christ, the incarnate Word, upon the cross.

I surrounded the outline with flourishing acanthus leaf. While you may have seen these leaves adorning the capital of an ancient Greek column, they are more

GOD HAS PROMISED TO RESCUE AND REDEEM YOU.

than just an appealing motif, having been interpreted to represent eternal life on one hand and sin and suffering on the other. And as for the hymn's title, I painted it to look like alabaster to suggest the broken jar in Bethany whose contents prepared Christ for His burial (Mark 14:3–9).

The other colors in the piece are likewise chosen for their symbolic properties: purple, which evoked high status among the ancient Romans, points to Christ as "King of kings and Lord of lords" (Revelation 19:16); green, which signifies flourishing, reflects Jesus' teaching that He came to bring life, and life abundantly (John 10:10); and gold, which medieval scribes used to evoke the heavenly, is here used to symbolize eternal glory (Hebrews 12:2).

Once I finished the central piece, I exchanged the scriptorium for the woodshop and began carving the cross and frame. I found this change helped reinvigorate my passion for the project, which is just as well because the bitter cold was setting in. Given the cleaning crew's mishap (which is how I euphemistically like to put it these days), I was no longer carving during the summer months as planned, but through the dead of a Colorado winter.

Each frigid morning, I put on my Carhartt coveralls and jacket and stepped into the freezing woodshop to take up the work of my cross, my

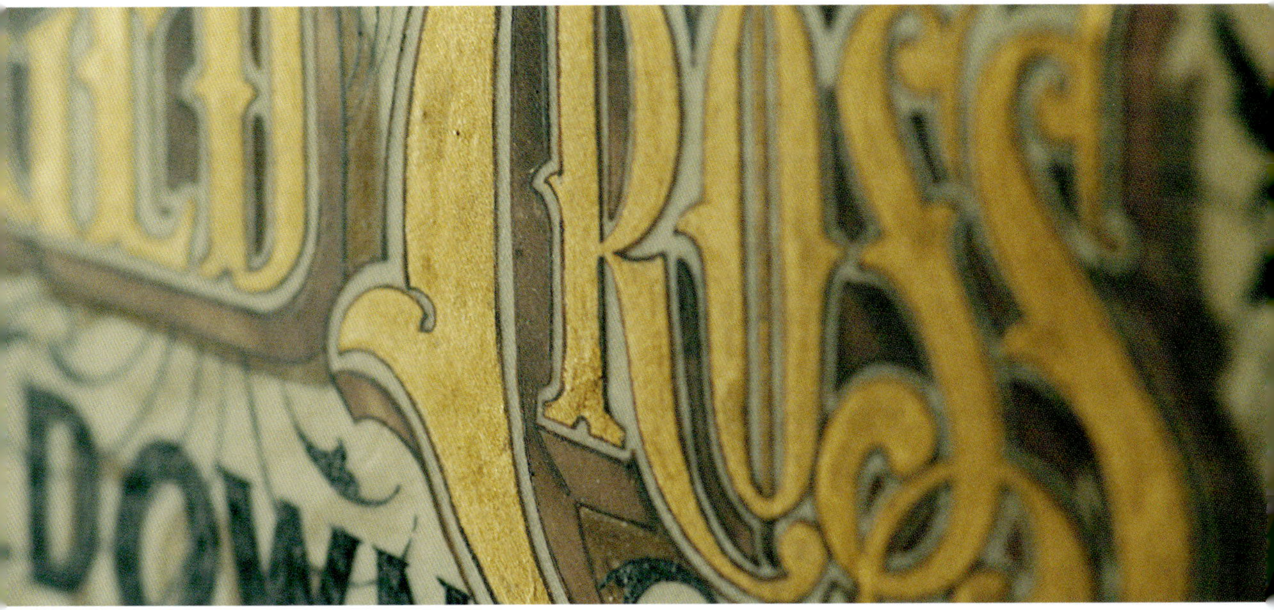

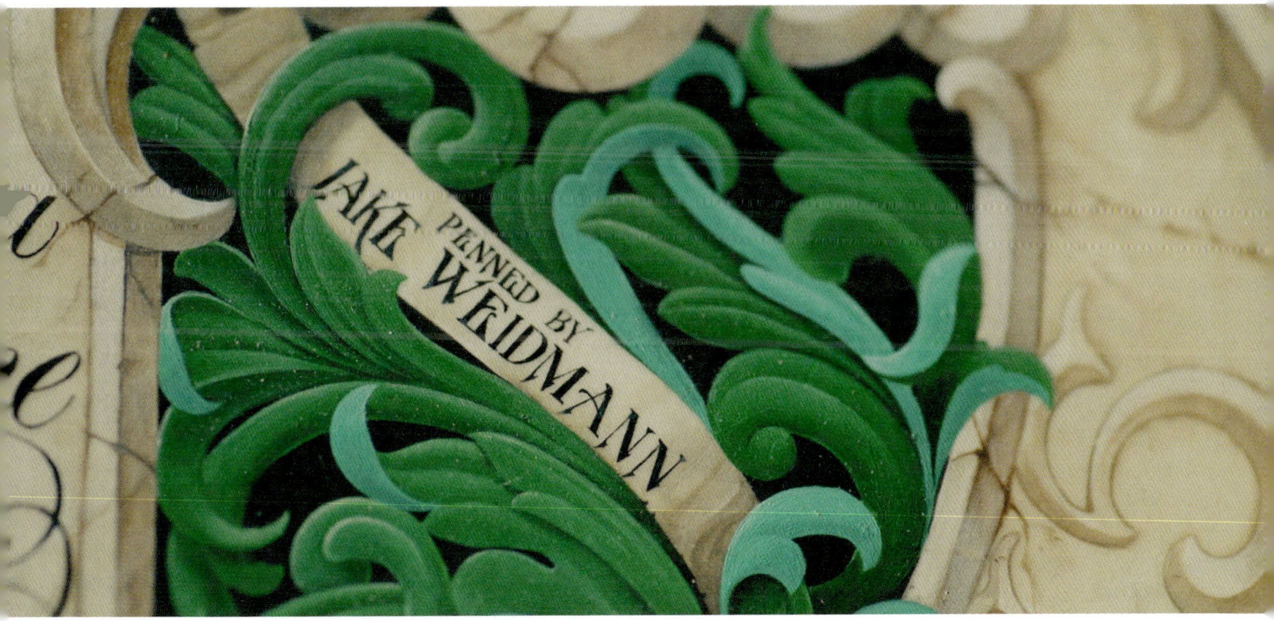
PENNED BY
JAKE WEIDMANN

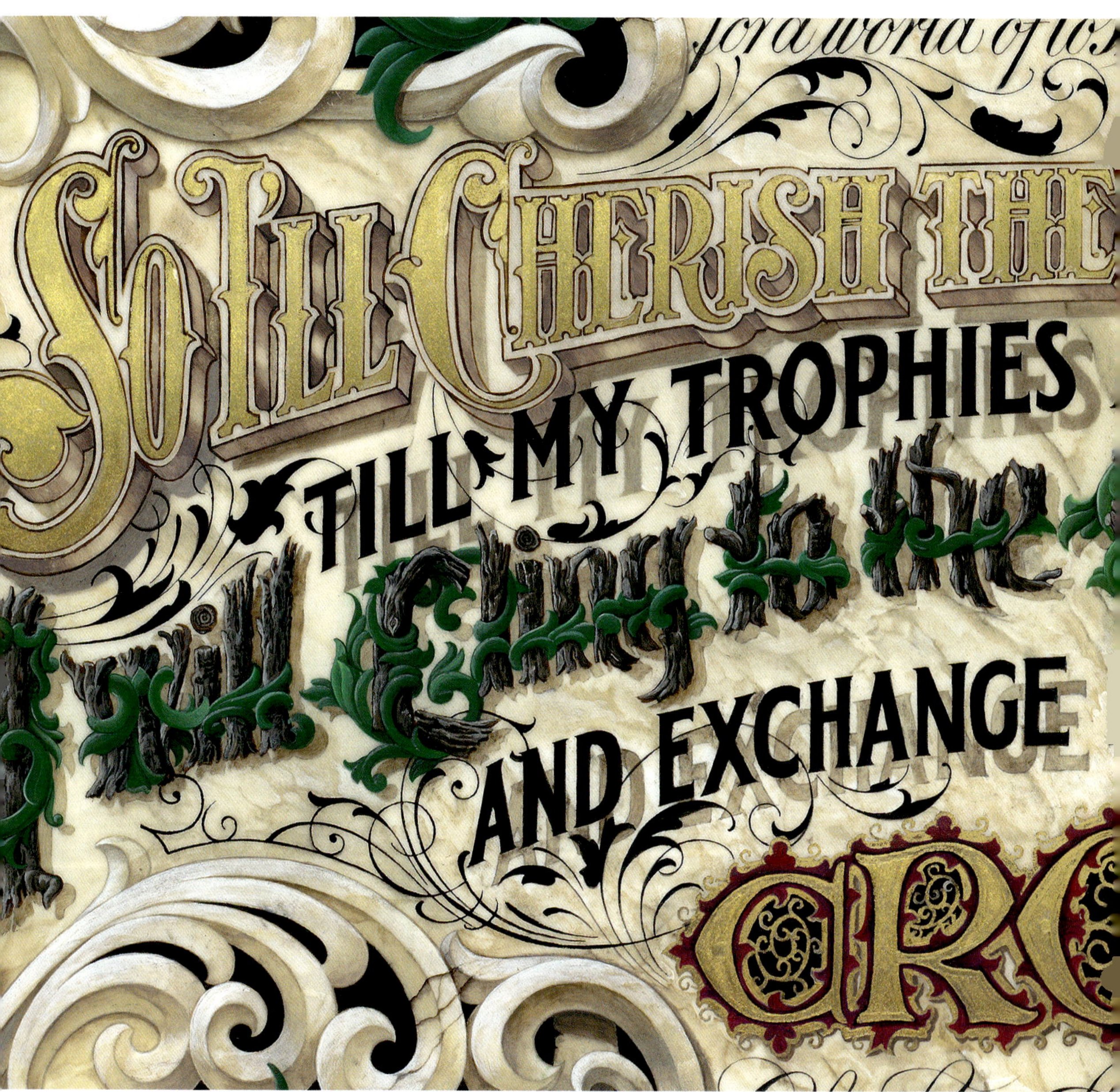
SO I'LL CHERISH THE
TILL MY TROPHIES
I will cling to the
AND EXCHANGE

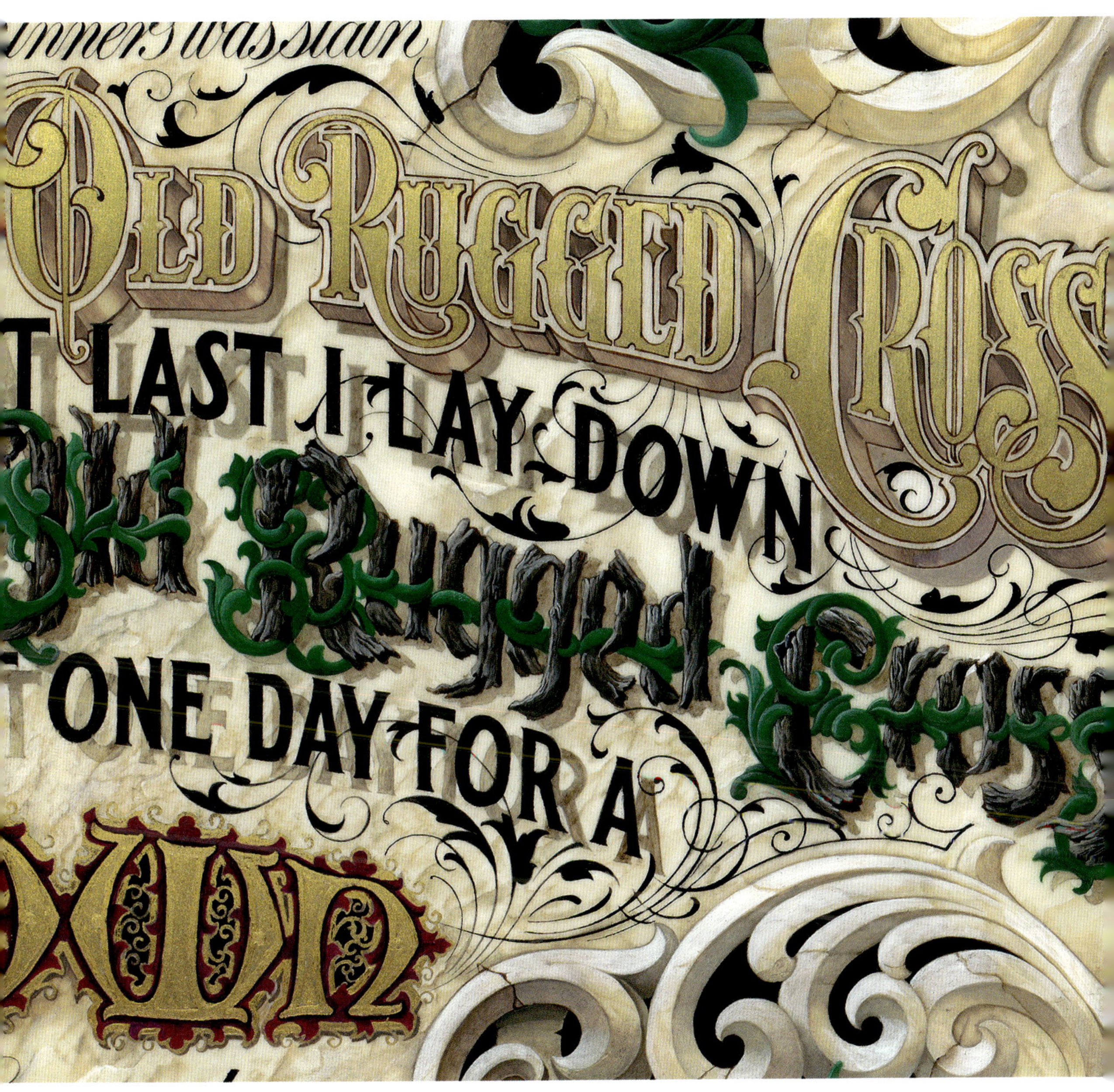
was slain
OLD RUGGED
LAST I LAY DOWN
Rugged
ONE DAY FOR A

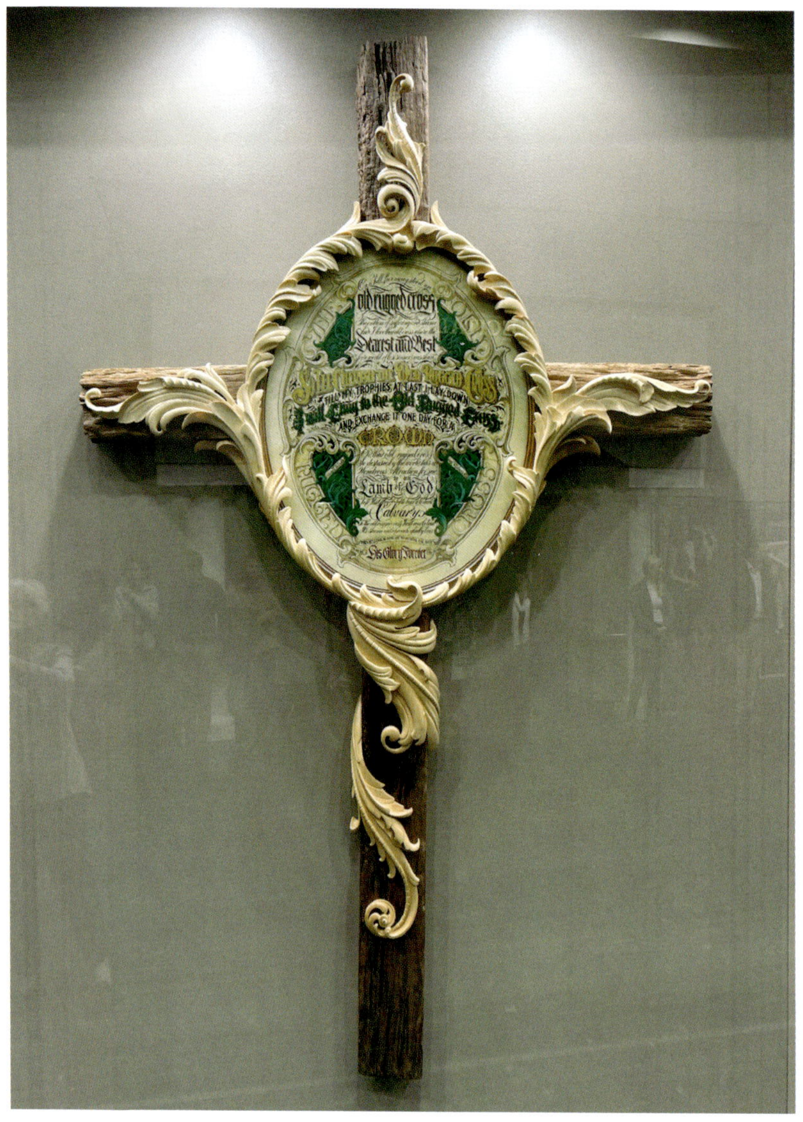

fingers growing numb as they clung to the carving chisels for hours on end. But far from despising my labor, I was deeply enjoying the work. With my goal in sight, the pain became less noticeable and, in some ways, even enjoyable as I came to associate it with a good full day of work. My frigid, calloused hands and tired shoulders were not a cause for complaint but rather a testament to the progress made.

As God has done throughout my story, I found that as I created in His image, He created something new in me. I began to understand more deeply the meaning of *passion*—or, rather, *His* Passion—and it was revealed to me in three ways:

- The first, *suffering*, might seem obvious. And in fact, it is the root meaning of the word, even if one rarely thinks of suffering when they say they are passionate about something. Yet through this process I found it less overwhelming the more willing I was to invite the Lord into its midst and embrace His purposes within it.
- The second is *endurance*, which, it turns out, is actually the original word's secondary meaning. Our Lord's Passion then is not a momentary fixation or affliction but an experience of prolonged endurance for the joy set before Him. If that is so, I should not expect any quick fixes either. Instead, I have been called to persevere with patience, even as a project gets derailed and my hard work seems to come to nothing.
- The third and final way relates to *devotion*. Again, let's return to its original meaning, which is "sacrificial prayer." While there are many things I have devoted myself to over the years, I have never been so passionately devoted to one creative endeavor. Day after day, week after week, and month after month, I was drawn back to the cross. I sacrificed my time, my hands, my energies, and even my suffering, prayerfully offering them up to the One who had offered Himself as a sacrifice for me. And He met me there, in the midst of it all.

On the final day of carving, Hannah called our children, Emma and Henry, to the garage door, and they prayed over me before I finished. I bent low and picked them up as they reached for me. Each in their turn prayed the sweetest of prayers over their daddy. Much had been suffered, much had been endured, but this work of long devotion was finally completed—fifteen long months after its inception.

May we learn then that suffering is not something to run from but an instrument the Lord can use to create something new within us.

The piece was intended for public display, much as Bennard's hymn was intended for congregational singing, and yet—like Bennard himself—I treasured the long days spent in solitude working away at it, little by little. It was truly my passion project. And as much as I was familiar with the hymn, the difficult process of its creation became a means of encountering God and the mystery of the cross more deeply than ever before.

To speak of picking up my cross as a follower of Christ has taken on a whole new meaning through this long and arduous artistic journey. Rather than some mere signifier of a Christian artist, the cross has recentered and reframed my life. It informs everything I do—whether that be creating, loving and serving others, or surrendering my gifts to God in prayerful devotion. It is true that I shall never know the extent of Jesus' suffering on the cross, and that itself is good news. But what I have learned is this: The suffering we endure as His followers can, however mysteriously, increase our appreciation for His. May we learn then that suffering is not something to run from but an instrument the Lord can use to create something new within us, making us ever more into the image of His Son.

fig 13 DETAIL OF WORK

The Old Rugged Cross, 2021. Calligraphic illumination on genuine vellum, 22 x 28 inches. Verse by verse, this beloved hymn is designed within the context of a cross, each line composed of various calligraphic scripts to richly emphasize its meaning. The original is set in a seven-foot cross with carved acanthus frame as part of a permanent installation at Cedarville University.

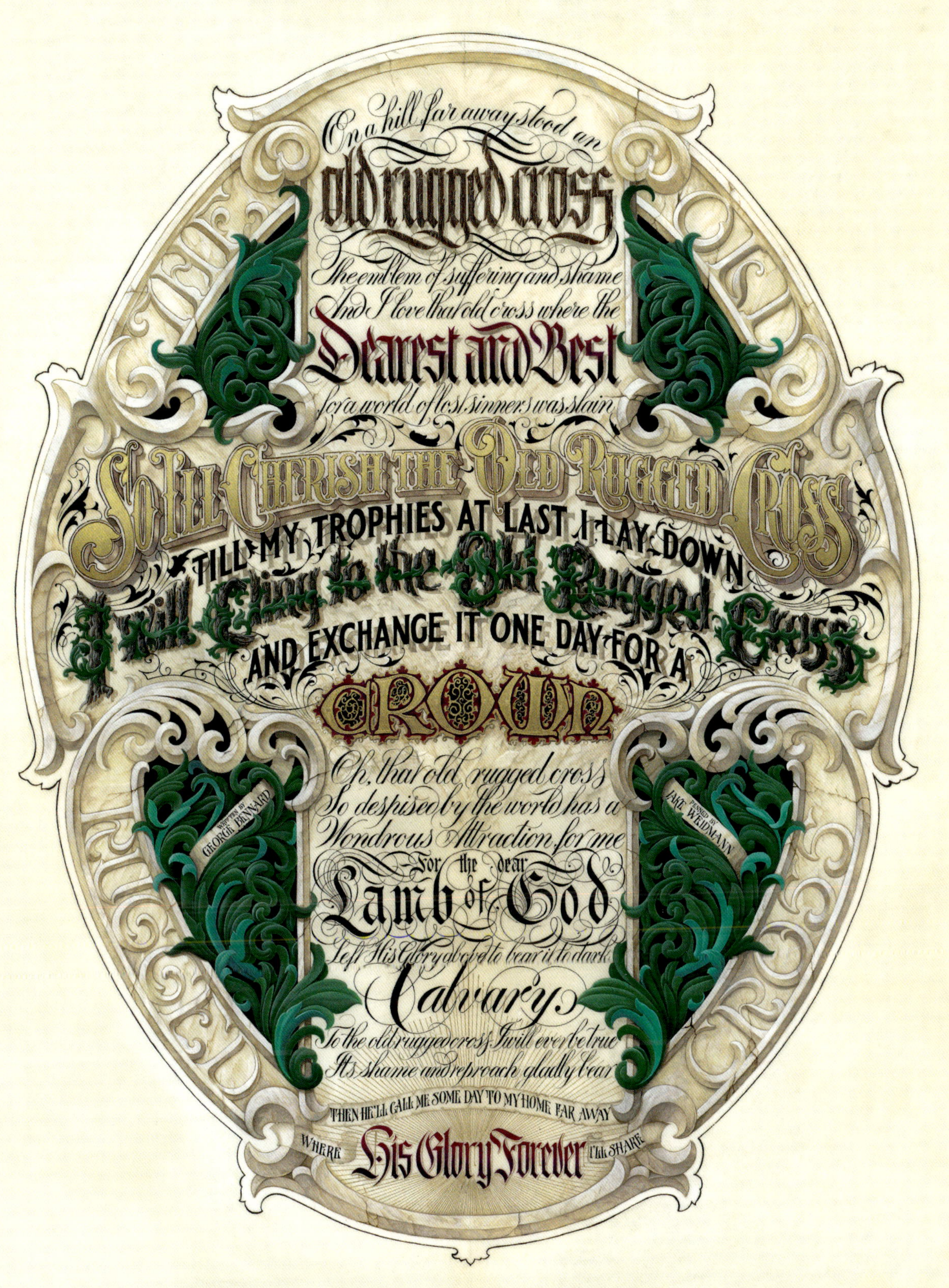
THE
OLD
RUGGED
CROSS
On a hill far away stood an
old rugged cross
The emblem of suffering and shame
And I love that old cross where the
Dearest and Best
For a world of lost sinners was slain
So I'll Cherish the Old Rugged Cross
TILL MY TROPHIES AT LAST I LAY DOWN
I will Cling to the Old Rugged Cross
AND EXCHANGE IT ONE DAY FOR A
CROWN
Oh, that old rugged cross
So despised by the world has a
Wondrous Attraction for me
For the dear
Lamb of God
Left His Glory above to bear it to dark
Calvary
To the old rugged cross I will ever be true
Its shame and reproach gladly bear
THEN HE'LL CALL ME SOME DAY TO MY HOME FAR AWAY
WHERE His Glory Forever I'LL SHARE
WRITTEN BY GEORGE BENNARD
PENNED BY JAKE WEIDMANN

CHAPTER EIGHT

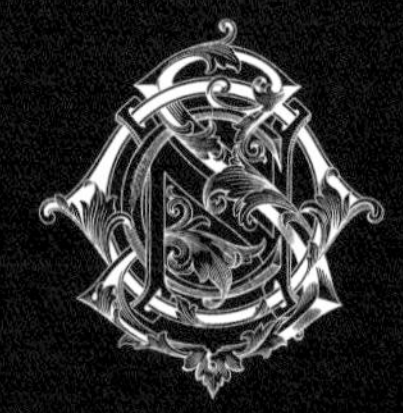

BE THOU MY

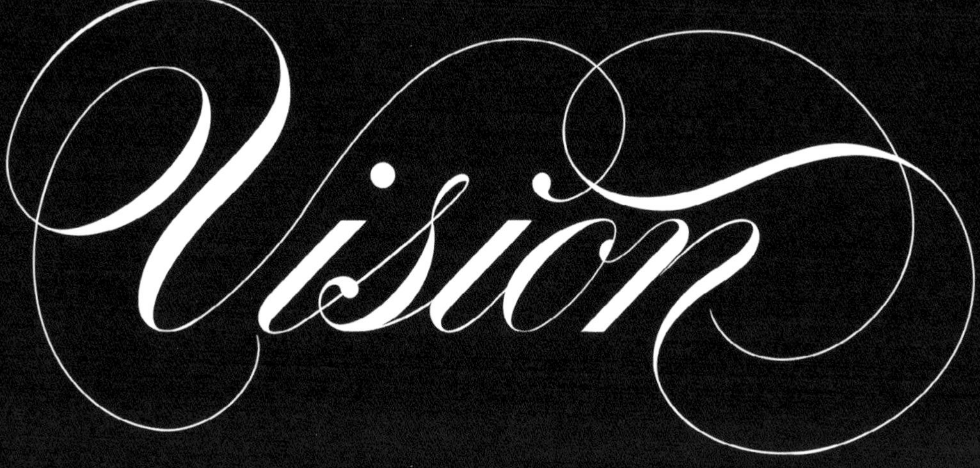

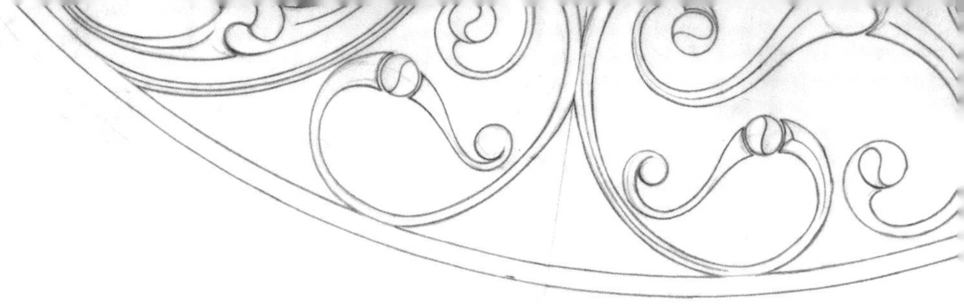

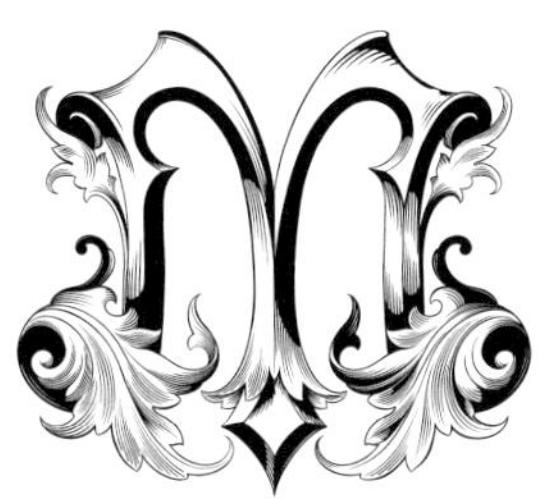

y art has taken me many places. In my travels I have seen wonderful and inspiring lands that stir my soul and broaden my horizons. I am, however, something of a homebody. A journey is more likely to take me on an unmarked trail through the Colorado foothills than along Europe's many cobbled streets. And yet, when I have been in the studio for long enough and cabin fever begins to set in, like Bilbo Baggins in search of adventure, I leave my happy hole of artistry and take to the open road.

There is something truly remarkable about traveling thousands of miles to a place I have never been, but where others have lived for millennia. It evokes a sense of connectedness to the grand story of humanity as I add my footsteps to the many who have gone before. And it never ceases to amaze me that wherever I travel, be it a splendid city or humble village, I find evidence of the insatiable creative spirit of man. From the Duomo in Florence to a farmhouse cottage in Oxford, from the opera house in Sydney to the runestones of Scotland, and from Notre Dame in Paris to the Western Wall, or Wailing Wall, in Jerusalem, the world is teeming with those who create in the Artist's image, whether they know it or not.

Those who do know have long shaped their lands to be both hospitable and holy. Their sacred spaces—chapels,

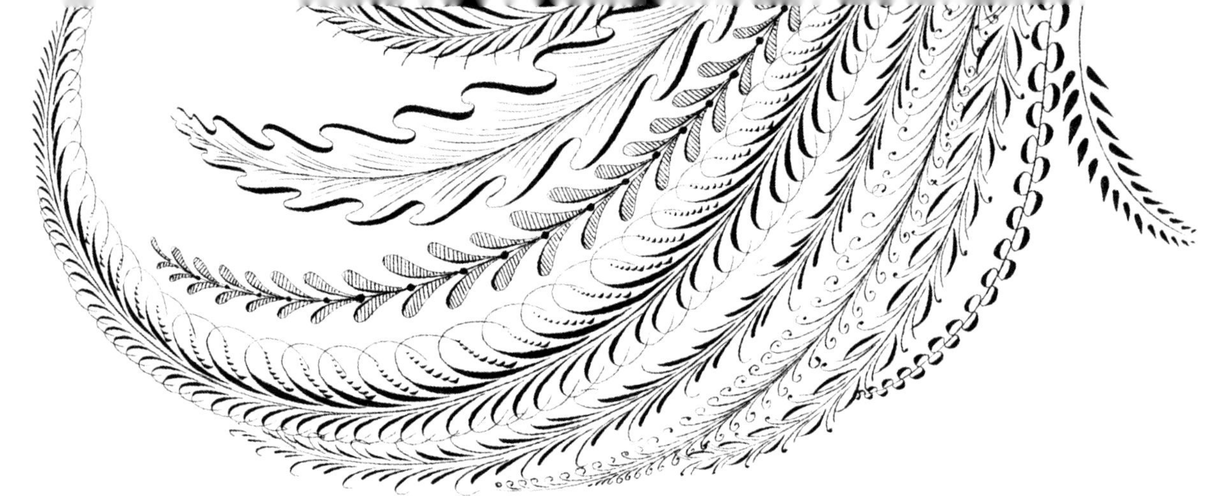

It's not just about the past but also our connection to it.

churches, and cathedrals alike—are a tangible reminder of the communion of saints, which draws upon Paul's teaching about the body of Christ (Romans 12:4–13; 1 Corinthians 12:27). So many faithful followers of Christ have gone before us. Throughout many centuries they have preached the good news and pursued holiness. They have ensured the survival of the Scriptures and filled their sacred spaces with a holy sound that resonates to this day. I am deeply thankful for them and their testimonies. But I know they are less interested in my gratitude than in my commitment to join their refrain in praise of our Creator.

Have you experienced something like this for yourself? Not all of us have the opportunity to travel widely, so if not, maybe you have a few places on your bucket list. And yet, even if the journey is closer to home, have you felt a sense of connection to those who have come before you? I wonder if that is part of the reason we protect historic landmarks or conduct archaeological digs. It's not just about the past but also our connection to it. Perhaps you've felt that even more distinctly at places where the faithful have worshipped for generations. I would encourage you to look and listen carefully; their faith is living still.

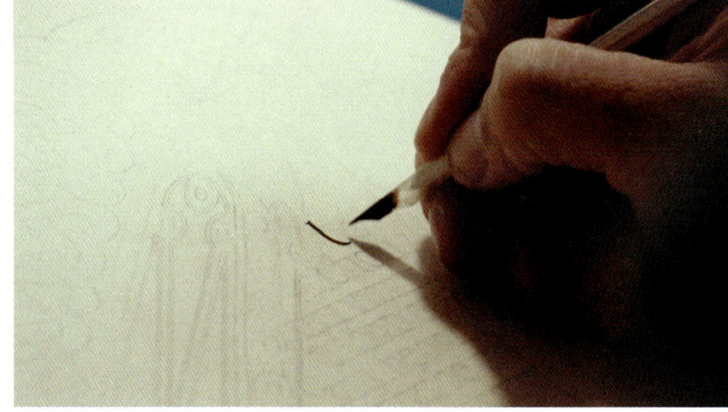

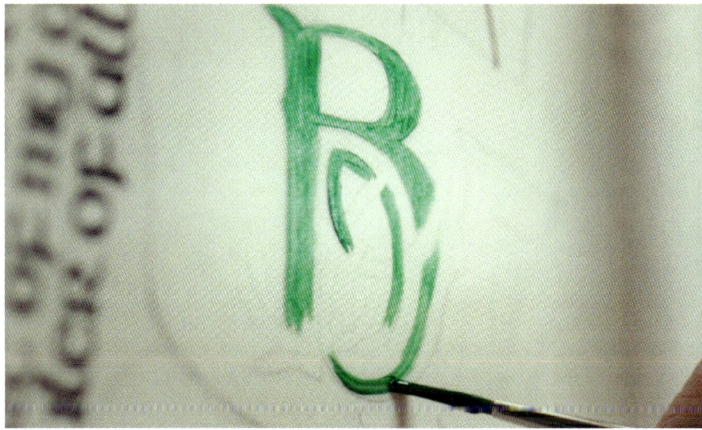

Ireland—unique in all the world—is home to many such places. Though it is perhaps an exaggeration to say the Irish saved civilization, they nevertheless number some of the greatest poets, musicians, authors, and artists in history. It's as if the very earth has been christened for the purposes of their creativity. Perhaps that is why it is so lush. (Well, that and the near endless rain!)

Years ago, Hannah and I had a chance to visit Ireland. We filled our days with hikes along its ocean cliffs and our evenings in pubs listening to old Irish men playing even older Irish instruments. While in Dublin, however, I made sure to see the Book of Kells, one of the greatest illuminated manuscripts in existence. It is rightly regarded as one of Ireland's national treasures. Housed in a museum at Trinity College, this priceless codex (a forerunner of the modern book) is believed to have been produced by a monastic community over twelve hundred years ago. Preeminent among its contents are the four gospels.

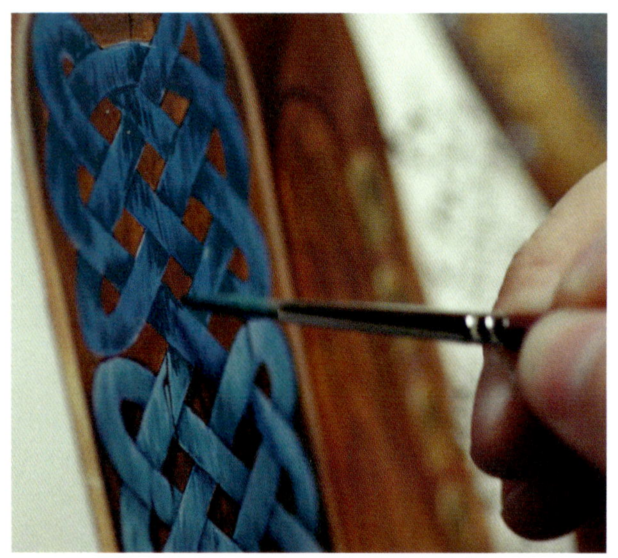

Upon entering the museum, we were introduced to the inner workings of a monastic scriptorium, including the techniques and tools of the monks' trade. As I looked through one particular display case, I was tickled to see several cut quills, sheets of vellum and parchment, inkwells and dapping dishes, as well as some gallnuts for making iron gall ink. I chuckled to myself; they were portrayed as implements of a bygone era, but I had them all sitting on my desk in Colorado. Had the case not been locked, I could have pulled all the materials from the display and leisurely jotted a quick bit of calligraphy there on the spot. Nevertheless, it was a welcome signpost. I was in the right place, and it felt like home.

Eventually, we were led into the room where the Book of Kells was displayed. Lit from above, here was the sacred relic for which I had made my pilgrimage across the sea. With arms behind my back and one hand clasping the other at the wrist, I leaned in as close as I could—nearly touching my nose to the glass. The intricate Celtic knotting, the vibrancy of the colors, and the crispness and consistency

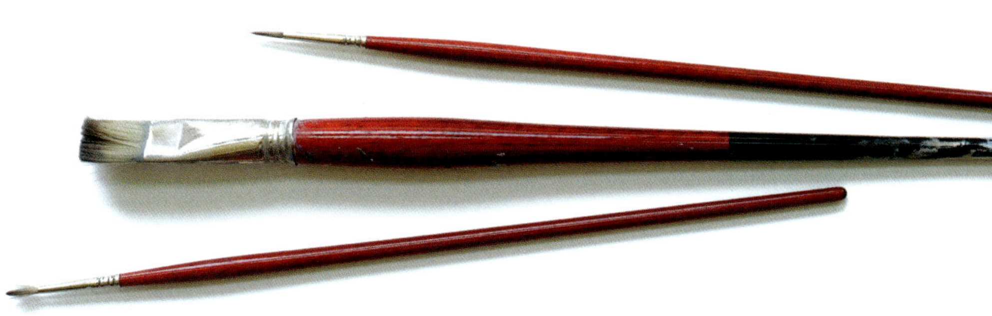

of the letters were all truly astonishing to behold. The twelfth-century priest and historian Gerald of Wales famously described the book as "the work of an angel, not of a man."[7] Having seen it with my own eyes, I could easily believe it. I traced each detail with my eyes, studying the letters to discern the subtle twists of the quill in the scribe's fingers as he wrote to form the serifs and ligatures. I could tell where his strokes began and ended, and even where he had retouched, which was evidenced by the slightest variation in opacity caused by the ink pooling more where the pen was last lifted from the page.

There is such intimacy in handwriting. And while I have been trained to see the slightest nuances in the form, I believe even the average person with an untrained eye can innately sense the life within the letters. How could anyone miss the devotion these scribes had for their subject? Every interlocking weave of their knotting must have bound their heart ever closer to the Word. It spoke volumes even in its hallowed silence: truly a creation inspired by the Creator.

However, the Book of Kells is not famous for its writing, per se, but for its exquisitely illuminated images. One of the most famous of these is found between the Gospels of Matthew and Luke and takes up an entire side of a folio leaf. In four quadrants, set within beautifully ornate frames, is an apparently strange assortment of creatures: a man, a lion, an ox, and an eagle. But this is no flight of fancy.

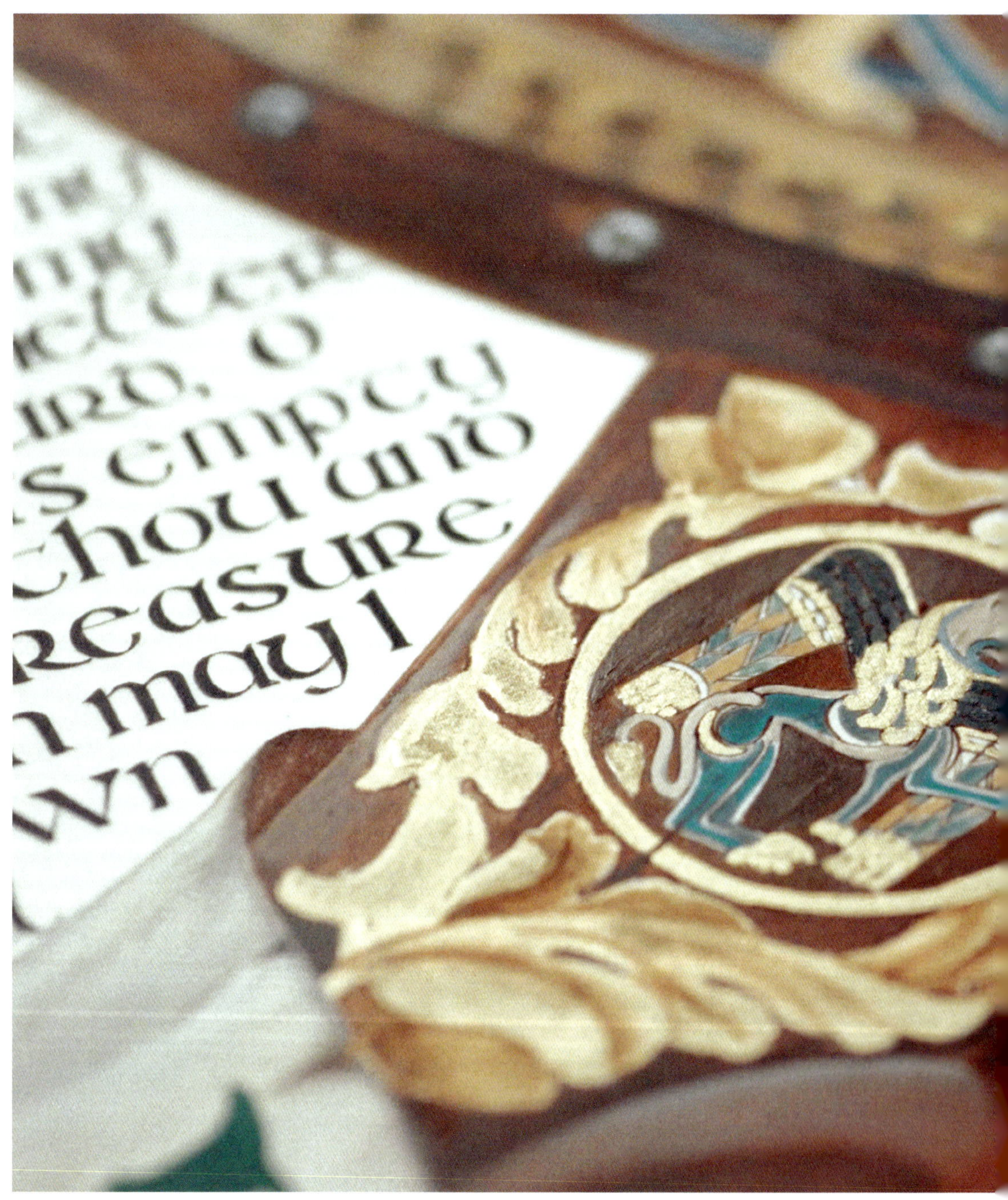
s empty
thou and
reasure
may I

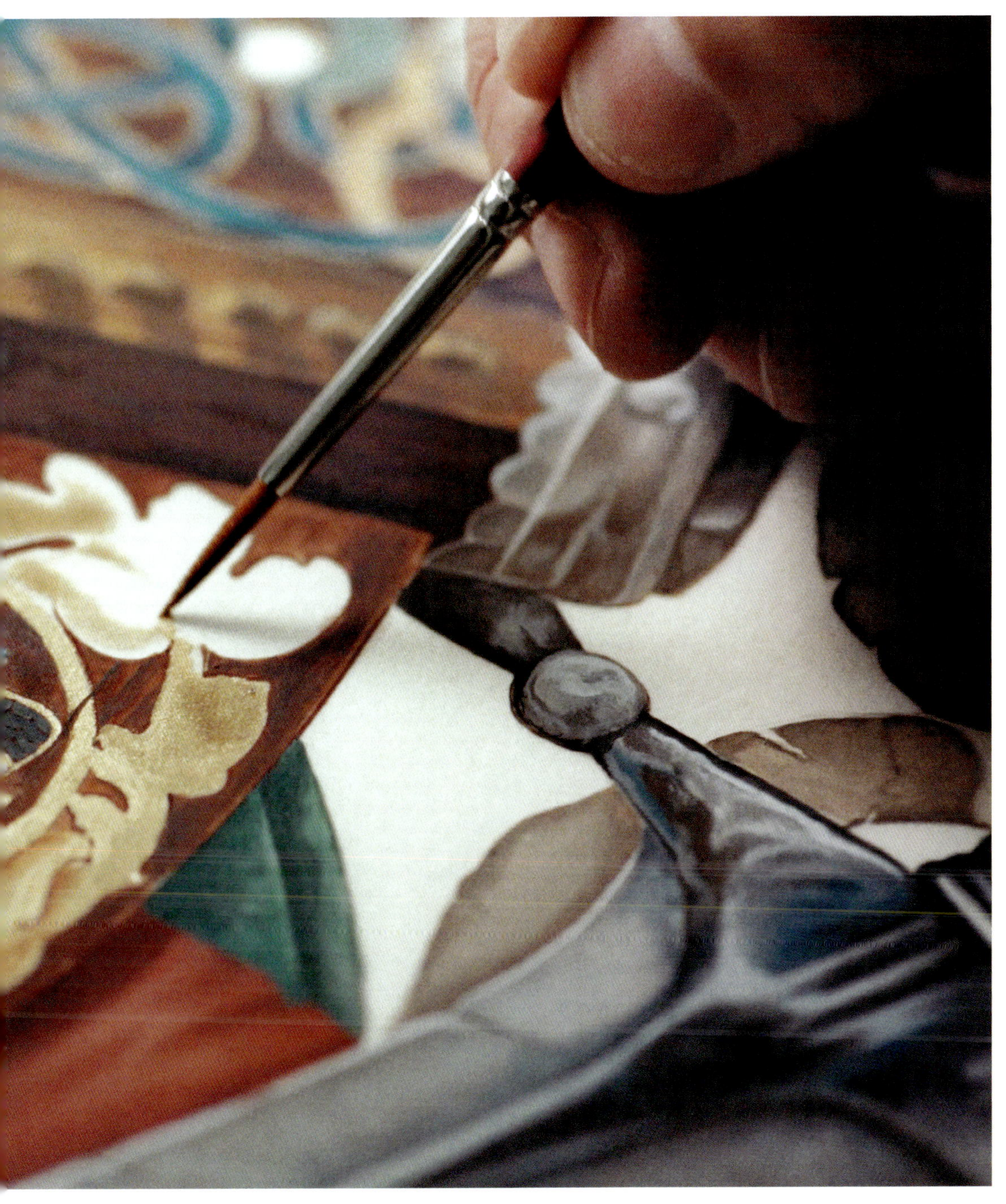

These four creatures derive from a combination of passages found in Ezekiel 1:10 and Revelation 4:7. And their significance is greater still. Drawing upon an exegetical tradition reaching back centuries before these monks put quill to parchment, the four creatures were interpreted to represent the four Gospel writers: the man, Matthew; the lion, Mark; the ox, Luke; and the eagle, John.

My mind reeled as I considered the many layers of history before me: the striking imagery shared between a Hebrew prophet in the sixth century BC and an apocalyptic seer within a generation of Christ—since swept across the Irish Sea to inspire a community of monks many centuries removed. And there I stood, over a thousand years later, taking it all in. I thought to myself then that someday I would love to take my place in this sacred interchange, to continue in the creative lineage they have passed down. *Lord, if only I was given the opportunity to join their communion.*

That opportunity came some years later when I was commissioned to illuminate the hymn "Be Thou My Vision." In preparation for the piece, I began to research its history, as I have for the others, only to find its story leads *much* further back into the past. In fact, it may well have emerged out of the same eighth-century monastic culture that produced the Book of Kells!

In its earliest Irish iteration, the hymn took the form of a *lorica*, or prayer for protection, which was inspired in part by Paul's description of the armor of God in Ephesians 6:10–17. As such, it shares some similarities with the well-known Breastplate of Saint Patrick, which may also date to the same period. The monks of this time were increasingly harried by Viking raids, so it is even more poignant that these prayers sought protection from enemies not so much of flesh and blood but of the spirit. They knew against whom they truly fought. And so I was transported to Ireland yet again, reliving the experience of those wonderfully illustrated pages and inhaling the salt wind of the Irish Sea, brimming with inspiration.

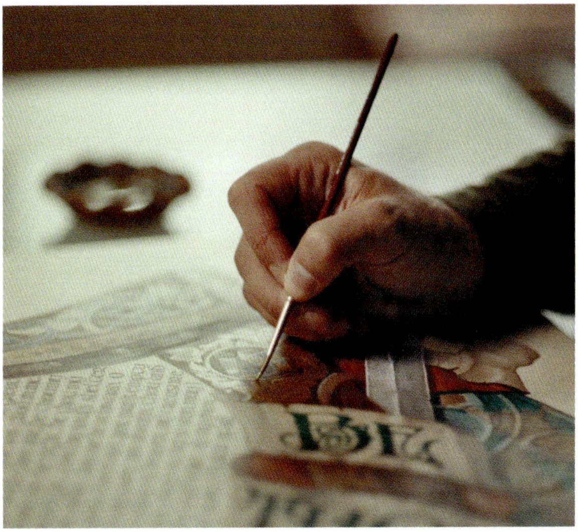

Nearly every culture has its own distinctive style of writing. It may vary through the ages as tastes change, languages evolve, or outside influences dictate. As I sought to represent this ancient Irish prayer, I decided it could be written in no other hand than that found in the Book of Kells itself: insular half-uncial. This beautiful, if slightly squatty-looking, text, with its truncated ascenders and descenders (ligatures that go above and below the typical height of a lowercase letter), is written with a broad-edged pen. This adds a lot of heft and variation to its form. These snug letters, closely written, create a pronounced horizontal line—like a row of soldiers standing shoulder to shoulder. Put several lines together in the body of text and you have the whole brigade on parade march. For this piece, I

> I TURNED TO IRELAND AND SETTLED QUICKLY UPON A HARP.

knew exactly which of my reserve I was sending into prayerful battle.

Words accompanied by pictures certainly complement one another easily enough, but to create an even tighter blend, I like to incorporate one into the other. I began playing around with some different contexts in which I could position the body of the text and turn it into imagery. Again, I turned to Ireland and settled quickly upon a harp.

The Book of Kells is not the only treasure kept at Trinity College; the instrument known as "Brian Boru's Harp" is there as well. This splendid instrument dates to the later Middle Ages and is the prototype for Ireland's national symbol. You may have even noticed its likeness on a can of Guinness. At once, I correlated my tightly regimented uncial with the harp's string and—*voilà!*—the perfect confluence of imagery and words was found. I must have drawn a dozen thumbnail sketches. As I turned the body of the text at a steep angle, justified within the wooden frame of the harp, the indication of the strings themselves was conveyed by the tight negative space between the consecutive lines. This steep upward angle draws the viewers' eyes repeatedly upward along a positive slope—suggesting a posture of heavenward praise.

The modern English rendition of the hymn, though a little different from the Irish original, still maintains the martial imagery in one of its verses. Even the

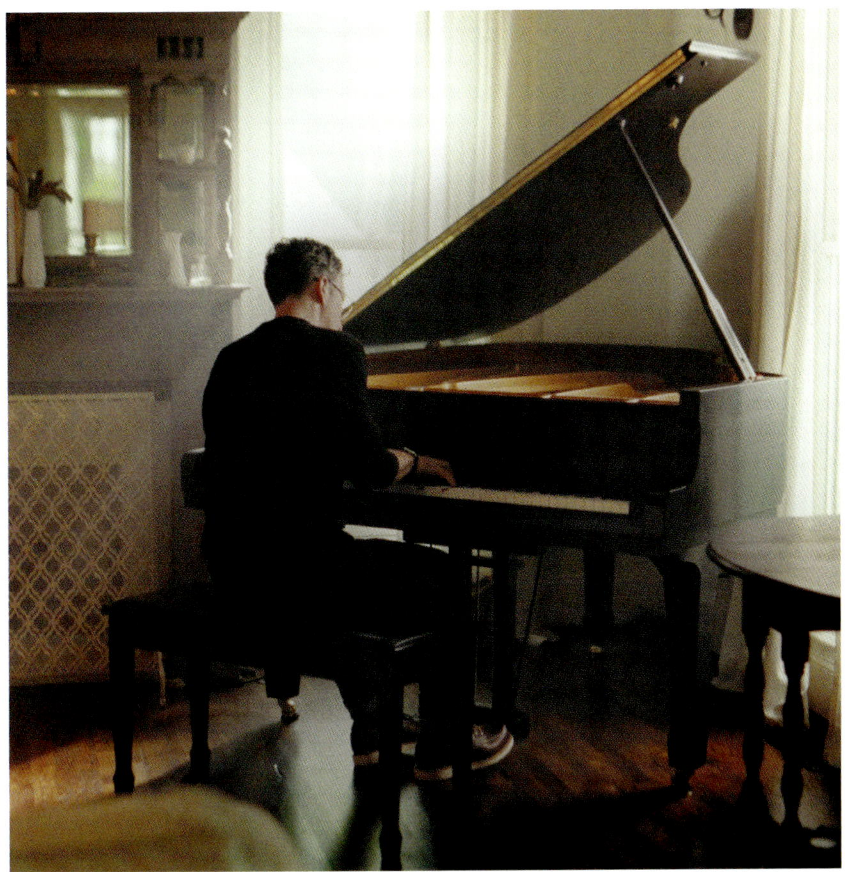

famous tune to which it was set a little over a century ago evokes a conflict between the powers of light and darkness. Entitled "Slane," it refers to the hill in County Meath where, as legend has it, Saint Patrick's lighting of an Easter fire in defiance of the pagan king Lóegaire ultimately gave him the freedom to preach the gospel throughout the Emerald Isle.

The hymn calls on God to be a "shield" and "a sword for the fight." So I started sketching a sword and shield within my thumbnail compositions, shifting and changing the elements until I found the right harmony between the component parts. There was also the question of the sword's kind and shield's shape. Again I turned to the annals of history.

A good friend of mine happens to be a blacksmith and has spent a great deal of time studying the history of swords. For an expressly Irish

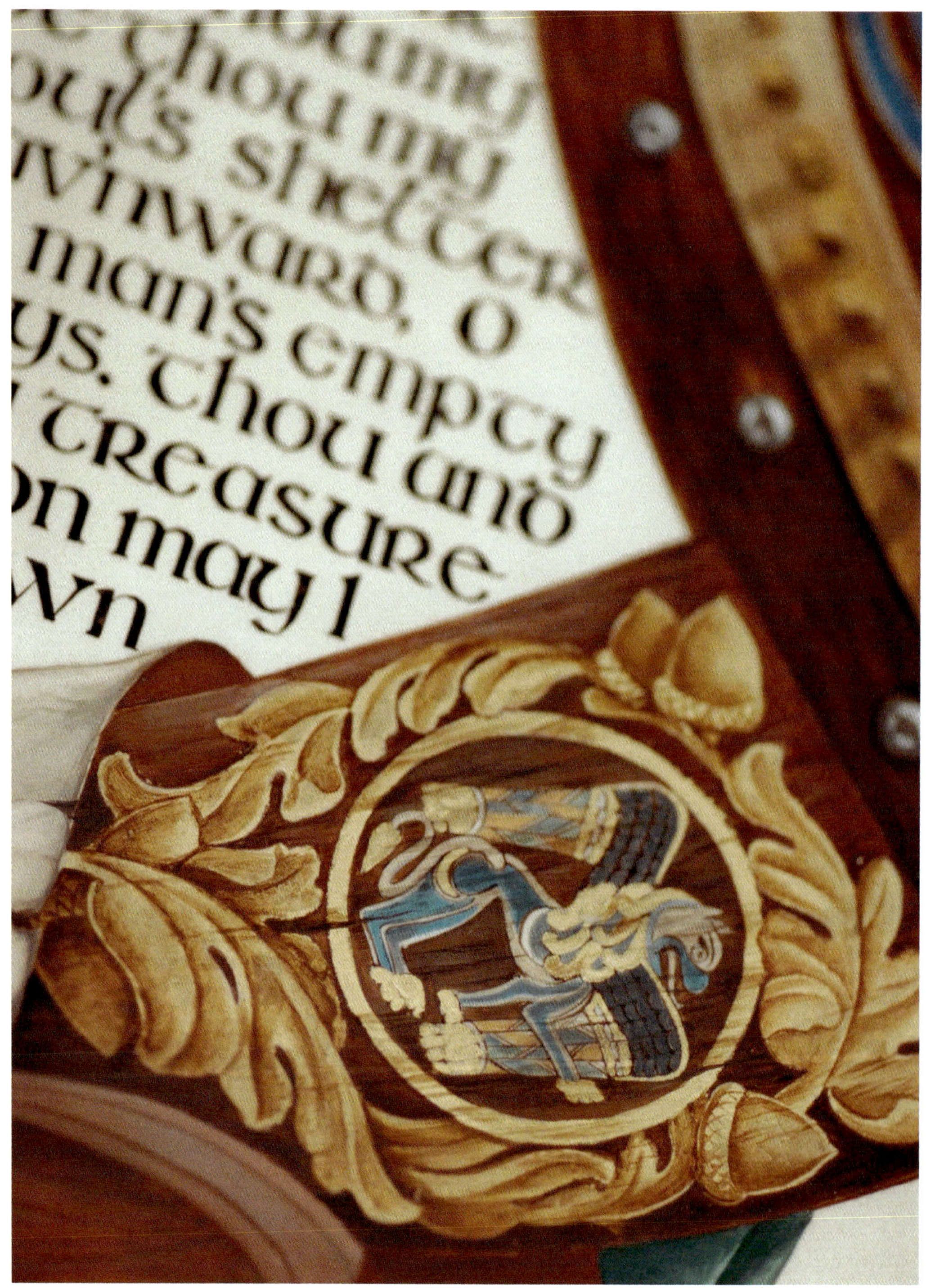
thou my
shelter
man's, O
empty
thou
treasure
may I

> WHEN WE CREATE IN THE IMAGE OF OUR CREATOR, HE GIVES US EYES TO SEE.

sword, he pointed me to the key-ring pommel sword. As for the shield, I stumbled upon an article online about an Iron Age Celtic shield recently exhumed from a warrior's grave, which was declared "the most important British Celtic art object of the millennium."[8] In light of the cultural interchange among the British Isles, I drew inspiration from both its ornate pattern and patina of oxidized bronze.

With my armaments gathered and my battalion of soldiers at the ready, I went to war on the final layout. In this to-scale drawing, I worked out the minute details of the composition down to the spacing of each letter. However, while it is important to create an exhaustive blueprint before the design is transferred to the vellum, concept sketches get you only so far. It's sometimes necessary to trust the greater strategy, even if some compositional questions remain. At a certain point you just need to take the creative battlefield and go from there.

It is a source of great consolation and encouragement to know we are not alone in this struggle. When we create in the image of our Creator, He gives us eyes to see—He is our vision. But He also brings others alongside to help us fight the good fight. For even as I sought inspiration from ages past, I found myself among a present-day communion of saints.

Nate and Christy Nockels are a husband-and-wife team and two truly anointed musicians. Christy is a world-renowned singer who has led the Lord's people in worship for decades. Nate is a skilled musician and accomplished composer. While I was still working on the layout for *Be Thou My Vision*, only a week or so into the process, Christy reached out to Hannah and me to see if we'd be interested in collaborating if an opportunity should arise. Upon a chance visit to our home shortly afterward,

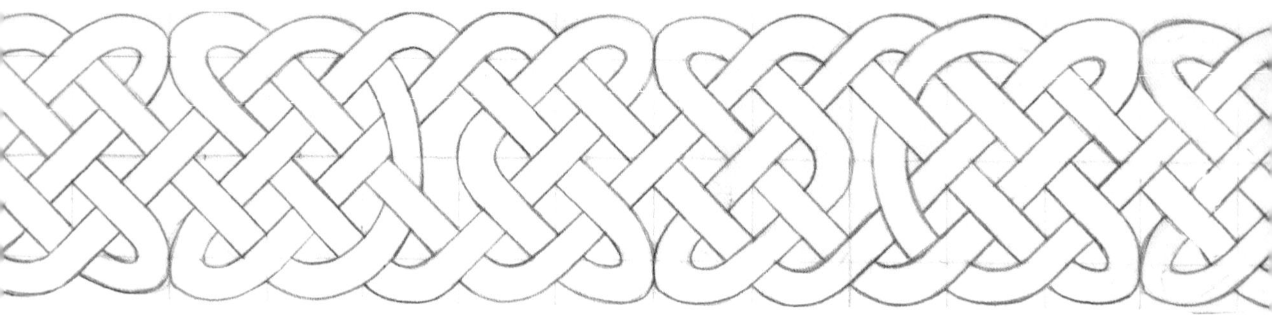

I WAS INSPIRED BY THE GLIMPSE OF LIGHT EMERGING FROM THE OTHER SIDE.

Nate and Christy accompanied me to my scriptorium to share my progress. Without hesitation, they offered to join me in the fray and combine our talents and our worship in the form of a music video.

In the weeks that followed, I shared with Nate about my vision for the piece and the rich history I had uncovered. Immediately he latched on to its Irish legacy, which set the stage for the musical accompaniment. He knew of a full-blooded Irishman named Paddy (of course!) who played an array of traditional Irish instruments. Nate asked him over to his studio to record him playing the Uilleann pipes for the song's opening.

When Nate sent me a few sample videos from the recording, I was overjoyed. I was at my desk at the time, transferring the layout to the vellum. It felt as if we were digging a tunnel from both ends, and I was inspired by the glimpse of light emerging from the other side. Furthermore, in addition to contributing this Irish flavor, Nate also sought to convey the ancient traditions represented in my piece by not overproducing the song and allowing some of the "grit" to show through. Even in collaboration, it was wonderful to see Nate create as the Spirit led.

As I continued in my work, the missing pieces of the composition emerged and fell into place. The strategy had succeeded. The sword,

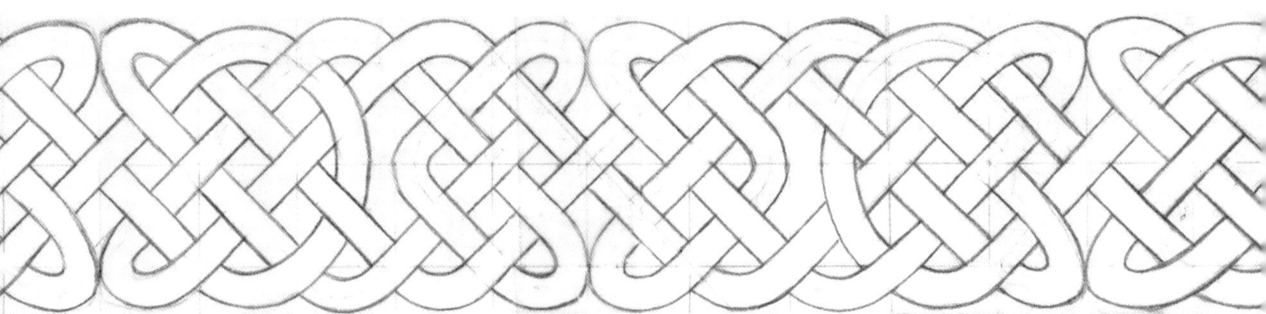

shield, and harp found their way into a dynamic orientation, which made the arrangement sing. As for the title, its placement was solved by a banner that I drew spiraling around the sword and the front portion of the harp, known as the *pillar*. I stylized the banner as if it were a standard rippling before an army on the battlefield.

With the project laid out before me, I finally saw the deeper connection between the hymn and the Book of Kells. On one hand, the hymnwriter prays for God's vision; on the other hand, the illustrator of the Gospel writers represents the very *vision of God*, as given to Ezekiel and John of Patmos alike. To honor this connection, I painted the four icons as ornaments on the harp, surrounding the words of the hymn. But there was one further illuminating discovery to be uncovered. According to tradition, Dallán Forgaill, the original Irish author of the lorica, was blind.[9] Be thou my *vision*, indeed.

This revelation brought together both the literal and spiritual significance of the hymn, if not also of the project as a whole. The hymn's author needed both kinds of sight, but he clearly sought one more than the other. The same is true of those monks who sought protection in battle. Yes, there was very real conflict throughout Ireland in those days, as there has been in the intervening centuries, though they did not seek swords and shields of iron but those of the Spirit. I pray that you likewise seek His sight, that the Lord gives you eyes to see the work He is doing within and around you, along with His protection against any harm, whether physical or spiritual.

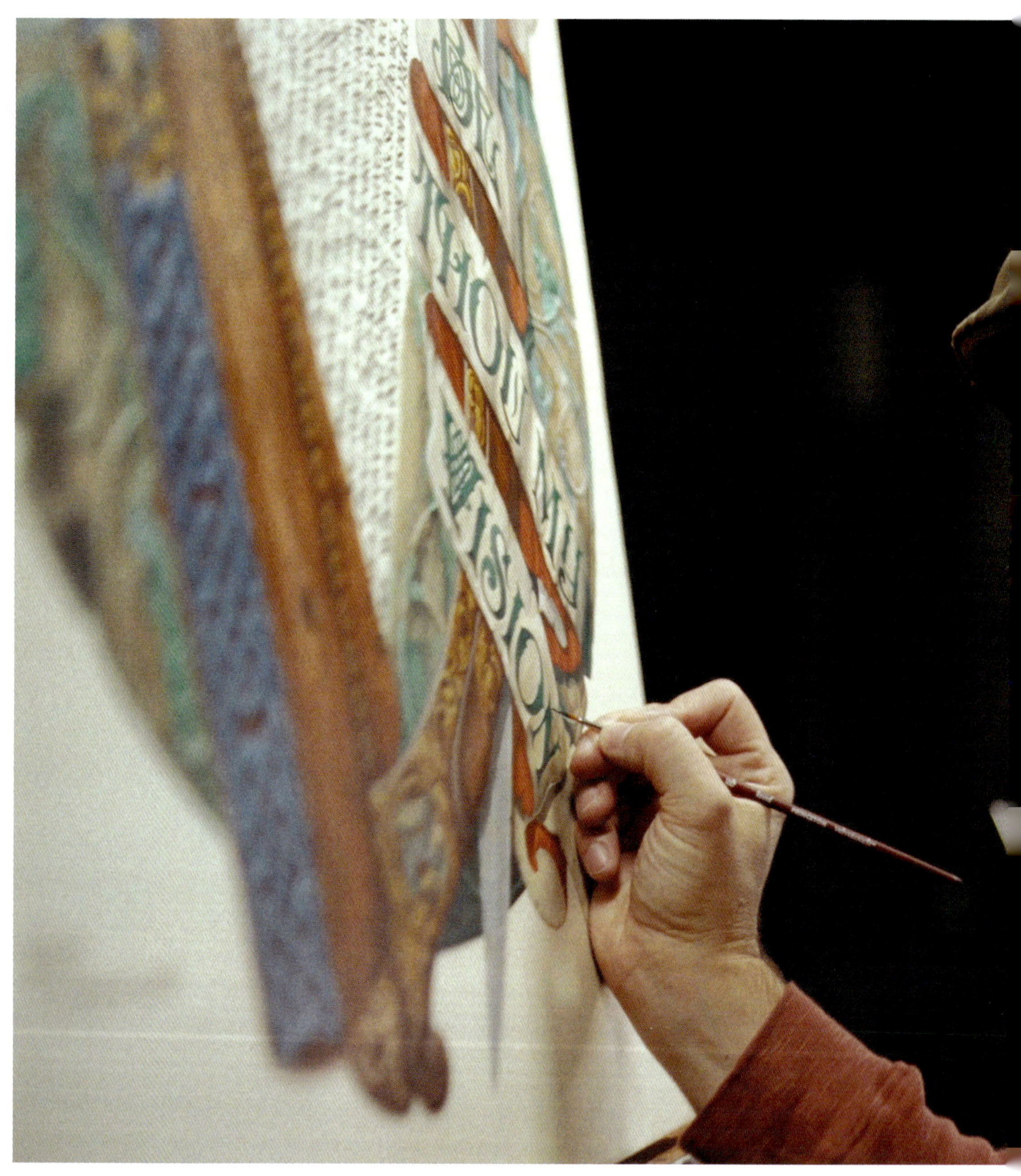

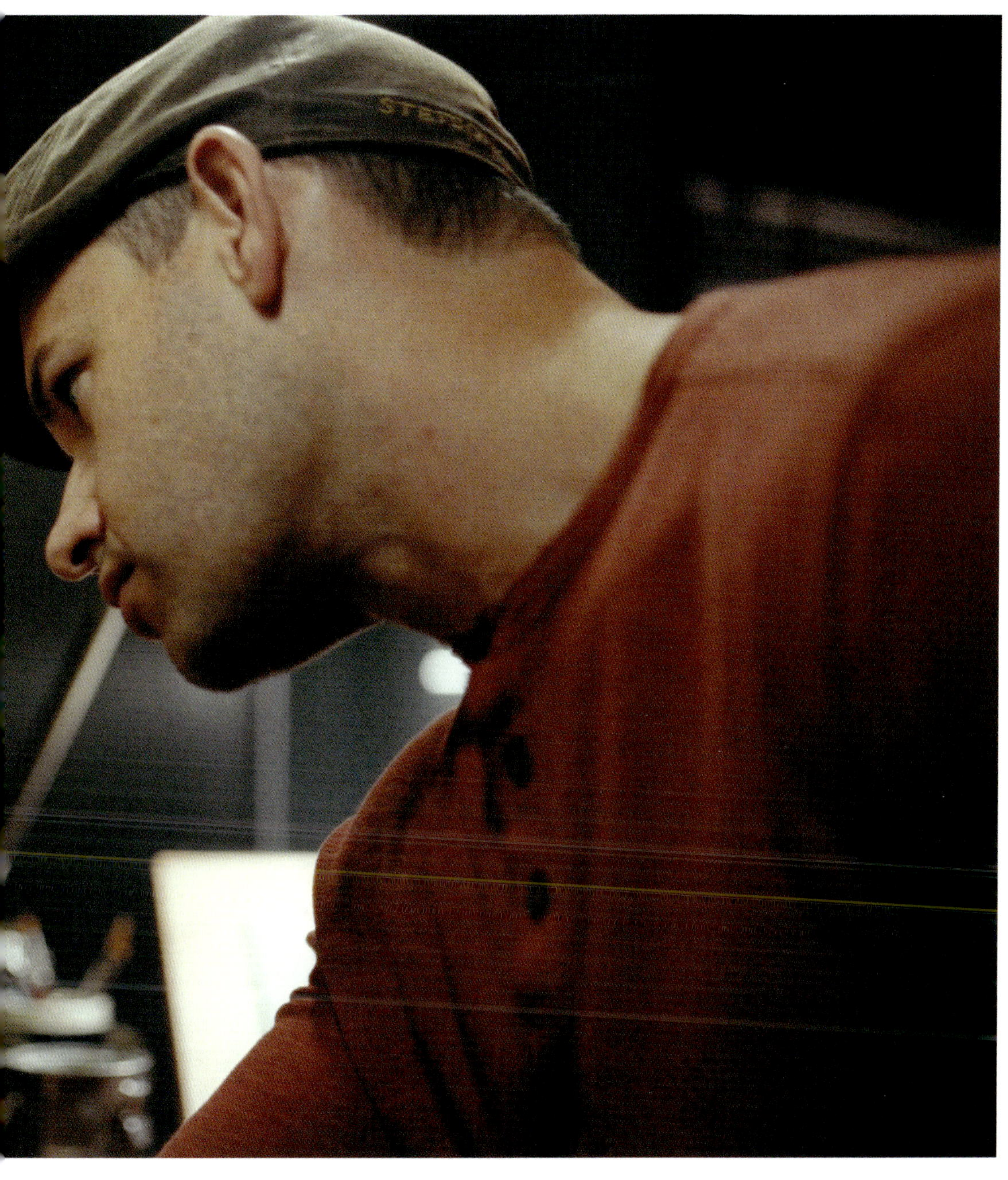

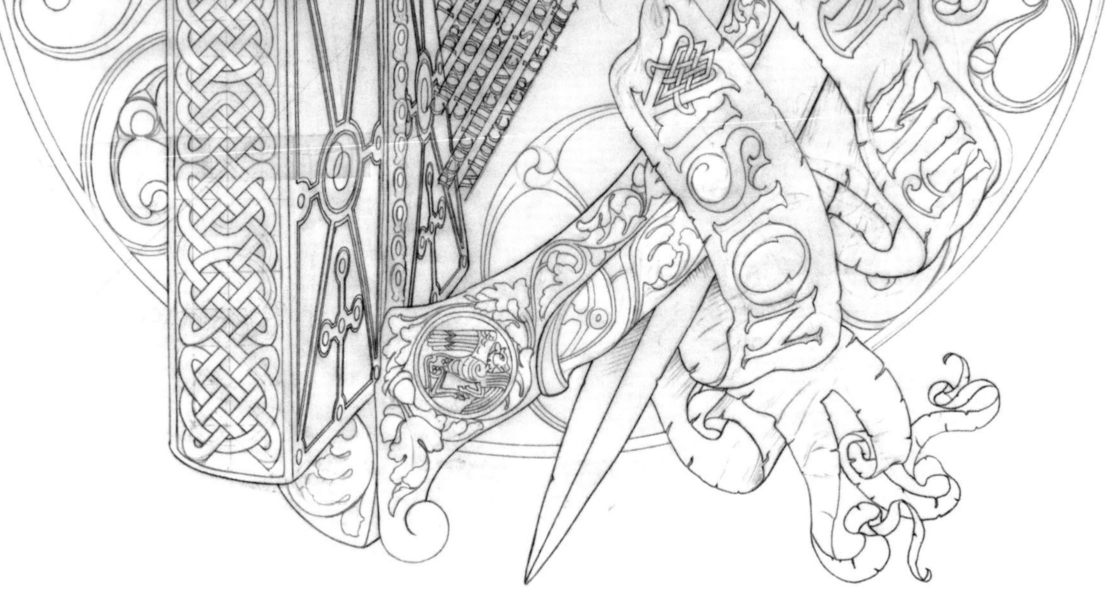

When we sing "Be Thou My Vision," we sing not just to see with earthly eyes but to see clearly from God's perspective. We desire clarity. Interestingly enough, this is the very same word used for a quill's preparation. One can't simply pull a feather from a goose and get to work. In order for my quill to be fit for writing, it needs to be *clarified*, or tempered, in hot sand. The process begins by carefully chopping off the root tip of the feather and pulling out the loose bits of keratin membrane from inside the stock. I then soak the tips in a vase of water overnight. One quill at a time, with the pan of sand heated to about 350 degrees Fahrenheit, I spoon in as much as the hollow shaft will hold and immediately plunge the tip into the scorching sand.

Timing is critical. Not enough time in the sand and the quill will not be properly tempered; too much and the quill will blister and burn. Just the right amount, however, and the tip of the quill will go from a milky white with slight striations running through it to an almost perfectly clear cylinder, like blown glass—hence, it being "clarified." Now the quill will better handle being cut into the perfect nib for writing and will better hold the ink and maintain its shape for longer.

Having made my own plunge, as it were, into the sands of time of faith tradition and church history, I, too, felt my vision clarified. I had enjoyed my journey into the past, but my purposes are in the here and

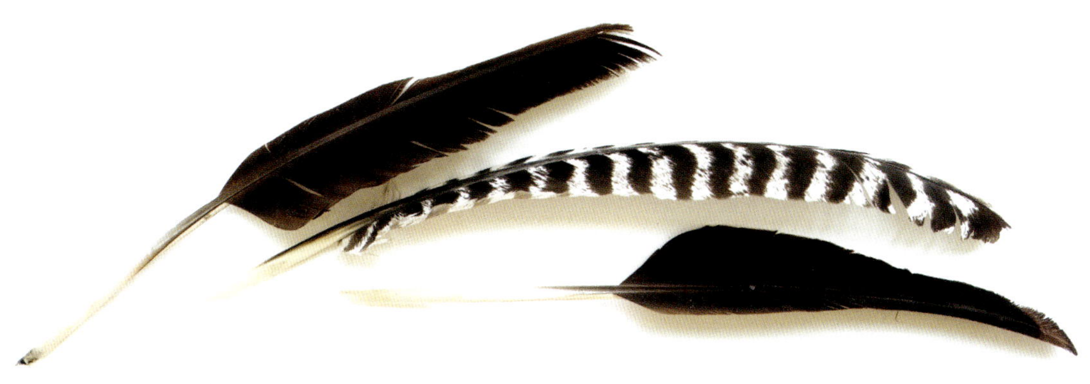

now. Creating within the great tradition of Christian artists does not mean forever looking back. To be truly faithful to their calling and to mine, I had to bring the hymn clearly into *my* present. And again, I did not do so alone. As I worked diligently toward the final illumination, Nate and Christy were completing their own arrangement and recording of the song. I was intrigued to learn that their journey unfolded in similar ways to my own.

Christy told me she had a hard time even approaching their hymn to begin with. She found herself putting it off repeatedly, feeling unready to bear the somber weight of its legacy. It was only through Nate's repeated urging and loving encouragement that she filled her voice with its melody. Still, she had been undone by the lorica. She recalled having to sing the last verse several times because she had been moved to tears. You can still discern the slightest quiver in her voice at that point of the song. It is my favorite part. It reflects the tenderness and beauty of Christy's heart, but also symbolizes the vulnerability we offer as artists to our King of heaven, praying He would be everything we need.

Through the skillful eye of our dear friend and videographer Luke Askelson, the collaboration was captured on film, with Christy and Nate performing the hymn in their home as I completed the illumination of the manuscript in mine. This joint offering was a true communion of saints, bringing past and present together in worship to the true Lord of our hearts.

As you set out on your next creative endeavor, look for opportunities for communion. Whether that means communion with the work of saints who came before or communion with artists with different specialties, trust that the unifying principle in your work is the gospel. Your love for the Lord. Your adoration of His Word. Your purpose to glorify Him. Even as you begin and you lack clarity on what the project will become, let the communion sustain you through the process. As you work together with fellow saints, you will gain a clearer vision for what the work of your hands could be.

fig 14 DETAIL OF WORK

Be Thou My Vision, 2022. Calligraphic illumination on genuine vellum, 27 x 21 inches. The traditional lettering (known as "Uncial," a traditional Irish script) becomes the strings of the harp that frames out these timeless lyrics of the beloved hymn "Be Thou My Vision." The original text is believed to date back to somewhere between the sixth and eighth century.

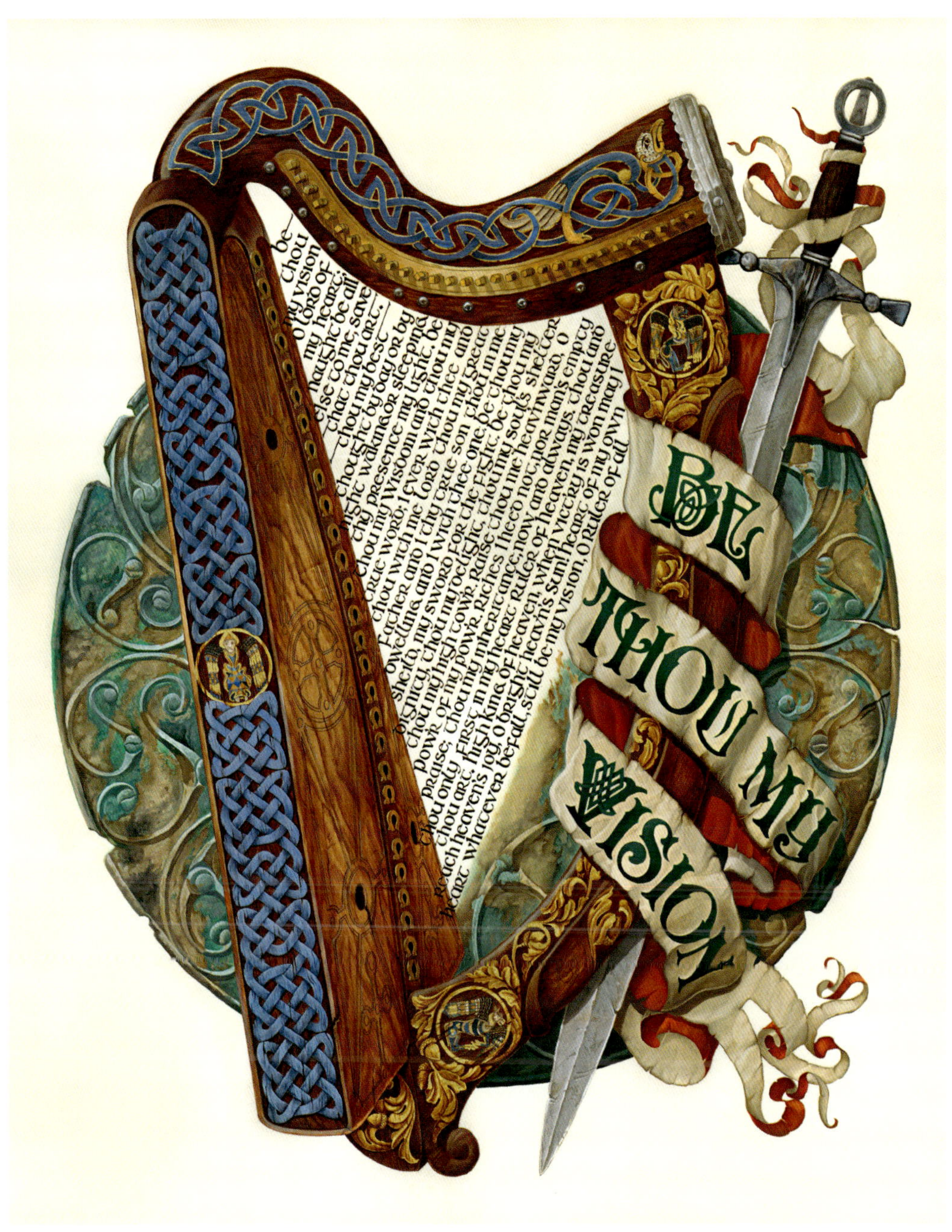
BE THOU MY VISION

CHAPTER NINE

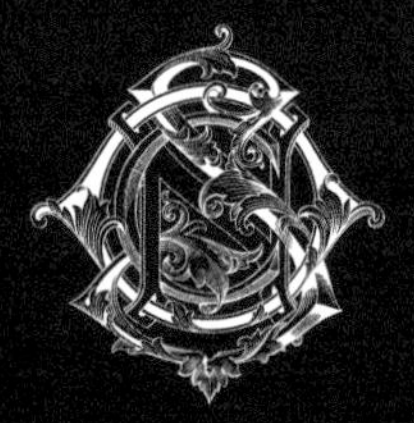

WAVE AFTER *Wave*

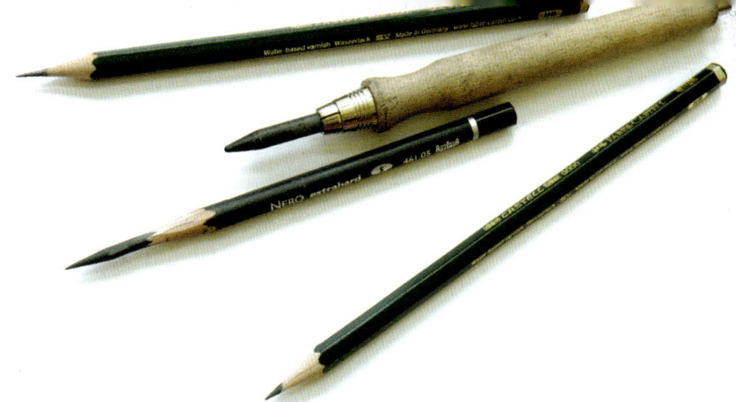

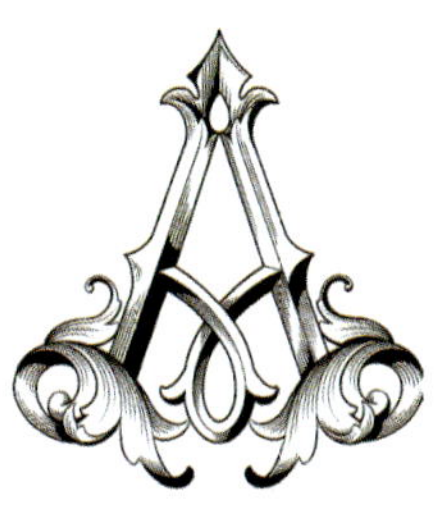dolescence is an awkward age for just about everybody. It sure was for me. I felt like a wobbly rowboat flung into churning breakers—the calm shores of childhood behind me, the ocean swells of adulthood ahead. How was I to become something seaworthy? Thankfully, my relationship with my parents was healthy, even if strained from time to time. Though I did not doubt their guidance, I felt compelled to set off on my own. I had several close friends, but they offered little in the way of guidance as we were all, so to speak, in the same boat. I found myself looking for some outside perspective, someone who could teach me the ropes. I longed to encounter a wise friend who had traveled beyond the horizon and could tell me what lay beyond the borders of the map.

How well do you remember this period in your life? (Maybe you're still trying to forget!) I imagine that many of us during this formative time were looking for someone who wasn't a parent or a peer—to look up to, to listen to, or to simply make proud. How many of us are still looking? Mentorship is so important to our formation, and it's a gift that we can give as well as receive. Perhaps you know of young men and women, caught amid the rough waves of adolescence, who are looking for guidance—whether they know it or not. I pray God would place on your heart those whom

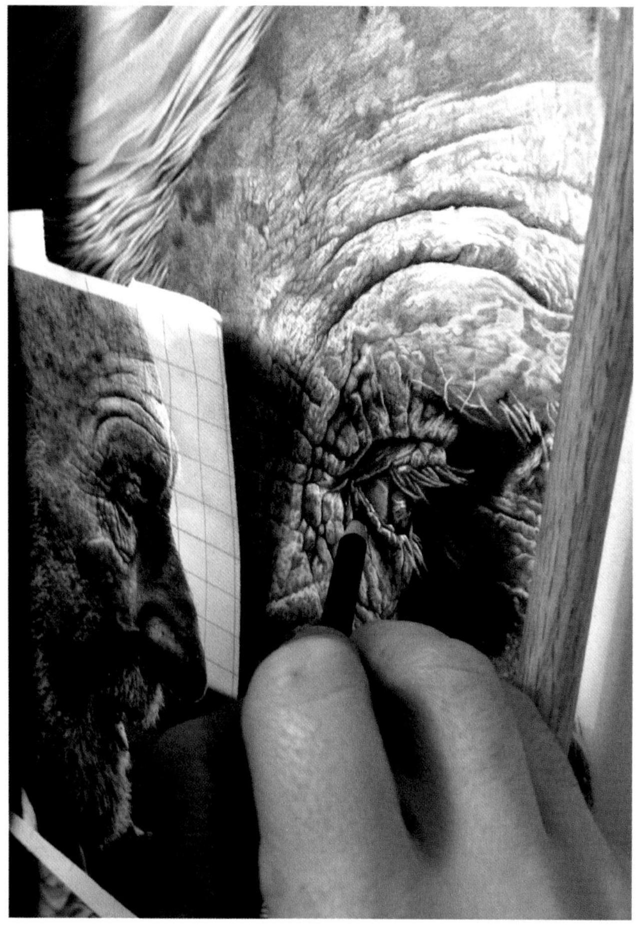

you might serve in this way. And as you do, I pray that you find others who would mentor you. No matter what our age or experience, we need all the godly wisdom and guidance we can get.

My adolescence, however, would not last long. Upon turning fourteen, I was given a task by my dad. I needed to select six mentors, each to represent a discipline of biblical manhood: a man and his God, a man and his wife, a man and his family, a man and his ministry, a man and his vocation, and a man and his friends. He told me I should choose them from among the men who played a major role in my life, such as fathers of my friends, youth pastors, or teachers. There were only two qualifications: one, I could not choose him as one of the six—as a primary point of the exercise was to seek wisdom from men who weren't my father; and two, I must pick my grandfather, so I might pass his wisdom on to the next generation. Over the next twelve months, I met with each of these mentors, having prepared a set of questions relating to their respective disciplines. The task would

Mentors have come and gone with the passing seasons of life, but I have never stopped seeking to learn from their wise example.

culminate on my fifteenth birthday, when I would formally enter adulthood.

That morning, the counsel of six, along with my father and myself, convened in a room at my parents' house. We discussed the culmination of the disciplines and how they each played a significant role in making us more into the image of Christ. My mentors offered wisdom, gave exhortation, and required accountability. That evening in a large room at our church each of them got up before a group of my peers to explain in summary how they had instructed me in the godly disciplines for which I was now responsible. Each in turn concluded with a prayer of blessing over me. What an extraordinary way to be ushered into manhood!

Instilled in me through that remarkable experience was a deep and abiding appreciation for mentoring, which has followed me all my days. Mentors have come and gone with the passing seasons of life, but I have never stopped seeking to learn from their wise example. I have had mentors for just about everything: spiritual mentors, academic mentors, business mentors, mentors for marriage, mentors in calligraphy, mentors in art, and yes, even a mentor for writing this book (thank you, Steve!). Submitting myself before the tutelage of others has not only made me more learned but eminently more teachable, which is just as invaluable.

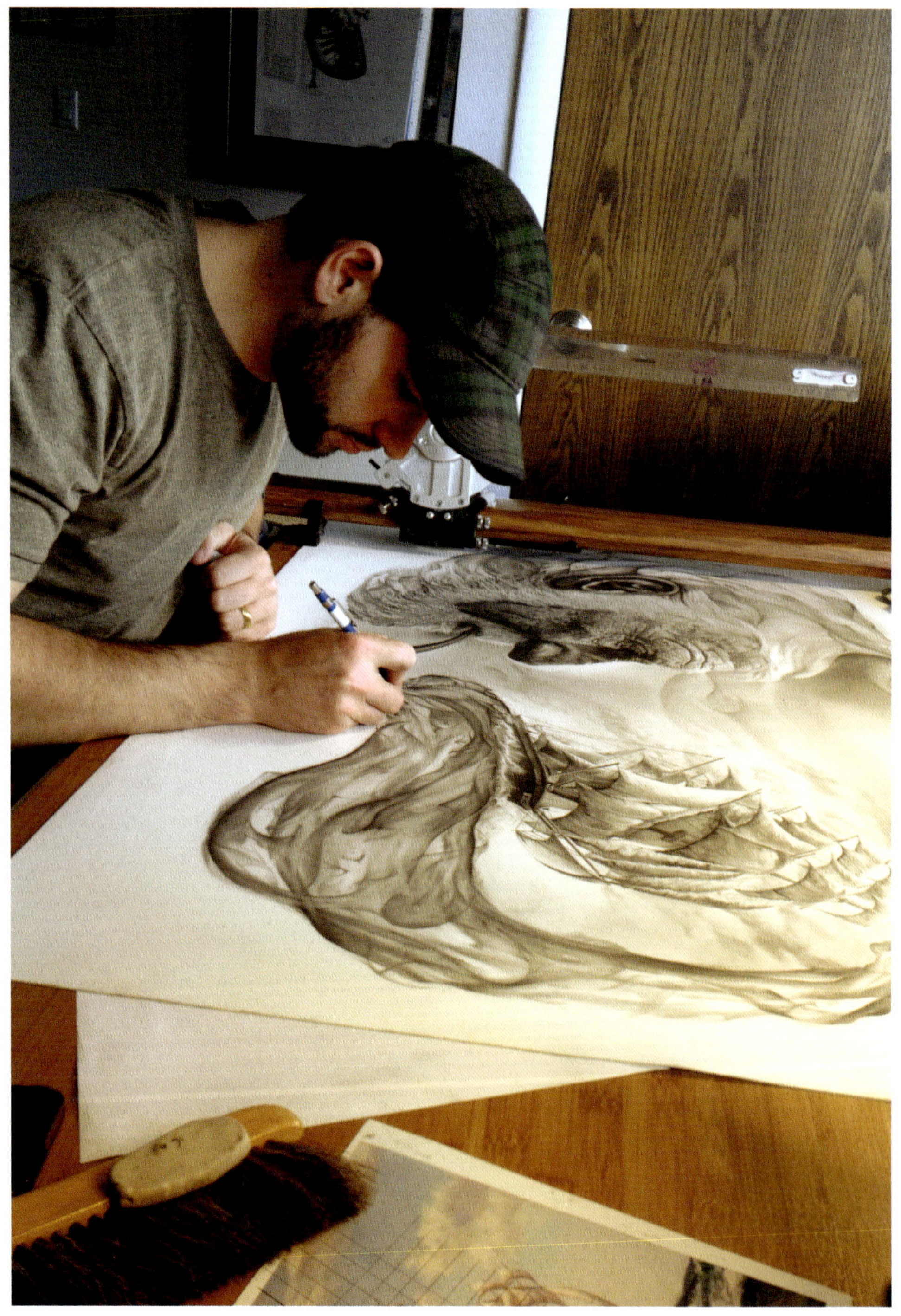

Mentorship, however, is also about legacy, about the way your experiences serve the next generation. Legacy is not in what you leave behind but in what you send forth. Your love, your wisdom, your good will all reach their greatest success when they are carried by those who succeed you. Several years ago I was able to sketch out—literally and figuratively—the all-important relationship between mentorship, legacy, and experience. It began with a little free drawing in my sketchbook of an old sailor, smoking a pipe and gazing toward the left side of the page. As the smoke rose up and out, I drew a small ship sailing on the plume. It was an interesting idea but felt incomplete.

I wondered where the smoke should go next. Thinking with a pencil in my hand is how my best concepts are born, so I scribbled out my ever-evolving thoughts on the page. The smoke grew and rolled up over the ship with my searching strokes. At first, I framed the ship alone in wisps of whirling smoke, yet the composition still did not satisfy. The sketch is to me what the hypothesis is to the scientist: It is to be either confirmed or denied. The pencil tip and the eraser are used in near equal measure at this early stage. Two strokes forward, one smudge back. And then, "Eureka!" My pencil wandered back to the sailor's head. Almost without thinking, I started blending the curls of the smoke into his hair and then into his beard. There seemed to be a narrative unfolding in the dynamic interplay of elements, yet I, the author, was not immediately aware of exactly what it was. I was intrigued how the blending of smoke and sailor made the old man appear ethereal, in spite of his grandeur in proportion to the ship. And a question started whispering through the rough pencil marks on the page. *What remains of us when to ashes we return?* Holding the book before me, I knew I had made a breakthrough. Here, potentially, was my next major piece.

Drawing is a helpful, if incomplete, illustration of the mentor-mentee relationship. At first, the eye constantly oversees and discerns the work of the hand. Yet over

> My sense of legacy only increased when I became a father, reminding me in more ways than one that legacy is something we *create.*

time, through faithful attentiveness, the hand internalizes the eye's watchful guidance through muscle memory. It learns to move fluidly without needing to submit itself nearly as often to what the eyes are seeing. Indeed, at this point the hand moves so fast there is no time to stop and ask for the eye's direction. But in a sense it doesn't need to; it already knows where it is going thanks to the many hours spent honing its movement under the eye's watchful gaze.

Now, while it is true that a mentor will never be as watchful as the eye, it is nevertheless true that mentorship is characterized by a kind of foresight that comes with wisdom. Even as they guide, the Christian mentor does not seek control, but rather intends for the practice of virtue to become an internalized pattern within the mentee. And throughout, a good mentor welcomes the transforming power of the Holy Spirit into the fold. For the Holy Spirit, even more than the most watchful eye, *is* ever-present, helping turn our sketches into full-fledged compositions.

And He did the same for me in this instance. The concept sketch of the old man being swept up in his own sort of pipe dream *seemed* complete. But as I studied my sketch further, I realized there was more to do. In the Western world we have been conditioned to view things from left to right since we read in that directional flow. The left, therefore, is indicative of the past; the right, of the future. And so, as he looked to the left, the old man seemed to be recalling his past adventures. It was fitting, but also conventional. Perhaps it was time to try something new.

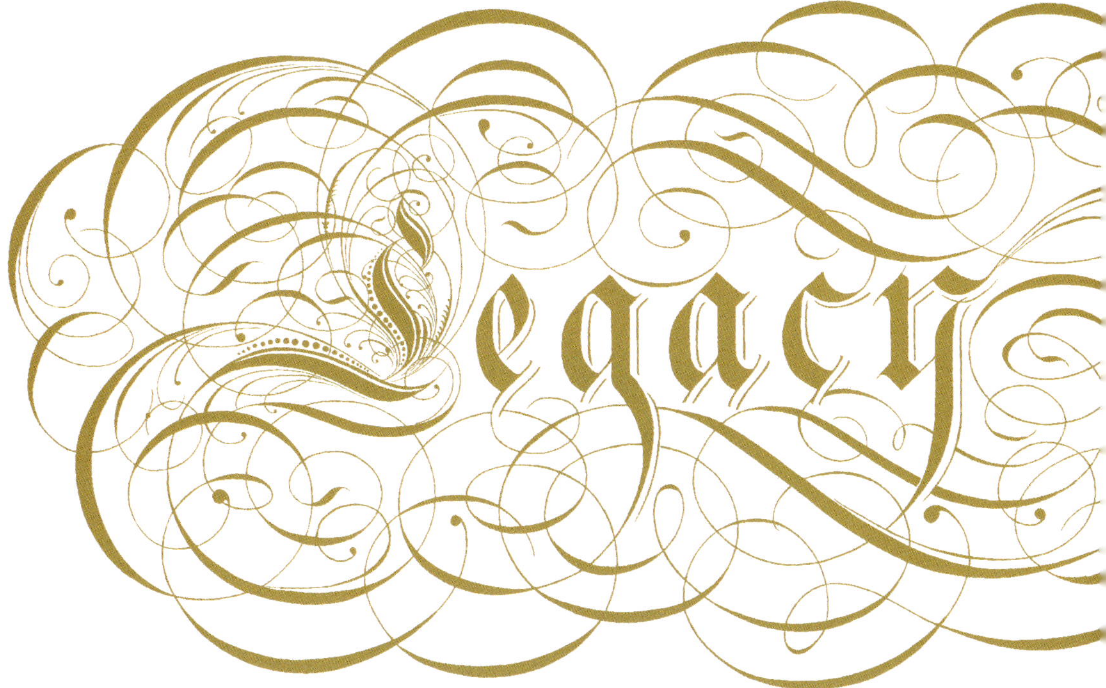

Because elements that move with the current have a greater sense of dynamism, I imagined flipping the entire design to see how it might change the piece's expression. When I did, I discovered not only that the ship seemed to be moving at a quicker pace, but also that the whole narrative had changed. Rather than an old man pondering his past adventures, he was now oriented to the future, imagining his legacy. Perhaps he was even dreaming of new adventures waiting on the horizon!

As an artist, I have always created with my legacy in mind. I hope my pieces resonate not only in the present but also in the future. For although my materials will only last so long, they point to the ongoing imperishable work of the Creator, participating as they can in His eternal truth and beauty. I also hope my story will prove beneficial to the next generation as much as I have benefited from the stories of the generations who have come before me.

My sense of legacy only increased when I became a father, reminding me in more ways than one that legacy is something we *create*. Fundamentally, of course, my children are flesh of my flesh and bone of my bone, albeit with the added beauty of their mother's eyes

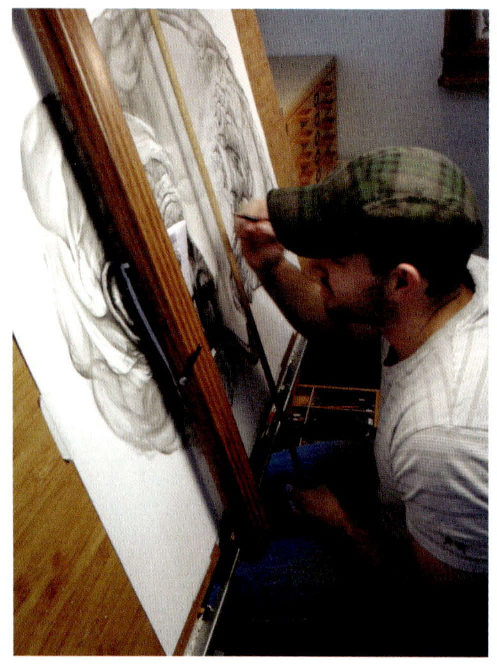

and smile. But as I watch them grow day after day, and year upon year, I think about what sort of legacy I am instilling in them. It's a weighty and wonderful thing to be a dad. Some days I wonder if I'm the right man for the job. But then I am reminded: As far as the Lord is concerned, I am the only man for the job.

Something of the same principle applies when we consider what it means to be a Christian. As brothers and sisters in Christ, we form a spiritual family. And over the centuries this concept has been deepened with reference to other relationships within the same: fathers, mothers, sons, and daughters—all in Christ. This family also has a legacy, which the Father has shaped and redeemed from the very beginning until the present day. And when He adopts us we become coheirs with Christ in that legacy, which lives within us as we continue to create in the image of our Creator, trusting He will take the best of what we make and make it better.

A legacy is something not easily won but is the gift of hard-earned experience. Returning to the drawing, I find myself reflecting on the many times I have received that gift from those whose faces have been weathered by life's many storms. How often has their wisdom steered me from rocks that would otherwise have torn my hull asunder? How often have they oriented my bow toward the coming waves

> A LEGACY IS SOMETHING NOT EASILY WON BUT IS THE GIFT OF HARD-EARNED EXPERIENCE.

lest I take on water and capsize? They have always provided a steady hand at the tiller, guiding me through waters both calm and treacherous.

I thank the Lord for the men and women in my life who have helped chart my life's course. Through their watchful eye and integrity of character they have formed me in immeasurable ways. I hope my life and artistry are a faithful testament to their rich legacy.

One such person is the man I introduced in chapter 2—the one in the grand conference room, with whom I shared *Suffering Servant in a Single Stroke*. Not only did he give me my start as an artist, but he and his dear wife have poured generously into Hannah's and my lives. Indeed, they have become spiritual parents to us. Whether in our callings, businesses, marriage, or parenting, there is hardly a facet of our lives that does not bear witness in some way to the richness of their legacy.

And where would I be without my many mentors in calligraphy? John DeCollibus first inspired me and is now a dear friend—able to make me laugh harder than anyone I know. Michael Sull, also a dear friend, wrote me my first letter in ornamental penmanship; his love for teaching instructs me to this day. And last but not least: the late great Rick Muffler. He invited me into the Master Penman program and changed the course of my life.

How about you? Who has mentored you? Whose legacy has shaped your own? Who has offered timely advice, even given you a necessary word of warning? Perhaps they have been a constant source of hope and encouragement, offering their presence at the very time it was most needed. As some come to mind, I would encourage you to say their names aloud, or even write them down if it helps. Perhaps you may be prompted to reach out and thank them for the ways they have formally, or informally, mentored you. I pray that you are reminded of just how much others have invested in you, loved you, and blessed you as part of their legacy. I pray, too, that it reminds you of the ways the Lord has worked through their lives to shape yours. You are part of His legacy also.

A Portrait of Wisdom

With the drawing's composition locked in, I decided to begin on the final piece. The weathering of the old man's face was critical to convey both wisdom and experience. The look in his gaze had to contain both memory and foresight. It is a tragedy that Western culture has taught us to dread old age, when old age is so often accompanied by wisdom—wisdom that benefits not only the wise but also those who heed their words.

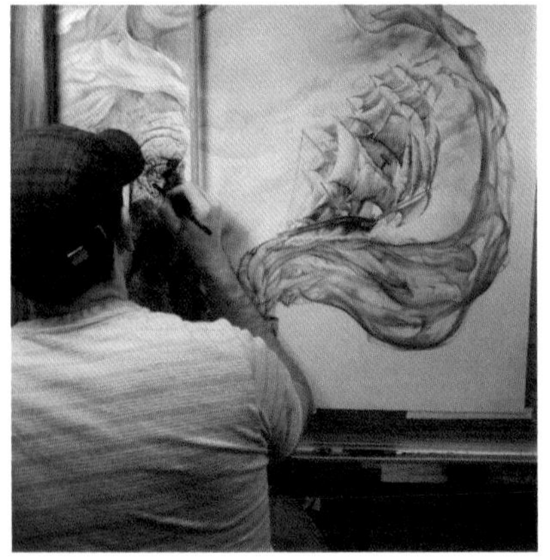

As I composed the smoke turning to water under the hull of the ship, I rendered them tumultuous in order to convey the rough waters of life. As for the waves, they were to look as though they were testing the very integrity of the ship's hull—crashing against it in a violent spray. Although we may wish for fair winds and calm waters, in our heart of hearts we must know it is the tempest that forms us. This is how we are tested. This is how we build strength of character, purity of heart, and steadfastness of faith. Indeed, even as I have relied upon mentors to keep me afloat, in their wisdom they acknowledge that much can be learned only from my own experience. Not every storm can be escaped—nor should it. After all, what piece of art displayed within these pages has not emerged from one challenge or another?

And speaking of challenges, there was the matter of rendering the smoke, which needed to morph into the hair and beard in a convincing manner. This, however, was a more pleasurable challenge, as I love drawing surreal transitions of this nature. I went whisker by whisker, dissolving them into the smoke with my soft pencils and blender, and then coming back with my finest eraser and even some white charcoal to bring out some highlights. I enjoy creating the illusion of something that looks real but cannot be seen in real life. Yet I trick the eye only to enlighten the soul. In this instance, I drew upon the theme of "ashes to ashes, dust to dust" as found in the *Book of Common Prayer*. Our lives, as it is said in James 4:14, are like "a mist that appears for a little time and then vanishes." Yet this brief temporality is contained within a longer-lived circularity, in which legacies are passed down from one to the next.

With its many textures—the wrinkles of the skin, the burl wood of the pipe, the whiskers of the beard, and the elliptical ring of whirling smoke—*Of Smoke and Sea* has to be one of the most fun and entertaining pieces I have ever had the pleasure of creating. A simple sketch opened the door to an expansive narrative: The rough waters that pass beneath you today become the wisdom that shapes the person you will become, a wisdom to offer to others on their own journey.

My hope for you, friend, is that you come to see the rough waters in your life as a means of character formation and legacy building. I pray you would be blessed as I have been by the loving guidance received. Allow others to pour into your life. Seek the counsel of the wise. Learn from others' successes as well as their mistakes and be grateful for them.

Moreover, I pray that as you become more teachable by seeking the guidance of those around you, you would ultimately learn to be attentive to the Holy Spirit Himself—that Spirit and soul, like eye and hand, would eventually work in perfect coordination.

And in turn, seek out those around you who are hungry to learn and desperate for guidance. Teach others out of your foibles and failures. Oftentimes they are of even more value than your triumphs! We all will have the opportunity to both receive and give wisdom. Strive to do both with all humility and grace. And finally, live within the greatest legacy we have in Christ Jesus. Be transformed into the likeness of His image—the very image of the Creator Himself. Such is to live into the very legacy of our Father in heaven and send it forth for a thousand generations.

THE ROUGH WATERS THAT PASS BENEATH YOU TODAY BECOME THE WISDOM THAT SHAPES THE PERSON YOU WILL BECOME, A WISDOM TO OFFER TO OTHERS ON THEIR OWN JOURNEY.

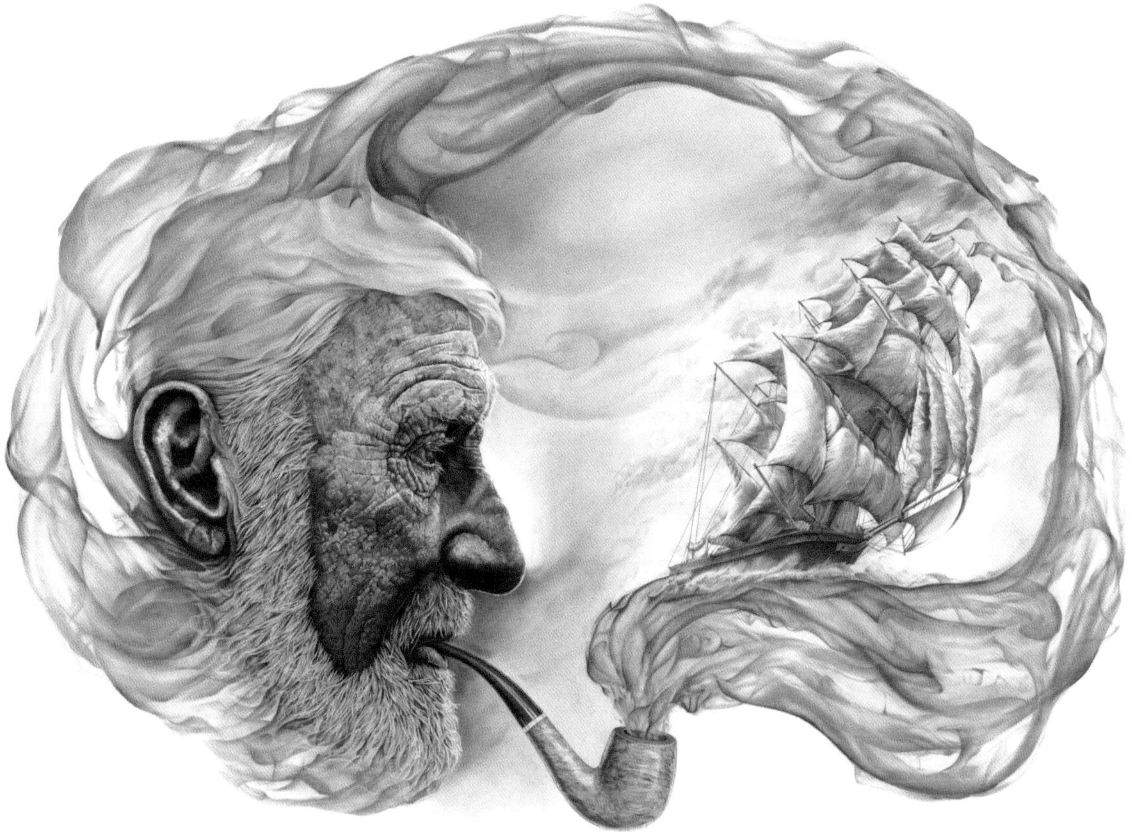

fig 15 DETAIL OF WORK

Of Smoke and Sea, pencil and charcoal on paper. This piece is brought to life through swirling tones of charcoal and graphite. More than an illusory transition of smoke to sea to man, this piece speaks to the cyclical motion of life.

CHAPTER TEN

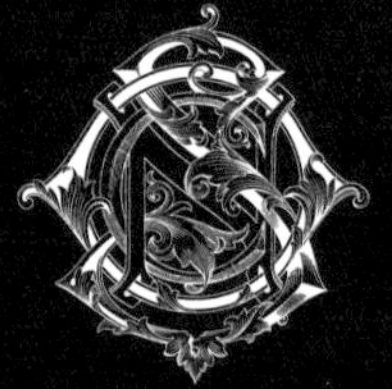

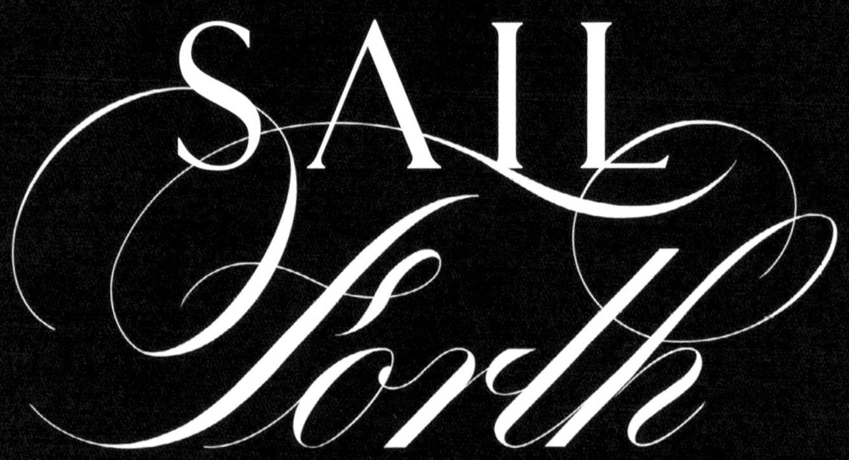

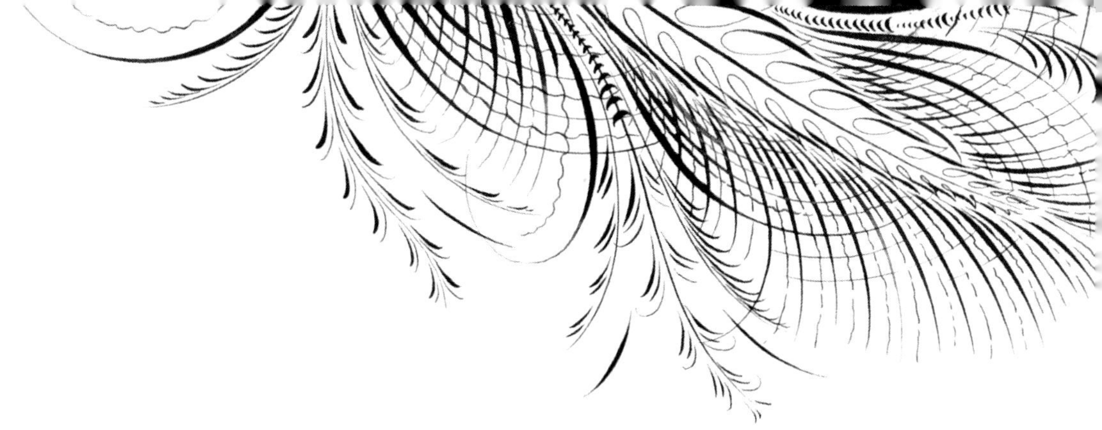

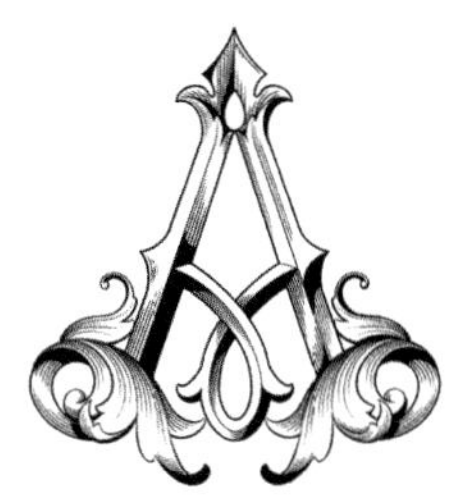

rt has led me on an amazing journey. It has changed me physically, spiritually, emotionally, and yes, creatively. From the ashes of my family's home, through the awkward years of my youth, to the affirmation of my calling, the discovery of my wife, and the birth of my three children—art has played a central role. And as the years go by, it has only continued to make its presence felt in every aspect of my life. I have prayed for my art and my art has become a prayer—an unceasing prayer (1 Thessalonians 5:17) that I will offer as long as I have breath in my lungs and strength in my hands. And when these fail, I live in the sure and certain hope of the resurrected life to come. May my prayer continue even then.

Writing this book has been an offering of thanksgiving. It has brought to mind all that God has done in and through my art, and I am overwhelmed with gratitude at His unceasing goodness and faithfulness. I cannot help but praise Him from whom all blessings flow. He has placed His creativity in my heart and used it for His good purposes and mine.

But much like the old man in *Of Smoke and Sea*, I am uninterested in dwelling too long in the past. As a creative, I am called ever onward. In the words of Walt Whitman, I hear a rallying cry:

Sail forth—steer for the deep waters only,
Reckless O soul, exploring, I with thee, and thou with me,
For we are bound where mariner has not yet dared to go,
And we will risk the ship, ourselves and all.[10]

I thank the Lord that I will not continue this journey on my own. Hannah, my children, my parents, my siblings, my friends—all go beside me; as do my patrons, mentors, and the communion of saints both past and present. But even more importantly, I know the Lord will be with me always. He is my vision and guide. Even now I hear the Spirit's whisper in my ear: "*Sail forth!*"

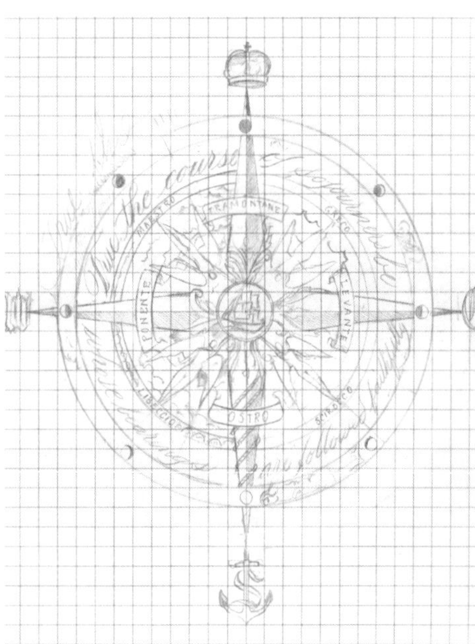

God's call to journey with Him as an artist is perhaps best exemplified in *The Sojourner's Rose*. For even as it contains many symbols reflecting the nature of this journey, it is a work that has itself embarked on a remarkable odyssey of its own.

It all began some years ago when I was commissioned to create an icon for a conference. Christian leaders from across the globe were coming together to seek a biblical way forward in a culture unsure of its bearings. The image of a compass rose immediately sprang to mind. Although compasses were once employed by later medieval cartographers to help sailors navigate the Mediterranean, I sought to put this compass to a different purpose. I wanted it to speak to the experience of Christians who, having their citizenship in heaven (Philippians 3:20), experience the world as sojourners, following God's lead and depending on His provision as they wander through this world. As such, I decided that each aspect of the rose would be imbued with the significance of spiritual direction.

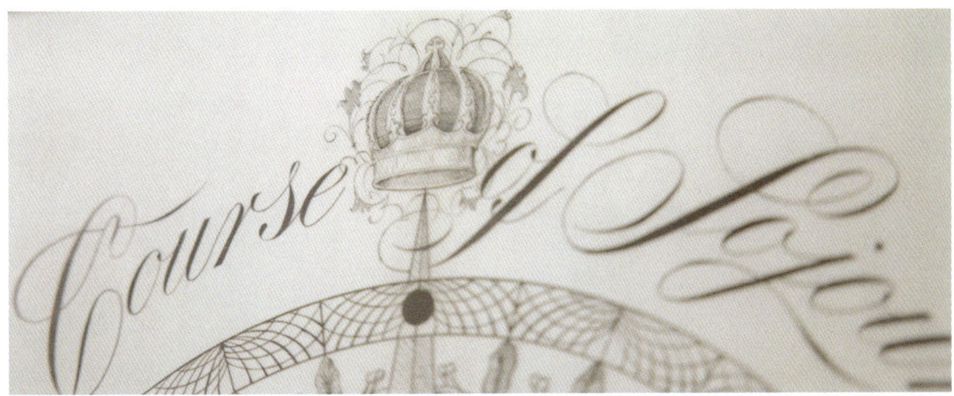

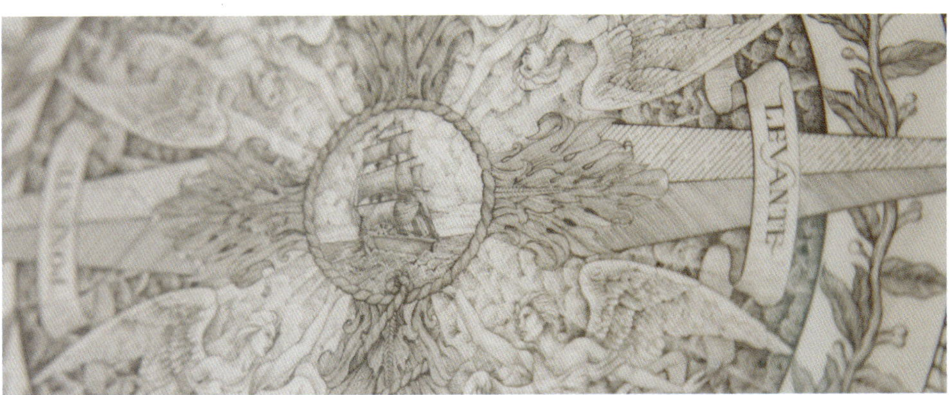

Finding all the symbols and working out their placement in a rigid outline makes for slow work. It felt like doing a jigsaw puzzle, only I had to cut the pieces as I went. I spent several days making multiple iterations of quick thumbnail sketches to grasp the bigger idea. I would sketch prospective symbols, shaping them with my pencil lines to try to make them fit within the composition. If unhappy with their integration, I would erase that portion or tear the page from my sketchbook entirely. Ironic as it is to say, I struggled at first merely to get my bearings.

One of the greatest challenges in creating a new piece is the elimination of possibilities. When the page is blank it represents an almost unlimited number of images that might fit within those two dimensions. By putting a single line down, I have

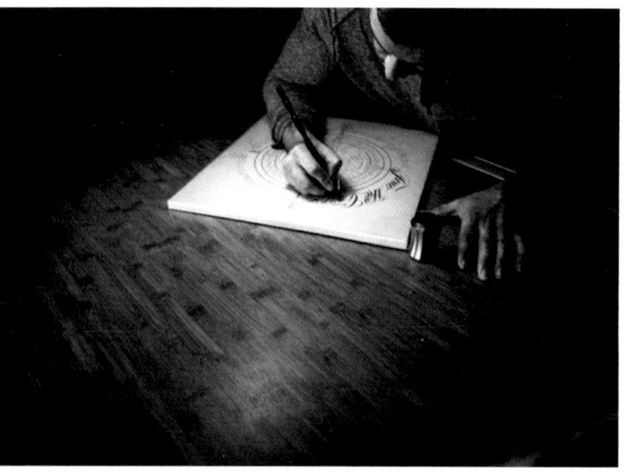

consequently eliminated a multitude of options. When I add another, another multitude follows them into the void; and so on and so forth, until the composition can be nothing other than that singular image filling the page. The loss of these innumerable possibilities must be outweighed by the satisfaction I feel in discovering the one that appears before me.

Finding our calling is not dissimilar. Within our life's bounds God has given each of us particular gifts, which marks the first line. He has given each of us the respective desires of our hearts—and there's the second. He has made us for such a time as this and has put us in such a place as we are—the third and fourth. Now add to this your family history and relationships, as well as your strengths and frailties. All of it culminates into a singular image of *you*, fearfully and wonderfully made (Psalm 139:14). And yet, as unique as you are, you nevertheless reflect His image—as we all do, even in our great and wonderful diversity.

God only knows the billions of possibilities He decisively eliminated when He formed you in your mother's womb. But what you can be certain of is the great satisfaction He takes in His creation. Let me remind you again: When our Creator looked at His creation He saw that it was *very good* (Genesis 1:31). It may be that you feel lost or dissatisfied with your calling. I know that I have and still do from time to time. I might compare myself to others and think my calling is less important, but—ultimately—does it really matter what I think? God has formed me and you for a purpose. If we sit around and mope about it, we may never discover just how much He can do with what we, in our limited understanding, have deemed so little.

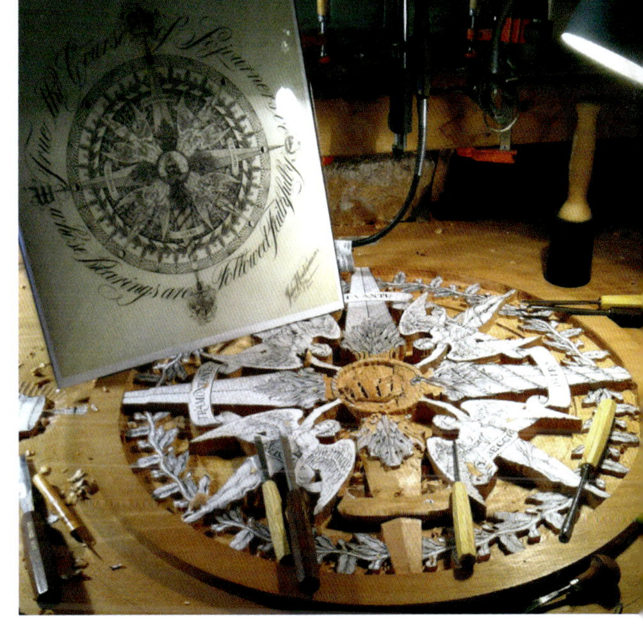

Returning to the rose, my process of elimination eventually yielded favorable results. Distilled on the surface of the page was the best of the dozens of options I had explored. I solidified critical aspects, such as the cross of Christ, which was formed by the spire of the four major winds, and the sojourner, depicted as a ship in its center. From there the composition truly started to blossom. I drew four cherubim subdividing the four cardinal directions; the cocked wings of the angels perfectly subdivided the four points. The hands of the angel would hold a continuous banner bearing the names of the eight winds as they were originally coined: Tramontane, Greco, Levante, Sirocco, Ostro, Libeccio, Ponente, and Maestro.

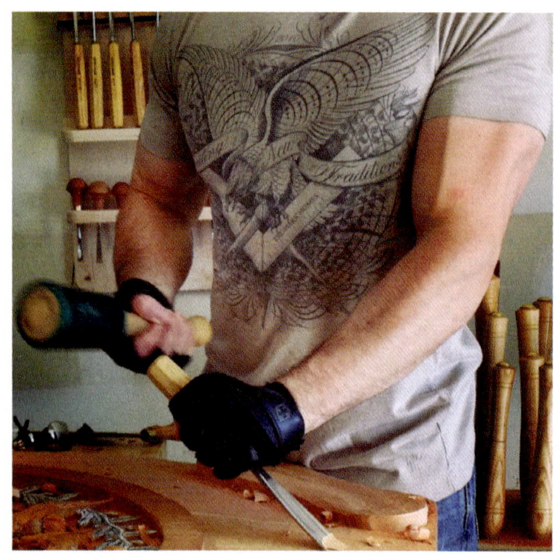

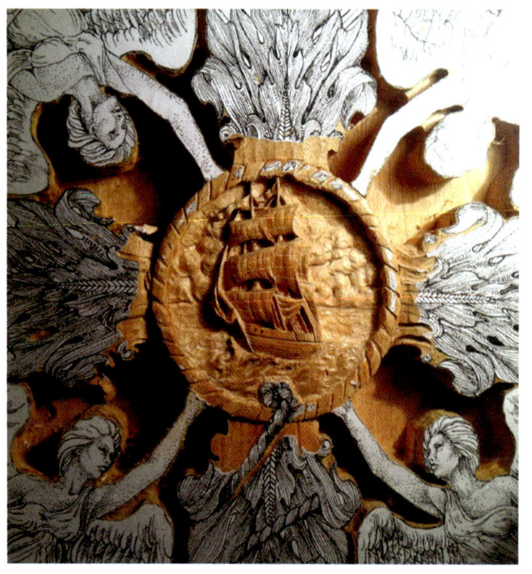

I found myself in the rush of a creative flow. My hand struggled to keep up with all that my mind had finally unlocked within the composition. I was spinning the sketchbook around on the surface of my drafting table, twisting my body to the left and the right as I drew with all haste the blooming design in radial symmetry. I was not racing the clock but my own thoughts. I did not want to slow or stop my hand from moving lest I should interrupt the flow as it channeled through the ever-decreasing point of my pencil. Working concentrically from the inside out, I eventually reached the outer ring of the compass. I dropped my pencil in the gutter of my sketchbook and leaned back in my chair to take it all in. In rough strokes, the culmination of this creative flow finally lay on the page.

Over the following two weeks I refined my sketch and scaled it up a bit. On a leaf of choice vellum in pen and ink I had established a brand-new icon from a familiar

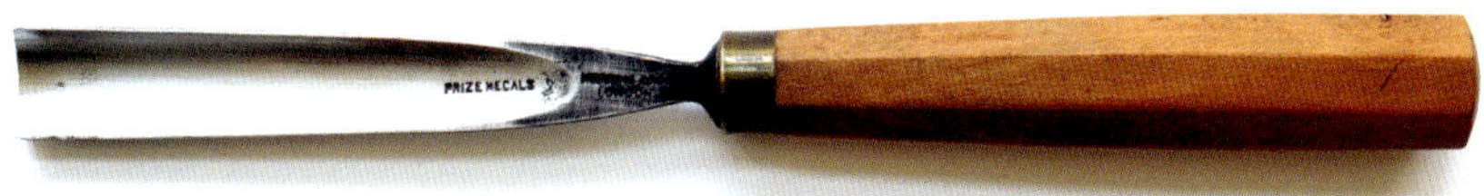

framework. When the conference came, I was given the opportunity to unveil my piece from the stage and share the spiritual meaning of its symbolism.

Some months passed, and I thought the story of *The Sojourner's Rose* was complete—forever logged away in the archives of my portfolio. Then one day, out of the blue, I received a phone call from a stranger. He introduced himself as a friend of a friend and told me that he had heard about the piece and all that it signified. He loved the design and its meaning, but he also wanted it at a larger scale. As the conversation continued, and one thing led to the next, I discovered he not only wanted it bigger but also hand-carved in high relief! The task would be monumental given the detail involved. He said he was up for it if I was—so off I went.

Along your journey, wherever your calling leads, you may encounter people like this. They see great potential in you, even if you don't recognize it in yourself. And sometimes their prompting, no doubt encouraged by the Spirit, is necessary in helping you realize that potential. Such was the case here. Reproducing *The Sojourner's Rose* as a wood carving wasn't remotely on my radar. Even if it had been, I could not have taken the massive amount of time needed to create it if it hadn't been commissioned from the beginning. Never underestimate the powerful way God can move through the people He brings into your life to aid you and send you quickly on your way.

With the advantage of having drawn such a detailed and complete

> AS YOU ASPIRE TO BE REMADE IN YOUR CREATOR'S LOVING HANDS, CHOOSE THE PATH THAT WILL SET YOU FREE, NO MATTER THE HARDSHIPS INVOLVED.

design in the two-dimensional art piece, I already had my carving plans in hand. The difficulty, as I had experienced with *The Old Rugged Cross*, was realizing the two-dimensional form in a three-dimensional carving. A process of elimination was again at play. But rather than purging possibilities, I was doing away with real material. I began with a single block of Honduran mahogany measuring 40 by 45 by 3½ inches. Chopping away at this pristine, furniture-grade hardwood, I felt more vandal than artist. But on this occasion, creation required destruction.

There is a valuable lesson here. As I have discovered in my own life, God's creation has often involved the destruction of my heart's idolatry. How often has He chipped away at the overburden of my pride? How many of my plans, made apart from Him, now lie as sawdust and shavings on His workshop floor? What engrained sinfulness has He painfully scraped from me? And what more is there left to cut out? God's pruning of my character is itself a holy art form. And He will not stop until the image of His Son is revealed.

Perhaps you know what it is to experience the pain of God's creation within you. A hard heart, if it will not soften, may require breaking before it is made new again. Bad habits and addictions, if they are to be set aside, can require long symptoms of harrowing withdrawal. Friend, this is the work of redemption. Grace is never cheap. Suffering, as we have noted before, can and will be redeemed, when set at the feet of the Crucified. As you aspire to be remade in your Creator's loving hands, choose the path that will set you free, no matter the hardships involved.

Carving the relief, though ultimately enjoyable, was also painfully slow at times. While great big chisels and heavy blows from the mallet made quick work of the preliminary shaping, as I got closer to uncovering the forms buried in the wood, I progressed down to smaller and smaller chisels, some even a millimeter or two wide. The tiniest of cuts are often as critical as the large ones. The pressure was at its greatest when I was carving the angels' faces. One slip and I could knock off a nose and ruin the whole thing. But I did not arrive at these faces only to be proven a lummox. No, every cut of every curled shaving had prepared me for these last critical details. I was a different carver now than when I imposed upon this block of wood.

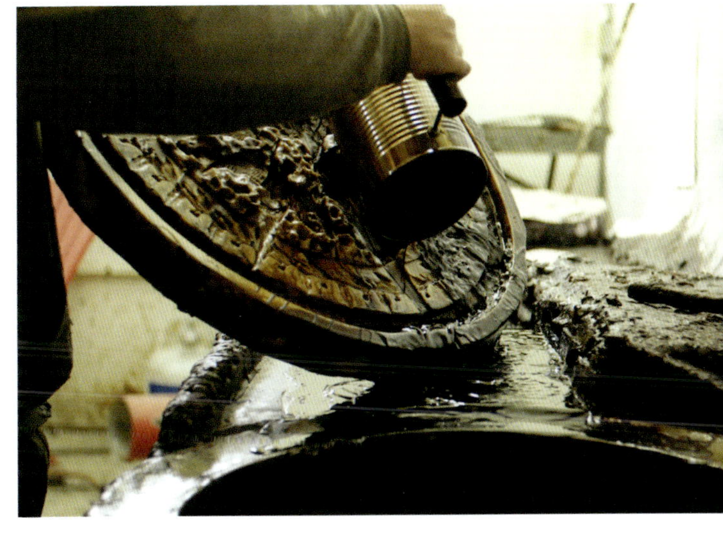

As God calls you onward, He also invites you to rise to the occasion. God promises He will not allow you to be tested beyond your ability (1 Corinthians 10:13—the

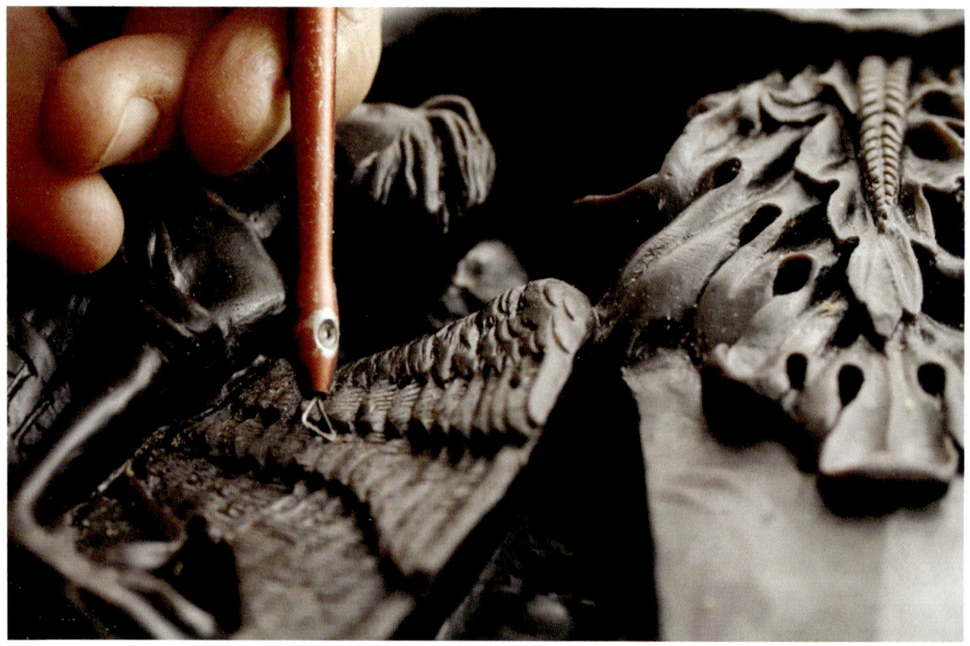

verb translated as "tempted" can also mean "tested"), but growing in your calling means you will be able to handle greater and greater tests as you proceed. With the completion of the wood carving, *The Sojourner's Rose* and its symbolic message had been elevated to a whole new level—and so had I. But still the journey went on.

Not two years later, I received yet another unexpected phone call from the man who commissioned the carving. This persistent patron went on to tell me that as it hung in his office over the last several months, it had garnered astonished reactions from a good many of his visitors. This gave him an idea. He suggested I come pick up the carving from California and take it back home, where I would have it molded to make bronze castings. Surprised but undaunted, I set off cross-country with my compass—the two of us journeying together in more ways than one.

Finding someone willing to make the mold proved difficult. No one wanted to touch the carving for fear they'd break the fine details while pulling off the mold. At last, I met with one brave soul who had enough plaster under his fingernails to be worthy of the charge. But that doesn't mean it was easy work. After producing a beautiful mold with not a splinter out of place, he confessed he'd lost more sleep over

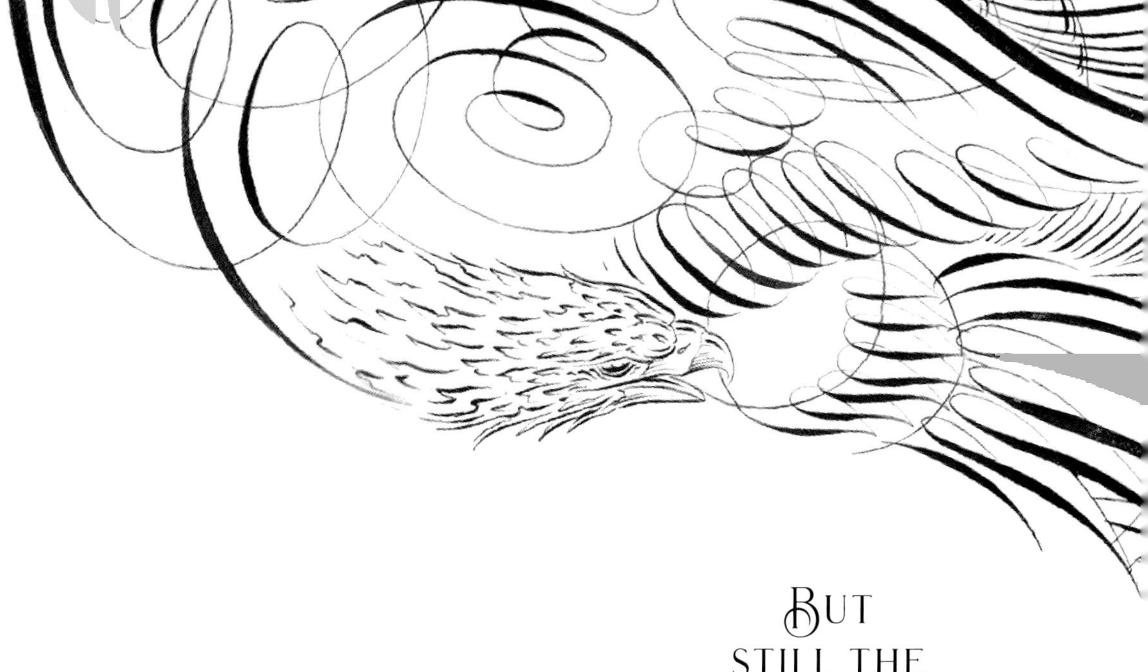

BUT STILL THE JOURNEY WENT ON.

this project than when molding a sixty-foot-long public art piece the year before. At long last the mold was done; now on to the foundry!

Through a method called "lost wax," which has been employed for hundreds of years in cultures around the world, a bronze casting was eventually produced. Every detail down to the fine grain of the smoothly sanded mahogany remains visible. Every feather in every angel wing. Every leaf on the laurel crown. Every script letter of the inscribed phrase. All was captured forever in solid metal. As I recall going to the foundry to see the first *Sojourner's Rose* blossoming from the fiery forge, I remember retracing all the steps and stages that had brought me to that moment: A visceral thought cast a shadow of graphite. A calfskin's illumination in pen and ink. Angels' faces carved in mahogany. A rebirth in bronze.

The complete narrative of *The Sojourner's Rose* is discerned by its symbols. The four spires of the compass evoke the cross of Christ, for by it we receive life and direction. The ship depicts the Christian sojourner, whose citizenship is in heaven. The sea it travels upon is rough, which reflects the trials of life we endure for Jesus' name. The ship's central place within the compass reminds us of the centrality of the cross to our faith.

As for the surrounding cherubim, they represent the heavenly host. With one hand they offer a hand of protection; with the other, a hand of direction—for we

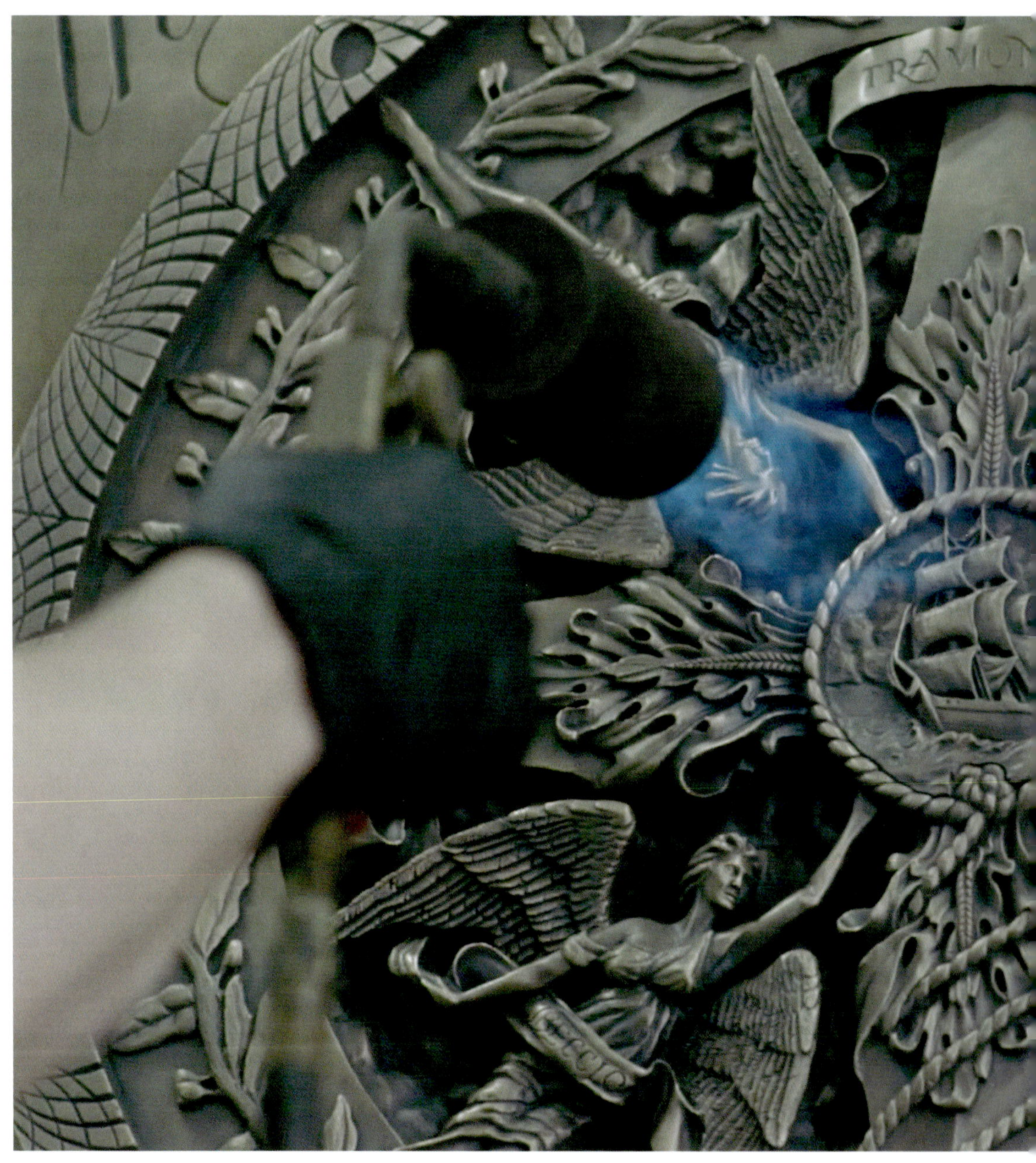

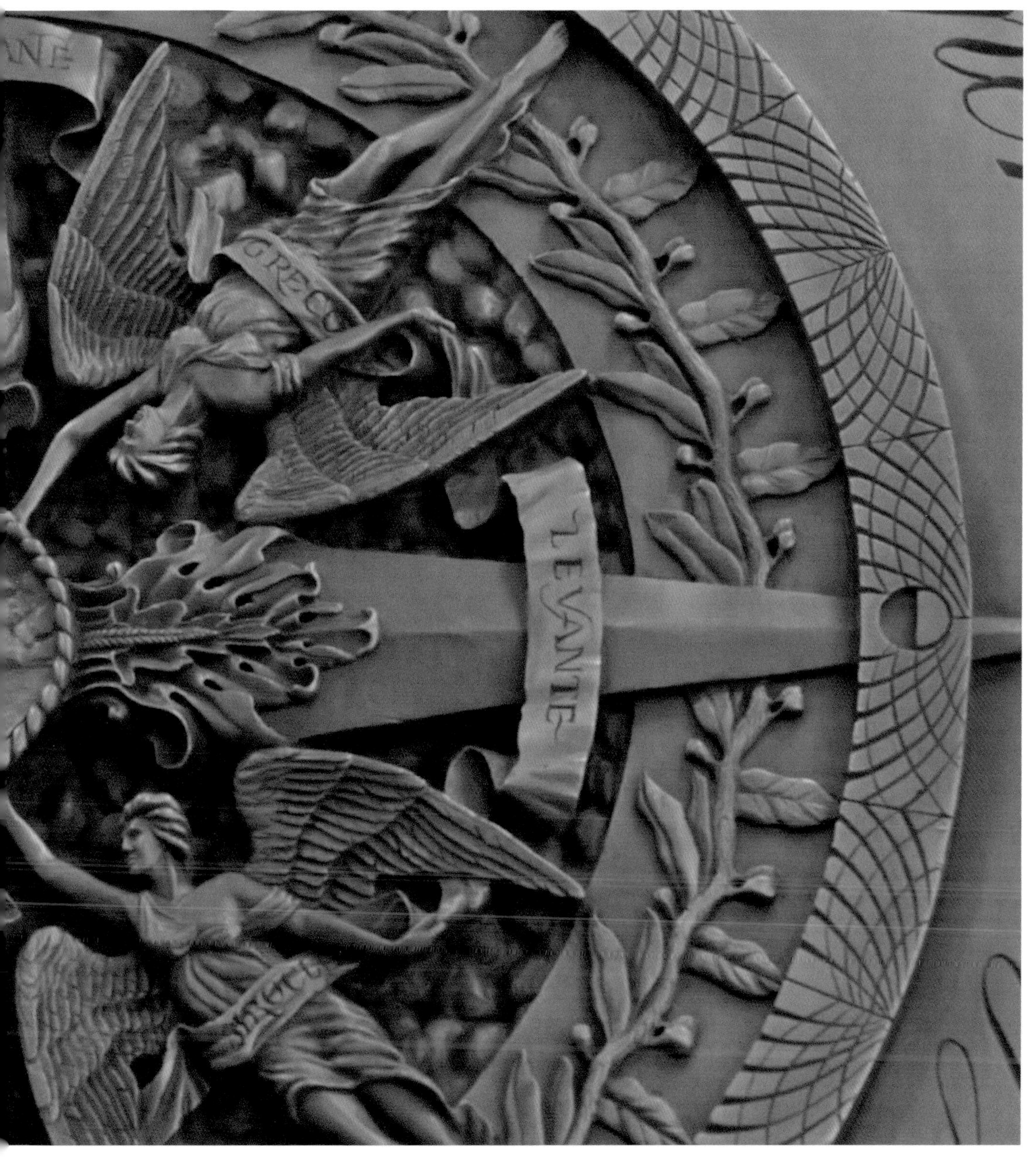
GRECO
LEVANTE

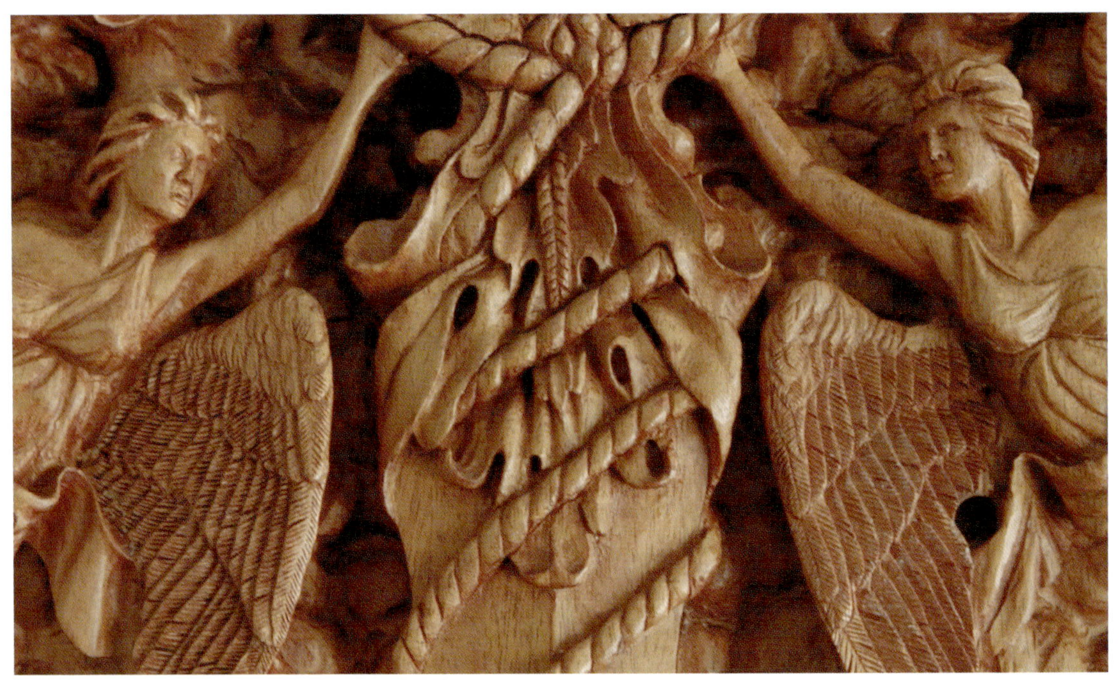

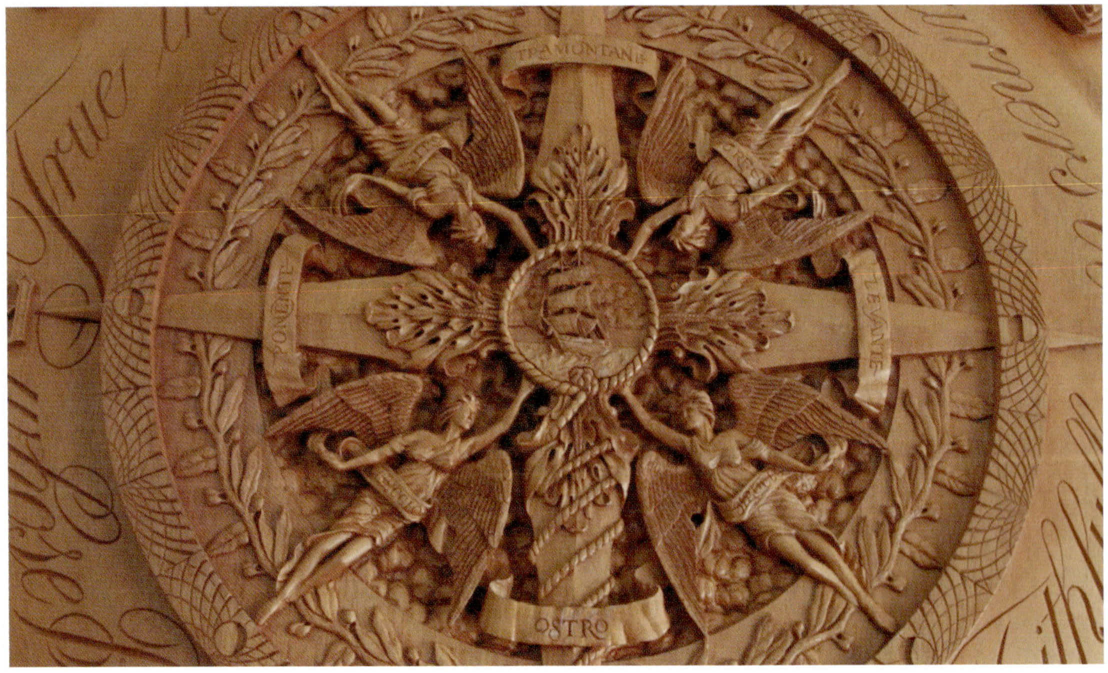
TRAMONTANE
PONENTE
LEVANTE
OSTRO

receive both from on high. Beyond this heavenly circle is set a laurel crown. This represents the imperishable crown of victory, which Paul said will be won by those who have run the race of faith (1 Corinthians 9:25).

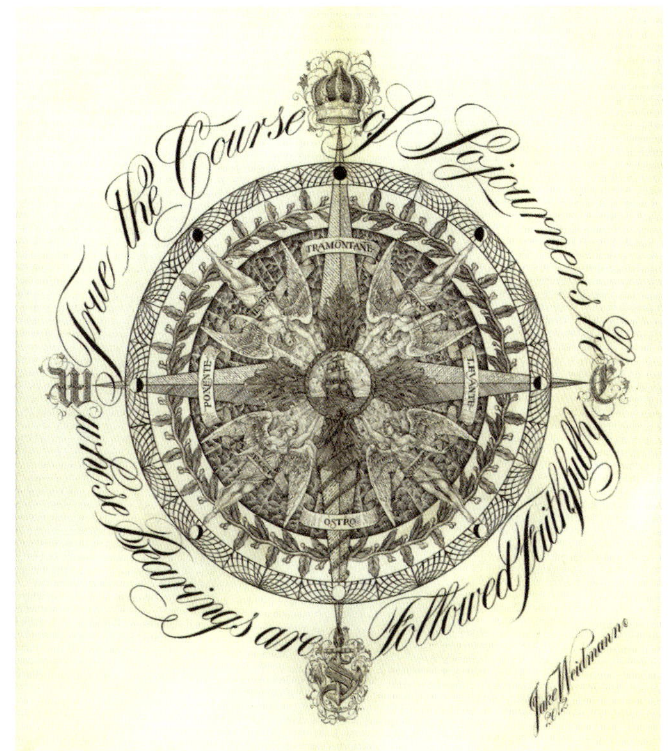

The bordering rim, for its part, contains the eight phases of the moon, which themselves are aligned with the eight winds. This is a reminder that God has placed us where we are for such a time as this. But we are not simply listless upon the waves, for at the tip of the south spire is an anchor, which tells us to be forever anchored to the foot of the cross—at once penitent and filled with abiding gratitude for the mysterious work accomplished upon it. Atop the north spire, however, there is a king's crown—*the* King's crown, because the kingdom of God must ever be our true north. Last, but by no means least, the piece is encircled by the following charge: "True the course of sojourners be, whose bearings are followed faithfully." It is remarkable to me that this work, intended as a universal icon by which any Christian pilgrim might spiritually orient themselves, might itself have traveled so far. I cannot help but wonder: *Where will it lead me next?*

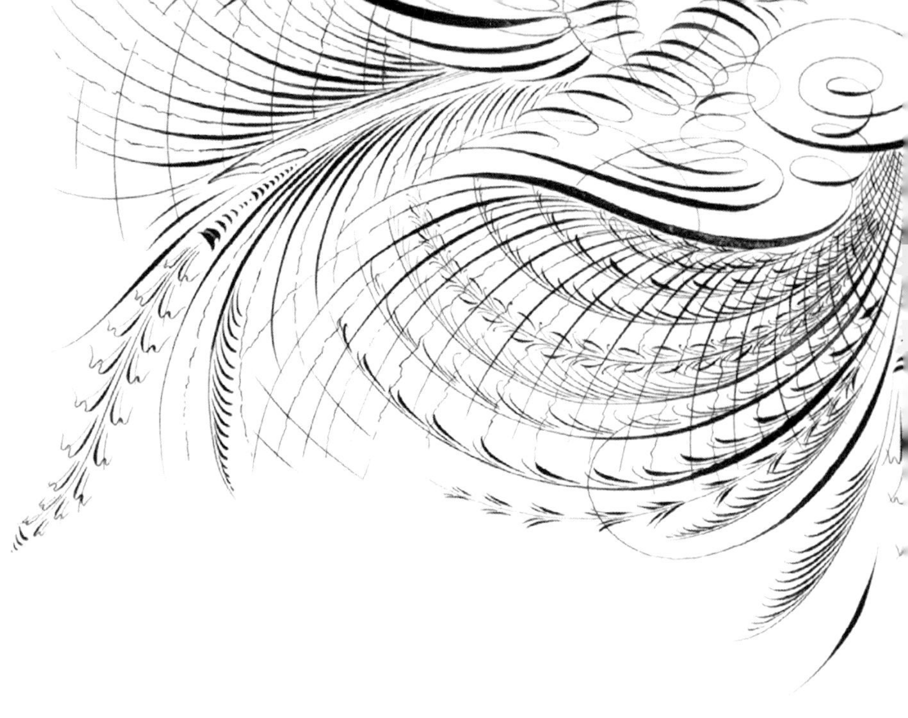

In Hebrews 12:1–2, Paul exhorted us to "run with endurance the race that is set before us, looking to Jesus, the founder and perfecter of our faith." The Spirit inspires and encourages us to push toward, transforming us into the glorious image of the Lord as we pursue our heavenly goal (2 Corinthians 3:18). Although our initial act of faith might seem as faint and ill-defined as a few pencil marks on a sketchbook's page, like the evolving iterations of the *The Sojourner's Rose*, God will give it ever increasing substance. He will increase our strength and perseverance so that we might reach our destination.

I had not anticipated the piece's many transformations. The same can easily be said of the changes God had wrought within me. At some point along the journey, counter to all my expectations, He even made me something of a leader. For as I have faithfully sought to create in His image, I have found myself not only captaining my own ship but making a way for others who have traveled in my wake. I am becoming aware all the time that the more effective I am in my own work, the more others look to me as a leader. This has taken

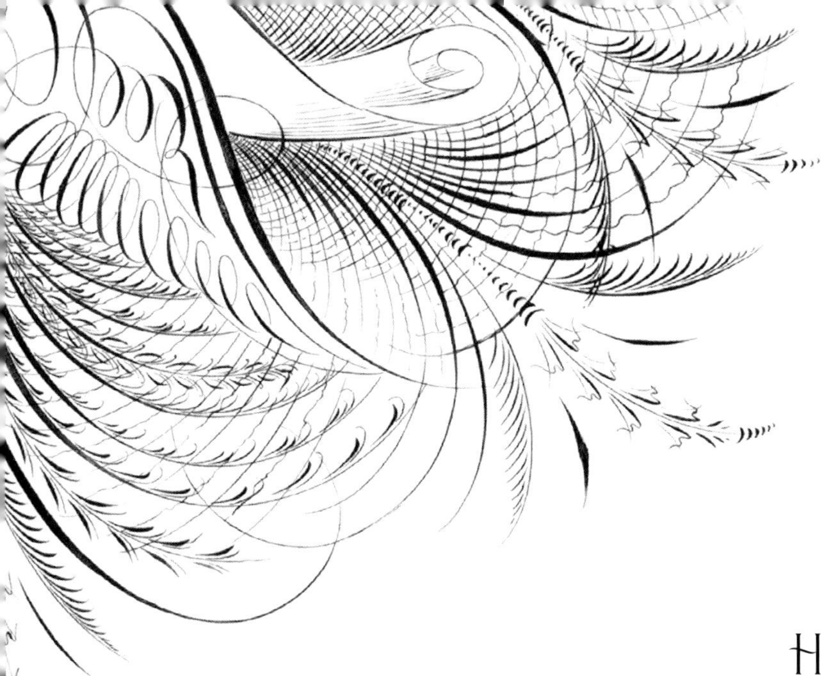

He will increase our strength and perseverance so that we might reach our destination.

some time to understand and longer still to own. All my life, I have had little to no desire to lead. It simply isn't the artist's way. Instead, I've felt a bit like Forrest Gump, from the movie of the same name, who just gets up and starts *running*. The sheer boldness of his action inspires others to follow and even to ask him for all manner of advice. It is as if the certainty of his purpose precipitates others' certainty in theirs. I find this to be true in my own spiritual race. The weight of leadership would fall heavy on me if I ever thought I was the one ultimately leading. Instead, my effectiveness to lead comes down to my faithfulness to follow Christ.

So, when you do set off purposefully on your journey, don't be surprised if others start following you. But insofar as God has called you to lead, I pray you seek to demonstrate, not dominate. After all, it is not so much about us as it is about the One who creates within. As Christian artists we are rather like the needle on a compass, ever drawn to the magnetic pull of the Spirit.

And so, at least for a little while, we have journeyed together. Me, in a sense, leading the way—the self-confessed artist. But you must know as well as I that I have been steered by forces greater than my own. This book, as I said at the outset, is really about my Creator—that is, *our* Creator. Each piece that graces these pages, and every circumstance that brought them to life, points to His ongoing creative work in me. And so, if you are to take anything away from this journey, know that it has been all for His glory. But if there is one further thing I might ask of you, it is this: Friend, when you create—and *I know you can*—do so in the Artist's image, the One in whom you have been fearfully and wonderfully made. Offer it all as a sacrifice of praise. Who knows what He will make of you!

fig 16 DETAIL OF WORK

The Sojourner's Rose, 2012. Pen and ink on vellum. 17 x 15 inches. Weidmann represents through symbolism born of scripture the pilgrimage of the Christian sojourner through this life in the icon of a compass rose.

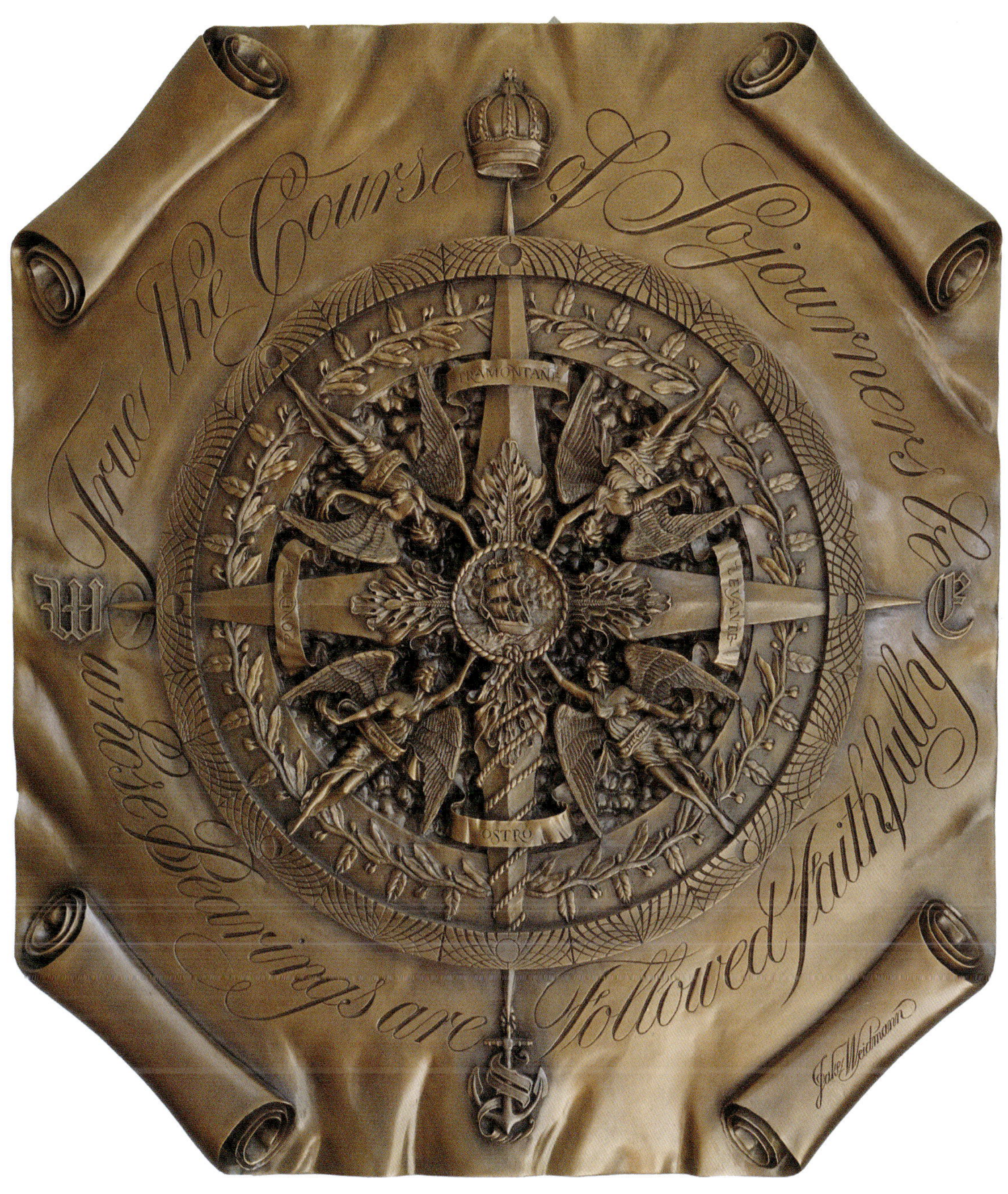
True the Course of Sojourners Be
whose Bearings are Followed Faithfully
TRAMONTANE
LEVANTE
OSTRO
W
E
Jake Weidmann

CONCLUSION

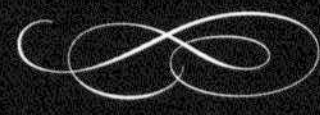

THE MAKER'S PRAYER

Great art Thou, Jehovah—Elohim, the eternal Creator.

Great art Thou, Jehovah—Elohim, *the eternal Creator.* I rejoice in the beauty of Thy name. Let my heart echo the refrain as the seraphim sing, *Holy, holy, holy is the Lord God Almighty!* Join with me, Thy created son, and I with Thee, my Maker be. Lead me by the power of Thy Spirit. Teach me to create in accordance with Thy will. Bless the works of my hands, O God. Give me ears to hear the truth Thou hast spoken. Give me eyes to see the fullness of Thy beauty. Give me breath to speak the goodness of Thy name. Be my strength when I grow weary. Be my guide when skill runs out. Be my wisdom when talent fails me. Be my assurance in times of doubt. Take joy in me as I create with Thee, made more in the likeness of Thy Son. Receive unto Thee my work as prayer and meet me when my head is bowed. When effort is spent and day is done, let the works of my hands sing Thy glory. Let the lasting change not be the mark on the page but my soul forever conformed to Thy image.

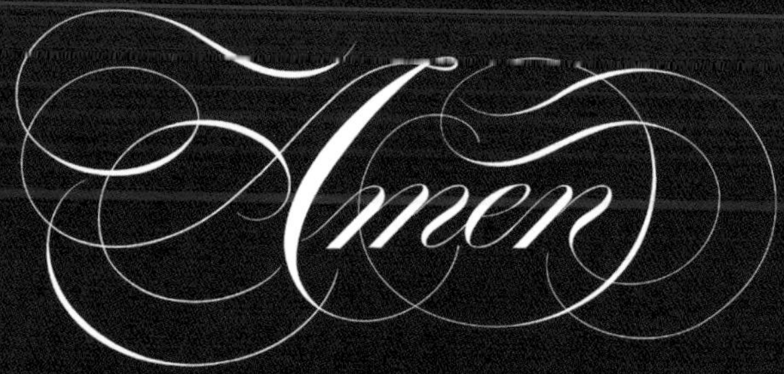

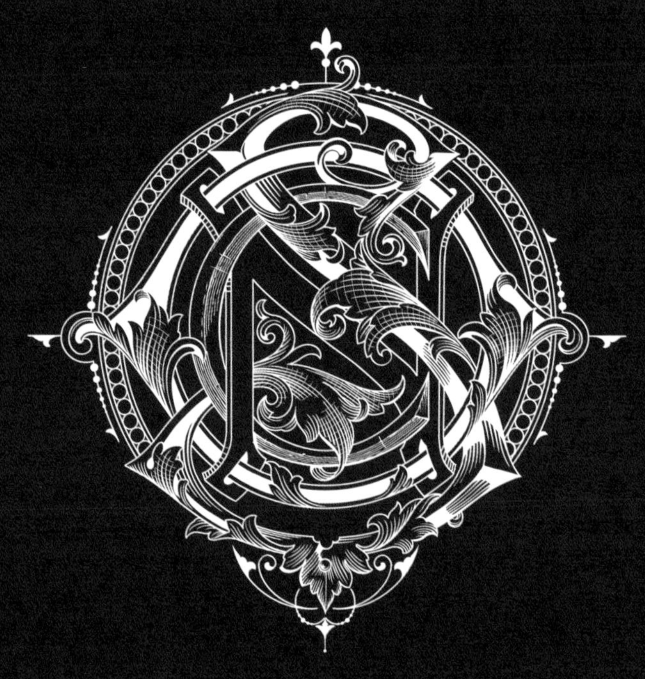

ACKNOWLEDGMENTS

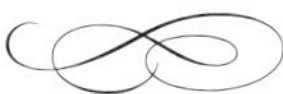

HANNAH: In you I have found at once my artistic muse, my grand collaborator, my confidante, my dearest, most wonderful friend, the mother of my children, and the one whom my soul loves.

As with everything else, I could not have done this without you. No one is privy to my work and to my struggle as you are. And I'm convinced that no one could have borne it or me with as much patience, grace, and love as you have. This book stands as yet one more creation of mine replete with your fingerprints. You have made my life more beautiful in countless ways. I love you endlessly.

EMMA, HENRY, AND ELOISE: Your lives are and forever will be my favorite works of art. Your laughter filled the house in the season of writing these words. So much of its richness is because of you. Thank you both for sitting with me in the studio and for the times we were apart, always being excited when I emerged from long hours behind its doors. I hope that one day when you read these words, they conjure up fond memories of our daily lives and the ways God was at work in your little years. I love you with all my heart.

MOM AND DAD: You're the first ones to champion my work and, what's more, a heart for the Lord. From letting me paint murals on my bedroom walls to commissioning my first art piece, you've encouraged me from the start. I can't thank you enough for the ways you've encouraged me, believed in the God in me, and prayed over me without end. Whatever fruit my life bears for the glory of the Lord is because of your prayers.

STEVE AND ELAINE MUSICK: Hannah and I reap harvests we never sowed; we enjoy the fruit of the vine we never watered; we more easily walk in paths of righteousness because a faithful few (you two) paved the road. Our hands are full of graces we could never afford. We do not give anything we haven't already received, and you've given your very lives for our sake and the sake of the gospel. Every Sunday since the world shut down in 2020, you've committed to gathering (and you take on the one-way forty-five-minute commute) to be with us. It's the line of our favorite psalm: "He gives us more than we can hold. Our cup overflows" (paraphrase of Psalm 23:5). Thank you for reminding us that heaven is closer than we think and should be experienced repeatedly.

Jenni Burke: You've been a trusted guide in the foreign land of publishing. I look up to you not only as a co-laborer but as a friend. Hannah and I have said time and again throughout this journey that you've given us wind under our wings to courageously take flight to horizons beyond our borders. We're better, more faithful followers of Christ because of you.

Lisa-Jo Baker: While you didn't work directly with me on this book, you're the reason it exists. Your initial message encouraged me more than you know. And while numerous relationships in the publishing realm have come and gone, it was never right, until right now. Here's to future endeavors together, starting here. Thank you for seeing me and boldly pressing Send. You brought this artist out of his comfort zone with your courageous kindness.

Danielle Peterson: Your exuberance for this book from day one has served as fuel for inspiration and encouragement. You've generously lent me your expertise for the success of this project and given me confidence to believe God was at work in these pages. You've edited numerous drafts and managed to find gems in the midst. You've called me higher in this work, and you've encouraged this novice to relentlessly pursue mastery. And while I'm nowhere near mastery, thank you for seeking and finding, and making me better at my craft.

Steve Watts: I believe you to be a diamond miner, for you have polished this rough cut and made it shine. All the right materials lay beneath the surface, but it was your questions throughout the writing process that served as the pressure needed to materialize a stone of remembrance. Our regular calls brought layers of depth and joy that are this book. Beyond you being my writing coach and first editor, I'll forever be grateful for our friendship and our long discussions of medieval history, the early church fathers, and the glories of vellum. Thank you for serving alongside me and turning this lump of coal into a treasure for the sake of the reader.

Tiffany Forrester: In a foreign land, I was relieved to have found that you and I speak the same language. So much is new to me in the process of publishing my first book, and I found immense comfort when I discovered we spoke the same dialect of design. You've been the bridge for this analog artist to cross over and share his message with the masses in a land I've never known. While I can't say publishing feels familiar to me, it no longer feels foreign. Thank you for helping me feel at home here.

The Thomas Nelson Gift Team: To the many hands that have lent themselves to this book, I couldn't be more grateful. I trust God has used its message to touch the hearts of those immediately surrounding it, the way the Holy Spirit so skillfully does, before it makes its way into the marketplace. In the same way skillful workers brought their gifts to bear in building the tabernacle, you have lent your offerings to the building of this book for the glory of God. The generosity of your gifts laid here offers the reader an abundance of beauty to feast on. You've made this book a dwelling place for His presence.

Pete and Janet Richardson: Your questions are like answers. The way you ask is a guiding force that perpetually leads me to the heart of Papa God. You envelop Hannah and me in wisdom and hold us as family. We better understand heaven here and now because of you. Thank you for endlessly uplifting us, supporting us, praying for us, and being the family Christ defines. You love us as a son and daughter, and it's changed how we see everything else.

Curt and Nancy Richardson: During the writing of this book, you held my hands to the plow with the largest commission of my career to date. I am simultaneously writing these words and sculpting your family's legacy. The immense honor is humbling and gratifying work. Thank you for not only trusting me to do justice by the story only God can tell but for inviting me into your hearts as family. You pay me the highest compliment by commissioning me and loving me as one of your own.

TJ Klaijnbart: As one of my earliest patrons, you and Jorge have supported me in numerous ways, but most chiefly in prayer. You both prayed Hannah into my arms, and your encouragement of my work early on is the foundation upon which God built His faithfulness. We honor Jorge's memory by acknowledging that you both paved a way for me to walk in righteousness. I hope these pages do justice to your co-laboring with Christ by which I am forever changed.

Cathy Turner: I can't tell you how many times I thought of you and Dennis during the process of writing this book, and how I wished I could call Dennis on the phone and read him first drafts and ask his fatherly opinion. I like to think of imagination as prayer, and I imagine Dennis beneath the shade of heaven's walnut trees saying, "Attaboy, Jake!" You and Dennis furthered God's goodness in my life merely by your presence in my life. How I love you and hope to honor you both within these pages.

Luke Askelson: For more than a decade you have used your talents and skills to uplift mine. And once again, in this book you have done the same by the contribution of your amazing images from our many video projects together. I am forever grateful! You are truly gifted by God in all that you do as a craftsman, artist, and cinema-photographer. I count myself so blessed to have benefited from your gift. But far more than a great collaborator, you are a dear friend. I admire and treasure you for the talent you share, the heart you have, and the man you are.

NOTES

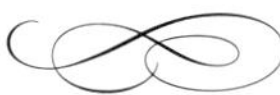

1. John Ruskin, "A Joy for Ever (And Its Price in the Market)," delivered at Manchester, Lecture 1, July 10th and 13th, 1857, Project Gutenberg, https://www.gutenberg.org/files/19980/19980-h/19980-h.htm.
2. C. S. Lewis, *The Last Battle* (New York: Macmillan, 1972), 162.
3. "John DeCollibus Calligraphy—Lettering," posted July 16, 2014, YouTube, 7 min., 11 sec., https://www.youtube.com/watch?v=XOaosF3s8uc.
4. Ruskin, "A Joy for Ever."
5. Howard Thurman, as remembered and shared by Gil Bailie, quoted in John Eldredge, *Wild at Heart: Discovering the Secret of a Man's Soul* (Nashville, TN: Thomas Nelson, 2021), 184.
6. Andrew Murray, *Humility: The Beauty of Holiness* (London: James Nisbet & Co., 1896), 14.
7. Gerald of Wales, *The History and Topography of Ireland*, trans. John O'Meara (Penguin Classics: New York, 1983).
8. Caroline Elbaor, "An Ornate Shield Found in a Celtic Warrior's Grave Is Challenging What We Know About Ancient Combat," ArtNet, December 10, 2019, https://news.artnet.com/art-world/celtic-shield-warrior-grave-1725090.
9. Ailbhe Mac Shamhráin, "Dallán Forgaill," Dictionary of Irish Biography, October 2009, https://www.dib.ie/biography/dallan-forgaill-a2367.
10. Walt Whitman, *Leaves of Grass* (New York: Random House, 1983), 348.